THE GAME BOOK

THE GAME BOOK

Game shots, wildfowlers, decoyers, stalkers and rough shooters alike will find a wealth of material here to fire their imagination and enhance their knowledge of their favourite sport.

Frederick Forsyth reveals why he prefers pigeon decoying, Max Hastings sings the praises of pheasant shooting, Jonathan Young of *The Field* puzzles over the trickiest shots imaginable, Will Garfit ends up in the hot seat on a partridge drive and Robin Scott of *Sporting Gun* relives his country past on a very special family shoot.

More than sixty contributors share their experiences of countless forays – from shooting grouse on the moors, ptarmigan on the tops, snipe in Ireland, woodcock in Norfolk and pinkfeet in Scotland to stalking red deer, fallow and roe wherever they roam.

THE GAME BOOK

A Shooting Anthology

Compiled by

CHRIS CATLIN

SWAN·HILL
PRESS

Copyright the individual contributors © 2007

First published in the UK in 2007
by Swan Hill Press, an imprint of Quiller Publishing Ltd

British Library Cataloguing-in-Publication Data
A catalogue record for this book
is available from the British Library

ISBN 978 1 84689 016 1

Design and typesetting by Paul Saunders

Printed in England by MPG Books Ltd, Bodmin, Cornwall.

Swan Hill Press
An imprint of Quiller Publishing Ltd

Wykey House, Wykey, Shrewsbury, SY4 1JA
Tel: 01939 261616 Fax: 01939 261606
E-mail: info@quillerbooks.com
Website: www.countrybooksdirect.com

The Game Book

Almost half a million people in Britain enjoy shooting game or other live quarry. Combine their numbers with the many thousands of clay pigeon shooters and you can see why shooting claims to attract more participators than just about any popular sport except golf or angling.

Shooters can draw on a wealth of sporting literature, which – as one of this book's contributors points out – tends to fall into two types: 'How to do it' and 'How it went'. Both are amply represented here, although I admit to preferring the sort of writing that even a seasoned enthusiast can appreciate, in reflective mood, after a good day's shooting. Hence the title of this book.

My hope is that *The Game Book* will appeal to anyone who has ever felt the urge to pick up a gun, call their dog and set out to shoot something for the pot, the game book, or both.

Here I must acknowledge a huge debt to that great shooting writer, Denys Watkins-Pitchford. It is now more than sixty years since 'B.B.', as he is popularly known, compiled *The Shooting Man's Bedside Book*, a classic selection of stories and articles that has inspired so many of today's shooting writers.

Like B.B. I aimed to collect some of the best contemporary writing about shooting in all its forms: game shooting, wildfowling, decoying, stalking and rough shooting. More than 60 writers and six sporting artists were approached – and every one of them agreed that all royalties from this book should be used to help more young people get to know our sport.

My thanks go to all the contributors, their publishers and our readers for supporting this initiative.

Chris Catlin

Lincolnshire, 2007

Acknowledgements

THE EDITOR WISHES to thank the publishers, editors and writers who gave permission for various articles and extracts to appear in this book.

He gratefully acknowledges the support and encouragement given by the editors of IPC's shooting magazines – Robin Scott of *Sporting Gun*, Jonathan Young of *The Field*, Camilla Clark of *Shooting Times* and Will Hetherington of *Shooting Gazette* – and by James Marchington of *Sporting Shooter* and Mike Barnes of *Fieldsports*.

Thanks and acknowledgements are due to Merlin Unwin Books for extracts from Laurence Catlow's *Private Thoughts from a Small Shoot*; to HarperCollins for an extract from *Country Fair* by Max Hastings; to *Gray's Sporting Journal* for Jonathan Young's article, *The Most Difficult Shot*; to Crowood Press, publishers of Lewis Potter's *The Art of Gunsmithing – The Shotgun*; and to Richard Shelton's publishers, Atlantic Books.

Contents

2 *Wildfowling*

5 *Shoots and Gamekeeping*

8 *History, Humour and Memories*

Illustrations

The Game Book features sketches by ASHLEY BOON, KEITH SYKES and
WILL GARFIT.

Other illustrations are taken from paintings by ASHLEY BOON, SIMON
TRINDER, BERRISFORD HILL and ELIZABETH HALSTEAD.

CHAPTER ONE

·

Game Shooting

Pheasant Memories

RICHARD BRIGHAM

DIRECTLY AUTUMN begins to sweep the countryside clean of its lingering summer lushness, my thoughts invariably drift back to some of my earliest game shooting days. Situated a few miles east of Norwich, the farm where my mother was raised was old-fashioned in the nicest way, unchanged by time, clean and 'green' long before the word became fashionable.

There was very little crop spraying, hedgerows and woods were managed sympathetically and vermin was kept in check. It all added up to a healthy environment for all forms of wildlife – including some very wild and challenging pheasants!

Getting there was not quite so idyllic; an early start was needed to beat the worst of the rush-hour traffic. True, there were far fewer cars in those long-lost days, but as I drove around Norwich, the unavoidable nose to tail crawl seemed to take forever.

Eventually, I would escape the early morning rat race, duck under the old railway bridge and thence to the familiar country road. Snakelike, it wound through sleepy villages where the pace of life became visibly slower. I always used these remaining miles to unwind before reaching the farmhouse on the hill, with its warm red-brick barns, outhouses, duck-pond and traditional country garden.

The pheasants, nearly all from wild stock, were tended by my Uncle Joe. He was quite happy to spend most of his time on the farm, and when not working was always to be found patrolling the fields and woods, a gun under his arm and a well-worn feeding bag slung across his back. Very little escaped his notice. He would scatter grain in strategic places, work a few traps and snares and keep a constant eye out for vermin.

The early morning chores completed, Joe would join my grandparents in the warmth of the kitchen to have breakfast and discuss plans for the day. Although invited, I was far too excited to even think of eating, my stomach already churning with the butterflies of anticipation. By the time breakfast was over, everyone had gathered in the stackyard and we loaded up, the tractors pulling the two carts belched smoke, and off we went for the first couple of drives.

The first job was to work out a maze of thick, berry-laden hedgerows, fresh plough and late stubble on undulating ground which led us across a gentle valley towards the Big Wood.

A covey or two of English partridges would always scream from the hilltop across the valley, hugging the contours and hedge-hopping before flaring skywards as they spotted the standing guns. Any stray pheasants would be rounded up from the remaining areas of rough scrub, thick hedges and bushy dykes, and pushed towards the wood. Its fifty-odd acres of managed woodland, besides providing all manner of timber for the farm, were good for three cracking pheasant drives.

As we faced the beaters on the first drive, which brought the boundary end back over a narrow ride, snap-shooting was the order of the day. Everything was pushed back to the heart of the wood ready for the two main drives before lunch. On several occasions I was lucky enough to draw one of the hot spots. And what spectacular shooting it was, with the approaching birds visible for a hundred yards or more! In the manner of truly wild pheasants, they would climb up through the towering beeches, hurtle out towards the line with whirring wings, and glide over us at their very highest.

Anything cleanly taken would fall far behind in that peculiar slow-motion way of the high bird, bouncing on the meadow grass with an audible thump. The drumming of wings, chortling of rising birds and shouts of 'Forward!' mixed with the tapping of sticks against the huge boles of oak, ash, chestnut, hornbeam and beech. As all these thrilling sounds rang through the trees they seemed to hang on the autumn air. Bags were never excessive, but the quality of the shooting was superb. It just wouldn't have been possible to take a bird too low.

Magic of this sort makes time fly, and all too soon it was lunchtime. With the sun already sneaking low across the sky, time was far too precious for second helpings before we headed out again to make the most of the short afternoon. Thick double hedges at the opposite end of the farm were worked towards another large wood, where the day reached its climax at The Plantation.

Its length bisected by a single ride, the plantation needed two drives to cover its long rectangle of mature woodland carpeted with heavy undergrowth. Waiting guns were stationed at the far end and well back along each side, while a couple of walking guns dropped off to cover anything breaking back. If all went well, everyone got some shooting.

One day I will always remember. Grandfather, well into his eighties, racked with arthritis and only just able to shoulder a gun, joined us for the final drive. On probation, I had been stationed on a hot corner beside him. I was lucky, and without wasting a cartridge managed to drop every one of the half-dozen birds that burst over me, including two left and rights. It was magical. As each bird crashed down on the fading stubble, out of the corner of my eye I could see the old boy smiling. And then, just before the end, a beautiful old cock came screaming over the ash tops. It was an effort for grandfather to shoulder the gun, but with a deft flick of his wrists he folded his bird, stone dead, directly overhead.

He was still smiling at the end of the day, content in the knowledge that he could still hold a gun straight. I like to flatter myself that the twinkle in his eye was also meant for a new generation of the family with the same passion for a sport which, sadly, he would soon be unable to pursue.

That was one of his very last pheasants, but I shall remember it always – a vivid picture of the old boy outlined against a weak November sun, stiff arms moving slowly but surely, taking the pheasant right under the chin with accustomed ease, as he had done so many times before.

Precious memories indeed!

Ballistic Pheasants

MIKE GEORGE

Is shooting high pheasants a science or an art? Having struggled with the ballistics of it all, I go for 'art' every time.

The fact is that you can construct a mathematical scenario for high pheasant shooting which takes into account the velocity and weight of the shot, the probable length of the shot string, the height of the target and, of course, its speed. You can then come up with what sounds like a magic formula.

It goes something like this … A good high-pheasant cartridge has a muzzle velocity of around 1,350 ft/sec. However, its average velocity over fifty yards is going to be nearer to 1,000 ft/sec and, by the time it arrives at a fifty-yard target, its velocity will have dropped to about 700 ft/sec. The shot string will be shaped like a flying sausage; through a full-choke barrel, the effective part of it will be about thirty inches across.

Here I am going to make an assumption that the length containing the really effective pellets will be about six feet, although there will be some faster and some slower, plus a few damaged flyers that might not make the target area at all.

Now for the bird. A really fast bird could, with the wind in its favour, be doing 60 mph. So during its time in the effective part of the shot cloud, it will have travelled a little more than nine inches. I must confess that a little 'guestimation' is involved. But Sir Gerald Burrard, who made practical experiments long ago, said that the distance travelled in the effective part of the shot cloud by a 40-mph bird at forty yards was about five inches.

This makes me think I am not far off, particularly as Burrard's findings were quoted unchallenged by the American experimenters, George Oberfell and Charles Thompson, who published a fascinating book on shotgun ballistics in 1960. Nor were they contradicted by the great British writer on shotgun technicalities, Gough Thomas.

Burrard and the American duo all said that shot string was not a major consideration when calculating lead. You should still get enough pellet strikes even if the pattern is not centred on the bird. At fifty yards through a full-choke barrel you should have 48 per cent of your pellets in your thirty-inch circle which, with $1\frac{1}{8}$ oz of No 6, will be 146 pellets.

With average luck, the vulnerable parts of your bird should be struck by at least four pellets, each with about 1.8 ft/lb of energy. That's well in excess of a lethal dose, so we could perhaps get away with a little more open choking, or a reduced shot charge, or a slightly less powerful cartridge. In theory, at any rate.

With all these figures we can also work out the lead, which would be about thirteen feet for a 60-mph bird, or about five cock pheasant lengths (beak to tip of tail feathers). We might also come to the dangerous conclusion that it would be difficult to miss!

Which is where a note of caution is needed from the redoubtable Sir Ralph Payne-Gallwey, Bart. His book, *High Pheasants – in Theory and Practice*, was first published in 1913 and still ranks as one of the classics on the subject. A new edition was published in 1996 by Tideline Books of Rhyl, North Wales.

Sir Ralph, an ingenious experimenter, went to extraordinary lengths to conduct his research including suspending targets from kites, sometimes with pheasants' skulls attached.

He concluded that there was a fair chance of killing an overhead pheasant with $1\frac{1}{16}$ oz of No 6 shot at a height of forty yards; practically no chance of killing at a height of fifty yards because the bird would rarely be hit by more than two pellets, and then with insufficient force to penetrate a vital part; and at sixty yards up no realistic chance at all.

His recommendations included using an ounce of No 7 shot, even for high birds, and taking them as an approaching shot rather than directly overhead. The best gun he ever saw, Sir Ralph tells us, always fired at high birds more in front of him than anyone else in the line.

His calculation of the correct lead for a 40-mph (or 60-ft/sec) pheasant was seven feet at thirty yards up, eight feet at thirty-five yards and nine feet at forty yards. But even then, he warned, it was impossible to measure feet and inches in the air in front of an overhead pheasant.

Of course, much of the theorising has another huge drawback. It assumes that the bird is flying a straight course, at a consistent speed, in still air. And no birds, high or low, ever do that. It also assumes that every cartridge-and-barrel combination patterns perfectly – and they don't.

The theory also takes no account of Sod's Law which, practical experience tells me, is one of the more important aspects of engineering and the physical sciences. For pheasant shots, in particular, it states that the moment you start thinking about the theory, you will be doomed to miss in practice. Perhaps that is what Sir Ralph Payne-Gallwey's crackshot friend had realised.

In a way, all this reinforces the idea that any shot taken at beyond forty yards with a 12-bore requires a tight choke, a powerful cartridge, and a high degree of judgment and skill by the shooter. With a 20-bore and a light load, the shooter has to be spot-on perfect every time.

Having twisted my brains with all the above, I finally found Burrard's tables and diagrams. He said that to kill a pheasant you need a pattern that puts an absolute minimum of 120 pellets with lethal velocity into a thirty-inch circle. Sounds easy, doesn't it? And so it is, until you have to master the art of placing that circle in just the right bit of sky!

Lucky Lapse

WILL GARFIT

You won't believe it, but yes, I left my gun at home again. I thought the lesson would have been learned a year or two ago when I turned up at the first shoot of the season and opened the back of the car, in which was no gun but my dog and a strimmer collected from the mower man on the way. 'Not very complimentary to your host's partridges,' laughed my mates.

On this occasion, a few miles from the shoot I looked over my shoulder. No gun on the back seat . . . panic! To return home would make me very late. I tried phoning my host but he'd left with no mobile.

Suddenly I had an idea and phoned Brian who helps keepering and is my right-hand man at Hauxton. Yes, he was still at home and yes, I could borrow a gun. I rally drove the ten minutes back to his house.

I rolled into the yard only five minutes late with apologies to my host who luckily was more amused than annoyed. The fellow guns on this smart shoot enquired as to whether my keeper's gun was a semi-auto in cammo colours. Luckily when I peeped in the slip it was Brian's old 30-inch Cogswell & Harrison side-by-side.

I was on the end of the line for the first drive. The main action was over the middle of the line but then a small group of redlegs came my way. I made a slow deliberate shot and the first bird flew into the pattern. I turned and took a second as it went out behind. It felt no pain. This gun was a joy to use and fitted me perfectly; at the end of the drive six birds were picked for as many shots.

On the second drive at number two I had one of the best pegs, being on the downwind end of the line. It was a long drive and partridges came from way back rising all the way as they approached the guns. The old Cogswell had a life of its own and jumped into action with

Exocet accuracy. We went sixteen straight before missing a high bird behind my neighbour.

I did not seem to do anything, the gun just knew where to go. The rest of the day I had a magic draw and was in the shooting. Those fellow guns who earlier laughed at my stupidity were becoming indignant at the injustice of the situation.

To have laughed all day at my missing with a borrowed gun would have been fun. However to find the gun shot better than my own and that I enjoyed a disproportionate amount of the sport each drive was not so funny. My neighbour's comment was: 'Are you going to offer your keeper a good price for it?'

The penultimate drive capped it all when out on the end of the line I was on the other side of an intersecting hedge. Normally the birds come over a tall hedge in front of the rest of the guns who stand well back. However that week the hedging contractor had misunderstood instructions and had flailed it down.

The result was the birds flew forward and banked downwind, out of shot of the line of guns who acted like flankers. The partridges then rose and came over the tall hedge on my right, which was the one that should have been cut low. A steady stream of partridges came in ones and twos and then rose to make great shooting for me. With embarrassment I appeared from behind my hedge at the end of the drive with two handfuls of birds and flanked by two beaters similarly laden.

At the end of such a good day Brian's old Cogswell had contributed an embarrassing ninety-nine birds of the total bag of 245 for the nine guns. So, a generous thanks to the keeper – and I may want to borrow his lucky gun again.

Ahead of the Game

SAM GRICE

No aspect of shotgun shooting fascinates and frustrates sportsmen quite so much as the question of forward allowance, or lead. Eavesdrop on any conversation at a clay stand, or after a game drive, and as often as not someone will be discussing how much lead the target should be given. And the chances are, there'll be no shortage of expert advice on the subject.

Defining 'lead' is easy. It means putting your shot string or cloud of pellets at the right distance ahead of a moving target. Everyone knows that the object of the exercise is to ensure that target and pellets meet.

It sounds easy, doesn't it? But by the time you've applied some tried and tested formula to work out the distance in yards, you've missed. You might just as well think of a number, divide it by your granny's birthday and add the date if there's an 'R' in the month. Everyone knows you must apply lead. The big question is: how do you do it effectively?

Basically there are five methods, along with variations and combinations. Some will work for you and others will not. My advice is to learn a sound basic technique on which you can build. You will then have something to fall back on if things start to go wrong.

Many shooters use a mixture of different methods without knowing what they are doing. When none of them work, they end up having a bad day. Their performance always tends to be patchy, largely because their technique is based on a hotchpotch of unrelated information and guesswork.

So, let's look at what is on offer.

- The Method: mount on the target and pull away in front.

- Swing Through: follow a 'smoke trail' from behind.

- Churchill: short and very fast mount and swing.

- Maintained Lead: the muzzle stays out ahead of the bird.

- Interception: an 'ambush' with no gun movement.

The Method

This is the basic style recommended by the Clay Pigeon Shooting Association (CPSA). It is an effective and simple technique on which novices can build. You mount the gun directly on to the bird, point straight at it and track it, then finally pull away in front of it before firing. The strength of this technique is that it provides accurate information on the target's line and speed relative to the shooter. However, if it is not executed correctly the gun can stop.

The key point to remember is that the gun, like the target, must keep moving. Once this has been learned successfully, a streamlined version can be adopted for game shooting. This involves mounting smack on the bird and pulling away without tracking. Timing and gun mount are crucial but this 'Mark Two' method really is excellent in the game field.

Swing Through

The gun starts behind the bird and is swung through the bird, firing when the correct lead is perceived. Simply imagine that the bird is emitting a smoke trail like a jet plane then swing along it and out the other side. The line of the bird is generally well established, so all you have to do is accelerate and swing through.

If you start well behind, you really will have to swing to catch up and get ahead. Sometimes it pays – if you are missing behind – to start a bit nearer the bird or even on the 'back edge'.

If you miss in front, you've swung too fast; if you miss behind, too slowly. To apply lead you have to swing at the correct speed. Trigger timing, too, is crucial. Fire too late, and you will miss in front; fire too soon and you will miss behind.

Coaches will tell you that 'lead pictures' vary from person to person – which is one of the reasons why recommending lead in terms of yards is counter-productive.

The Swing Through method is used with great success on driven and crossing birds. My main quibble is that it tends to be rather imprecise, mainly because muzzles and bird never move at the same speed. On a bad day the gun can be reduced to slashing desperately at the bird.

The Churchill Method

This method was just right for Robert Churchill's build – short, stocky and square – and his 25-inch XXV barrels. Short barrels are, of course, quick on and quick off, which is the essence of this style. The Churchill method is all about fast handling, fast mounting and fast shooting.

The swing and the mount really are very quick. It appears that you are shooting directly at the bird, leaving the very speed of the moving gun to achieve the lead.

The Churchill Method calls for a conscious swing on to the bird followed by what its originator called a 'subconscious' swing ahead. The left or leading hand is used very strongly to move, lift and direct the barrels. In his words: 'The hand must point the barrels at the bird throughout the process of lifting and mounting.'

Your gun must be a perfect fit to do this successfully. It requires a squarer stance than usual for overhead birds. The weight is placed on the left foot for birds on the left, and on the right for birds on the right. The body movement is firm and solid.

This style, when perfectly executed, can be quite devastating – but it doesn't suit everyone. Badly done, it can end in a prod and a poke some-where in the sky. Virtually no lead picture is perceived. And that can be a very real problem if you keep missing!

Maintained Lead

This can also be called a sustained lead. There are two starting methods. One is to start on the front of the bird, move in front and stay there, main-taining a measured distance ahead. The gun must move at the same speed as the bird.

The other is to start in front, measure off and stay in front as before. You need to have a good idea of the lead required for different targets, speeds and distances, but you will always see a moving gap. The result is that you feel well in control.

You may face problems with the line of flight and miss above or below, but on quick birds this method is very effective indeed – especially in a short window.

The advantage is that you can always 'plant' your pattern in front of the target. As the target never gets past your muzzles, it can rarely beat you. With practice, maintained lead produces a steady, measured shot which can create great confidence. The trick is to get in front, stay there and keep moving.

Interception

This is often known as the 'ambush' or 'chop 'im off' method. A snap shot is taken straight in front of the target with an almost static gun and virtually no swing.

An 'ambush' is very handy when there is little time to see the bird, say, in a hide with a very small window of sky. Perhaps this is why guns with inconsistent techniques always seem to be happier when shooting in woods. It is pretty instinctive and can be very successful in the right circumstances.

This is a technique to keep in reserve for a tight spot when the barrel movement is limited by trees and branches. Hares and rabbits, too, are often shot successfully this way. Lots of 'good ol' boys' use interception as a reactive method of applying lead. It is certainly short and straight to the point!

A word of warning on all the various methods: if you attempt all or several of them at once you are doomed to failure. I usually recommend The Method for starters and build from that. Eventually you will work out a successful style, provided you give it thought and practice. Consistency is all that is required. You may not kill them all, but you should kill most.

Proper Partridges

JONATHAN YOUNG

YOU KNOW WHERE you are with a shrunken pheasant or, to use its proper appellation, a modern partridge. The hill becomes alive with 'ay-ay-aying', 'hold on the left' and other general noises of assorted beaters and keepers. Then there's a burst of brown from the cover crop as the partridges play out their part and fly over the valley to the opposite hill.

Sometimes those little brown birds are surprisingly tall and we applaud politely (if inwardly gnashing) when one of our party despatches them with panache and only a little looking to right and left to make sure his neighbours have noticed the feat.

And then, at the end of the maize, kale or hemp (the rope type, not the smoking variety), the beaters flush the pheasants. They are so much bigger, so much slower, so much easier than the partridges. Except, as we all know, it's an illusion. The old pheasant motors, he curls, he dips – he's difficult.

And there lies the pleasure of the mixed day: you've just sorted out your swing and lead on one quarry when the game, literally, changes. And since I adore shooting in all its forms – ergo, I freely admit to loosing a barrel at a mullet earlier this season – my soul sings when invited to a pure 'shrunken pheasant' tall-partridge shoot of the sort that abounds in Dorset and other counties dangerously west.

But occasionally I get the call for a proper partridge shoot, of the sort our forebears described as manors before the phrase was hijacked by sinister men in south London with a penchant for lock-up garages and surgically-enhanced blondes. Here, the birds are shown over hedges: not any old hedges, but ones topped and lopped into a rough A-shape.

I had such a day in Lincolnshire a fortnight ago. As anyone who has tried it knows, it's a game that draws the nerves tighter than the denouement of *The Archers* on a Friday night.

The whistle for the drive begins and the gun immediately goes to the half-port. Nothing happens. You lower the gun to stand-easy. Then a couple of fieldfares spring up. Again the muzzles are readied. Again nothing happens. And then there's that wonderful sound of frantic flag flapping, up at half-port again and a blur of birds is showering, cascading, exploding over the hedge like brown fireworks.

At which point I used to do something so hopeless it makes my toes not so much curl as tie themselves in a full bow-line with a half-hitch for good measure. I used to ... (sorry, confessions are never easy) ... I used to consider my neighbours. A fatal mistake for your shooting, not for the partridges.

Shooting low partridges over hedges is best done in a three-second space. Unless the hedge is very high, shooting them as they first appear might involve skimming Mr Eley's finest chilled pellets over the heads of beaters. In ye olden days, beaters are reputed to have liked this sort of thing, especially if you were vaguely aristocratic and showered with sovereigns if a fustian rustic was added to the game-cart as 'walking wounded'. That reputation was probably due to the fact that *My Ways With A Partridge,* and other such Edwardian tomes detailing the forgiving nature of the pranged flanker, were written by the vaguely aristocratic and not by the old boy extracting half an ounce of pellets from his person. Today, that mythical spirit of bribed forgiveness has been replaced with a threatened thumping and a speed-dial to a damages lawyer.

So, you have to wait another second, in which time the partridges are high enough to kill safely and twenty-five to thirty yards out, so the shotgun pattern is at its best. With luck, you can then drop a pretty right-and-left to general huzzahs and cheering.

What you cannot do is hesitate and wait to see if said partridges are really going to continue heading towards you – thus becoming indisputably, legally, and morally yours – or whether they might have second thoughts, touch the tail rudder and swing more towards your neighbour to port or starboard.

That's why showering niceties on neighbours is such a heinous crime. Any dithering and the whole covey is over your heads, leaving the choice of smashing birds at close range (a real crime) or shooting behind, saluting them up the tail, and incurring the silent wrath of the picker-up behind who was a country mile to the left of the shot (and has moved forward, despite instructions) but still reckons you warrant a snotty look.

All of which most of us know in our hearts. Yet there are certain days – strange shoot, unknown guns, polished Labs – when you just don't have the confidence to get stuck in and be branded a poacher. Such a day happened last season and we shot, collectively, a cartridge-to-kill ratio that made the chances of winning the Lotto look two-to-one on. And we could all shoot! At least in theory.

Most of our fathers trotted out old proverbs which could be safely ignored but with this one they hit the mark with a perfect centre: he who hesitates is lost.

No such sin visited our Lincolnshire day. On the left was an old shooting mucker whose chief delight is stealing a bird just off my barrels – a pleasure only ever exceeded when I return the favour. He makes the Sundance Kid look as quick as cold porridge. On my right was a young Italian of gentle birth and high blood. He had never shot a driven partridge before but didn't seem the slouchy type. And so it proved.

Shooting in such company makes you shoot early – or you don't shoot at all – and the birds are nearly always killed cleanly in the head. And it's this type of partridge, shown over hedges and not as a mini-pheasant, that reveals the partridge as a truly glorious gamebird.

Pheasants

MAX HASTINGS

ONCE UPON A time the pheasant was an honoured bird, and not only by women who stuck its feathers in their hats. Until late Victorian times, sightings were uncommon enough for its gaudy plumage to rouse oohs and aahs. It remained less important, however, to country sport than its feathered brethren. Trollope's squires talked a lot about their partridges and grouse, rather less about their pheasants. Then came driven game shooting in the late nineteenth century. Sportsmen perceived the pheasant's utility. It is a heavy, lazy bird which accelerates upwards for a maximum of eight seconds, flies strongly for a while, then settles again. It is much more predictable and manageable than the grouse or partridge, does not stray far, and can be reared in large numbers.

When electric incubators succeeded broody hen coops, the pheasant entered the age of mass production. Today, we take it for granted. It has become a sporting commodity, sold by the hundred, shot by the million every season. The taste police tremble at the vulgarity of its colours. It employs the same couturier as the late Barbara Cartland. It is cursed with the silly eyes of a Church of England vicar cornered at a cocktail party and asked what he thinks about homosexuality. It makes the sort of parent who is always in trouble with Social Services. When it reaches the table my children revolt and say: 'Why can't we have chicken?'

That is the case for the prosecution. Yet stop a moment, and think where field sports would be today without the pheasant. Grouse are caviar, and cost about the same. The wild partridge has become an endangered species. His reared brethren are a joy to meet on a shooting day if they are flying high. But the pheasant has become the staple of English shooting sport – a supremely reliable, almost all-weather performer, at its best superbly exciting and testing. Grouse and partridges thrill us in coveys. We remember wonderful days, great drives. Yet the best pheasants stick in our memories as individuals, whether we hit or missed them. I think of a bird climbing on oxygen alone over the line, in Surrey of all places, twenty-five years ago. There were catcalls from my neighbours as it headed unerringly for me. I raised the gun conscious of forty-odd spectators, from the beaters to the pickers-up – and killed it. 'My money was on the pheasant,' said a friend sardonically, indeed almost crossly. But of course I was in heaven for five minutes. I haven't forgotten a detail of the occasion, even after all this time.

Likewise, painful details of a mirror incident in Wiltshire a decade later remain etched on my mind. I did not drop the bird. Assorted dukes, crack shots and celebs, none of whom I knew well, roared in delight. I was sure that I had touched that pheasant with the left barrel as it went away. Had I been granted licence, I would have spent an hour with my dog looking for it. I cared that much.

When packs of driven birds come over the guns, often they are visible only as shapes silhouetted against the sky. But to a rough shooter, each flushing pheasant represents a special moment to be cherished. In my twenties, I used to lope at a trot along Midlands hedges, a length behind my questing Labrador and two lengths behind a sprinting bird, praying that it would rise on my side and within shot. Say what you will, a low crossing pheasant at thirty yards is much more difficult than even a pretty high driven bird, especially if one is puffing and panting fit to burst. I seldom came home with more than one in the gamebag. Yet for me, that was cause enough for celebration.

Some people like to see pheasants in the garden. Those of us who cherish our borders would rather watch them feeding in the fields with the sun lighting up the cocks' colours, or mushing their tracks in fresh snow. When we lived in Ireland, where pheasants were rare things coveted by members of every local gun club, a roving shooter would follow a bird's marks all morning if he thought there was a chance of a shot. And if he caught the bird, he would more often stuff it than eat it. The shelves of our local taxidermist were lined with pheasants sent to be set up by proud sportsmen. Snipe and pigeon interested them very little. For a pheasant, however, they would ford streams, brave bogs and plunge through brambles.

Half a century ago, shooters used to say: 'Up goes a pound, bang goes sixpence, down comes half a crown.' Today, all those numbers have multiplied many times, save the last. Yet, measured against incomes, both live pheasants and cartridges have become much cheaper. And as for dead birds – we all see how many guns are unwilling to take their brace home. I preach the gospel of the casserole. It is the bones and sinews that can make a pheasant so tiresome on a plate. Braise it, carve the breasts free of every impediment, add cream, apple, celery, Madeira or Calvados, and return to the stove for a while. You have a dish fit for any dinner party, and you are doing your bit to preserve a vital principle of field sports, by eating what you kill.

The pheasant we all admire most is the one we never get to see over the guns, the bird Patrick Chalmers was thinking of when he wrote about the Christmas variety: 'A sage of fourth season, he knows the red reason/for sticks in the covert and "stops" in the strips/and back through the beaters he'll modestly slip.' Pheasants appear at their most winning when they squat looking nervously back over their shoulders, knowing they have been spotted. Then they scuttle away through the long grass with a low, creeping stride like that of Groucho Marx on an off day. Those are the ones which I hope get away, and usually do. Granted, the pheasant is a bit of a spiv. He lacks the honest yeoman qualities of the grey partridge, the Highland pedigree of a grouse. But our winter sporting days would be lost without him. Any shoot is the poorer that treats him simply as an industrial commodity.

All Aboard the Quail Bus

RICHARD PURDEY

OH FOR A POUND for every time I've been asked, 'Where's your favourite shoot?', or 'What sort of shooting do you like best?' I could have pocketed a small fortune! But for me, where shooting is concerned, variety is the spice of life. In eleven years as Chairman of James Purdey & Sons I was lucky enough to be invited to a wonderful variety of shoots, and in several different countries. Whilst comparisons may be odious, certain days do stand out, usually for no better reason than they were completely new, and probably once in a lifetime experiences.

One such unforgettable weekend was in February 2005, when an American friend and client flew my colleague Nigel Beaumont and me from Houston to South Texas, for two days all wild bob white quail hunting on his eight thousand acre ranch. We arrived in time for lunch on the Friday, after which we donned ranch issue day-glo orange hunting caps and vests, and suitably armed with the right make of 20-bore side by sides, sallied forth aboard the finest custom built hunting truck I'd ever seen. It was everything one would expect of Texas. It was b-i-g in every department, designed as the ultimate 'guns and dogs' bus, built to traverse the ranch's undulating tracks with everything man or dog could possibly need on a day's hunting, and with the ability to go off piste without getting bogged down in the prevailing soft sand of what was once Gulf of Mexico sea bed.

Mounted each side and ahead of the truck's flight deck-sized 'hood' were two jump seats. Nigel and I, having been deputed to shoot the first flush, sat on these. In the six-man cab rode the driver, and two dog handlers, one of whom was Steve, the ranch manager and equivalent of the head keeper, but looking and sounding for all the world like John Wayne! Steve was in radio communication with a pair of outriders, two ranch hands on horses, patrolling a mile or more away on either side of the truck to spot and report the movement of quail coveys

Behind the cab sat a block of ten steel cage dog kennels, four on each side and two facing aft. In each box, bursting with pent up energy and excitement, quivered six white pointers. 'All balls and muscle,' observed Nigel, accurately! Above the canine accommodation block, like a howdah atop an elephant, and reached by port and starboard ladders, was the observation deck, boasting an enormous sofa and two equally generously proportioned armchairs. In these, enjoying a panoramic view of the endless coarse grass and scrub, studded with mesquite bushes up to about 12 feet in height, sat our host and his son-in-law, waiting for us to show whether we could shoot a quail.

The truck ground its way along a track, dead straight as far as the eye could see, occasionally avoiding deep gouges in its surface. 'Feral hawgs,' said our host, 'do a lotta damage, though we trap and shoot plenty.' The upside of the wild pigs, it transpired, is that they enjoy rooting out and eating the rattlesnakes, another unwelcome and indigenous occupant of Texan ranches, and one which preys on quail, regardless of whether eggs, chicks or adults. In the relative cool of a February day, the snakes remained snugly below ground – thank God! 'You'all should come out these here parts October time if you wanna see some real big rattlers,' laughed Steve later, thoroughly enjoying my involuntary shudders!

Suddenly the truck veered off the track and we started to plough our way through tall grass, dodging the odd clumps of mesquite. We stopped, and Steve climbed out and lifted down two dogs from their kennels. The pointers started immediately to quarter the ground, frequently out of sight in the long grass, at times up to three hundred yards away before return-ing towards us. Nigel and I walked either side of Steve, guns loaded and ready. 'OK – we gotta point,' said Steve. We walked quietly up to the right-hand dog, which indeed stood in a classic point, stock still, a front paw raised, and the tail straight out, rigid with anticipation. Steve allowed the pointer forward. It moved two paces and stopped, on point again. Then, whatever it was that had alerted the dog had gone, and we walked on again, our breathing slowly returning to normal.

'He's on it agin,' said Steve, as the right-hand dog once more stood rigid just ten yards ahead of us. The pointer moved forward, nose pushing into the undergrowth, and whoomph! Out of their cover flushed eighteen quail, almost exploding into the air. Relatively tiny birds, a lot smaller than a partridge, the bob white quail is not only a fine flyer but a deservedly respected quarry. With whirring wings the covey dispersed in every direction. I shot at one on my right, twenty yards out and about twelve feet off the ground. I missed, then swung back to fire the left barrel at another straight out in front, which, much to my surprise in such an adrenalin-fuelled moment, dropped into almost waist high grass. Mean-time Nigel had bagged two with a nifty right and left to his left rear quarter. A good start makes all the difference to one's confidence!

The other dog handler now moved in for the retrieve, using our host's yellow Labrador bitch, both of them earning our admiration for having marked these birds so accurately in such long grass, finding all three swiftly and unerringly.

Now it was time for the guns to swap over and our host and his son-in-law took the jump seats. Nigel and I climbed to the howdah to enjoy our turn on the sofa watching these quail hunting veterans at work. We didn't have to wait long before a fresh pair of pointers put up a covey, and from our vantage point we saw how quickly both guns mounted and fired. Four shots and three birds. It didn't look hurried, but they were on to their quail far sooner than I had been. Then our host shot a lone quail which got up fifty yards in front of him. He hit it hard, it hesitated, then turned and flew a good hundred yards to the left and behind us before dropping dead into the grass. Once again the Labrador retrieved it, a great display of good teamwork by dog and handler.

Steve had heard from one of the outriders that three coveys were about a mile away from us in slightly more hilly terrain. All four guns rode the swaying howdah as our driver conned the truck as fast as he could to our new hunting ground.

During this interlude our host explained how he tried never to shoot more than three or four birds in a covey, and never shot at the same covey twice in a season if he could help it. This way coveys stayed intact and kept their territory, and with eight thousand acres to hunt there was the space to allow this careful rationing of the shooting. He went on to say how overgrazing was as much a curse of Texas quail country as it was for a grouse moor in the UK. His quail flourished, he said, because of good habitat management at the expense of more intensive grazing, and his investment in conservation measures, not least ensuring adequate supplies of water in a notably arid climate. Again we were able to appreciate just how much work, and cost, is involved behind the scenes to run a day's shooting.

Arriving at our new ground Nigel and I jumped down and retrieved our guns from their lockers as Steve brought on two fresh bird dogs from their kennels. This time Nigel took the right-hand side and I the left. We were walking up a dusty knoll when the left-hand dog suddenly pointed. Steve moved the pointer in and nine quail flew out from a grassy clump. This time I shot deliberately more aggressively and it worked. I downed two with two shots. Nigel also downed one, a nice shot on his right at a good height for quail, about twenty-five feet up. The retrievers went in, but of my first quail, which had dropped like a stone, there was no trace. 'Most likely gone down a hole,' said Steve. 'Tough little critters; you think you killed 'em, but when you go look for them they've run.' I hope it survived.

We moved further on, and the home team shot again with their usual efficiency, at a spectacular covey of twenty or more birds. Nigel and I then took over for the final flush of the day, shooting three more quail between us before the truck took us on the ten-minute journey back to the ranch house. The bag for our first afternoon was sixteen birds for thirty-five shots, with which our host pronounced himself delighted.

After a shower and a change of clothes we settled down for a great evening of good company, an excellent dinner assisting the easy flow of conversation, peppered with some improbable tales!

Over that weekend we came to see that quail hunting is not about big numbers, apart from the dollars required to own and run these wonderful conservation driven ranches, and that you don't have to shoot huge bags to have exciting and fulfilling days. The plight of the bob white quail is in many ways mirrored by that of the grey partridge. Changes in agricultural practice, use of chemical sprays reducing insect life, urban encroachment, even in Texas, are challenges to the ranch owner, and have motivated great conservation measures to save the bob white, and at least two generously funded chairs at separate universities in Texas are devoted to scientific research into quail and their habitats.

Pulling the trigger is but a tiny part of our sport: understanding our quarry, and how and why different shoots work the way they do, appreciating the work of so many others who make it happen, is in my opinion an altogether bigger and more satisfying part of our enjoyment. And after this experience I now see why Americans rave about quail as we enthuse about grouse!

The Early Bird

IAN MASON

THE PHONE RANG. His voice was clipped: 'Hello, Wilberforce here. Julian Wilberforce, Grouse Moor Owner's Charitable Trust … is that Ian Mason? We'd like to offer you a day on Wemmergill Moor. On the house, naturally… would the 12th be acceptable?'

Well, what do you dream about? Sadly for us paupers, grouse – like a lotto win – remain a sleep-time delusion. But still, September and October loom. Across the nation a groundswell of quiet preparation is underway. Breeks are being coaxed out of boxes and fusty bottom drawers. The more persistent of last season's burrs are teased away from tweed and a paint scraper taken to the largest clods of mud. A close inspection for moth damage and perhaps a trip to the dry cleaners? Perhaps not, they'll stand a few more days!

Then there's The Big Kit Hunt. Where did you stash those gloves, your 'lucky' pin feathers, hip flask, priest, gaiters, cartridge belt or favoured Tweed cap? Time also to bring a broad smile to the face of the manager of the local off-licence – the Wicker Liquor Basket needs fresh supplies of Shooter's Port, Famous Grouse, King's Ginger, and sloe gin.

There is also the cartridge question: the vexed issue of what to do with that rag bag of shells left over from the closing days of last season. Number 5s and 6s in every length and colour. Best use them up, but there again … why not splash out on a fresh thousand of the latest 'super load' from Hull or Gamebore?

It's also the time of year for many a marriage to hit the rocks. The wife is either sent packing – or she heads for the door anyway; the long-suffering and sainted woman realises that she cannot face another five months of an absent husband. On the rare occasions he does appear, he rolls home from the shoot supper with a gaggle of his *awful* friends (all *much* the worse for wear) along with half a game cart to be plucked, gutted and frozen. Cleaning his gun on the kitchen table *again* was the last straw!

So, assuming that kit is readied and The Memsahib placated – it's time to look forward to the shooting. In these pre-season weeks, I'm like a child on Christmas Eve. But I do have an admission to make; I enjoy my shooting a lot more once things have 'settled'. Let's face it, there are a host of potential pitfalls in the early weeks of the season.

First of all there's the weather. It's too warm and far too sunny (although the latter provides an excellent early season excuse for missing). Then there are all those pesky leaves. Autumn seems to come later every year. On well-wooded shoots just spotting the birds can be a challenge. Assuming you can see them, can you hit 'em? Those of you who have hacked away the cabinet's cobwebs to reach a shotgun that has not seen the light of day since February will face several problems. The gun is probably rusty and your swing almost certainly will be. The first few days in the field will be spent 'getting your eye in'. Perhaps it should be mandatory for all shooters to sharpen their skills with a few rounds of clays before heading for the covert? We owe our quarry an accurate shot and a clean kill.

Other skills may also atrophy during the game-free months. I break into a cold sweat on September 'partridge' days. It all stems from an unforgettable Saturday many years ago when I was a guest on a posh Kent shoot. On the first drive, the keeper blew his whistle and the birds came high and fast over a field of standing corn. I fixed a couple of quartering screamers on the edge of the 'covey' and was hugely satisfied to see my first two cartridges of the season rewarded with a right and left. They folded like a handclap and dropped sharply into the trees behind. My warm glow of self satisfaction faded rapidly when I noticed a crimson-faced gamekeeper heading down the line, propelled by those enormous strides only keepers and giraffes can manage. Huffing and puffing he fixed me in his sights. You've guessed it. My 'partridges' were young hen pheasants. My game recognition skills have improved, but the memory still haunts and brings a chill to early season days.

On much the same subject, August is an excellent month to make sure that the prescription in your shooting specs is bang up to date. Many times I've witnessed a fifty-plus gun peering skyward through lenses as thick as bottle bottoms, desperately trying resolve the 'partridge, pheasant' question. Alas, by the time brain has deciphered the fuzzy image and communicated the correct signal to trigger finger, the quarry is two fields away and still going strong.

Sadly, the earlier weeks of the season can also be the first opportunity for unsporting guns to flaunt their colours. These are men for whom restraint is an alien concept. Rather than leave October low 'uns to mature into sporting December or January birds, they blast away at anything with a leg off the ground. Fortunately, these people are few and far between, but it only takes one in the line to raise eyebrows and tempers. Restraint needs to be the watchword of the whole team during the season's opening days. With so many birds in the air, a bag can soon be filled with iffy flyers.

As September moves to October and smoke from bonfires shrouds the valleys, pheasants join partridges on the shooting menu. Marvellous – you no longer have to worry about dropping the wrong P. But where both species are put to wood, these 'mixed' days present their own challenge. Just when you've clinched the sight picture for one, along comes one of the other. It's like having midi or mini clays interspersed with dustbin lids. Still, if shooting was easy and the quarry predictable, where would the sport be? So, let's look on the bright side. It's time to get out, meet old friends, socialise, exercise, and if there are few blank pages left in your tattered game book, get ready to start filling them in.

The Most Difficult Shot

JONATHAN YOUNG

In the days when men who wore big moustaches were not, necessarily, friends of Dorothy, a London paper had a bright idea. The *Badminton Magazine* contacted the assorted marquesses, earls and Indian princes who had earned their spurs as the deadliest game-shots of their generation and asked them a simple question: what is the most difficult shot?

Today, some might consider the accolade goes to a jig of tequila, firmly strapped into a bandolier snaking round the minor foothills of a Brazilian go-go dancer. Indeed, I might have volunteered that one myself. But in April 1905 such things were unknown, proving that we have at least made some progress in the twenty-first century.

Our whiskery aristocracy gave their answers carefully.

Marquess of Granby – A genuinely 'tall' pheasant, 'sailing' with perfectly motionless wings, 'curling' and possibly dropping as well.

Earl de Grey – A high pheasant coming downwind with a drop and a curl.

Lord Walsingham – A bird which comes *straight* over your head at a moderate height, which for some reason (e.g. empty gun, thick wood in front) cannot be shot when approaching – you must then turn round and shoot under the bird.

Lord Ashburton – A pheasant, thirty-five to forty yards away, crossing and dropping with motionless wings.

Lord Westbury – Cock pheasant dropping with outstretched wings and curling away from the shooter.

Prince Victor Duleep Singh – A high dropping pheasant with the wind behind and wings practically motionless.

The Hon. A.E. Gathorne-Hardy – A pheasant which has come straight at you too low to shoot in front, and which you turn round to.

The Hon. Harry Stonor – A high cock pheasant flying down the line of guns with wings outstretched and motionless.

Major Acland Hood – A low partridge or pheasant on one's left.

Mr R.H. Rimington Wilson – Really high pheasants in a wind and with a curl.

Mr F.E.R. Fryer – A low, skimming pheasant against a dark background.

Mr R.G. Hargreaves –The second barrel at a flock of teal well on the wing. Ptarmigan driven round the top of a hill.

Mr T.S. Pearson Gregory – Pheasants coming down a hillside and skimming with a curl below. Driven grouse on a hilly country flying the same way.

Mr Arthur Portman – High pheasants floating off a hill with no apparent movement of the wing.

Mr W.H. Gilbey – A real, high pheasant with a curl on.

So, that's that. Most of our boys decided that the real test of a decent shot was the high, curling pheasant. If you could not deal with those, you had better retire from the lists, smelling vaguely of your mother's milk.

Do we agree? Well, their vote cannot be discounted lightly. Shooting was not a light-hearted game in Edwardian Britain; it was the epicentre of the social whirl. King Edward VII was a passionate participant in a travelling circus of shooting house parties. And he set a pretty unforgiving standard at his Norfolk seat at Sandringham. Arriving on Thursday and departing the following Monday, guests brought a retinue of personal servants, not least to carry the luggage. As well as guns, shooting sticks and cartridge magazines there were four dresses per day for ladies (obligatory changes for morning, luncheon, tea and dinner) and funny costumes for the evening's amateur theatricals. Presuming that one's valet had not had a hernia ferrying that lot into the Chinese Room (or whichever berth had been allocated), one would suppose that one's reward for all this rigmarole would be a decent encounter with his Majesty's game preserves.

Not so. At Sandringham and many other country houses, not all those invited made the cut to form the gun line. There you were, tweeds pressed, brogues polished, contemplating the brace of kippers at breakfast with no idea if you were to shoot that day or be reduced to polite handclapping and huzzahing as one of your rivals despatched the pheasants royal.

To avoid that ignominious support role, your gunnery had to be of the highest standard and there was no hiding from your cartridges-to-kills ratio. Not only were personal bags tallied meticulously (a practice still dominant in Spanish partridge shooting) but there would be, literally, a crowd of people watching your performance. So to earn that Olympian reputation as outstanding shots with views worthy of the *Badminton Magazine*, our heroes can safely be considered the Tiger Woods of their art.

Do we agree, though, with their choice? In the early twentieth century, shooting was a rather different affair. Our team were masters of the driven, native partridge, jingoistically called 'Englishmen' though branded in foreign climes the grey or Hungarian. Preserved from nature's redded tooth and beak on special shoots known as partridge manors, the English partridge were shown over hedges manicured into an A-shape. The game involved despatching your birds as far in front as possible as the covey burst over the hedges. Two guns were the norm and our heroes could kill four birds in as many seconds as regularly, and with as little fuss, as you and I pull on our socks. On grouse the old boys were equally deadly, knocking down neat doubles quicker than a Scottish gillie.

Tall pheasants were another business, as high-pheasant shoots were then relatively rare. Numbers, not quality, were the imperative. Shooting with triple guns was not unusual, and sometimes they used four. With two men acting as loaders, the Edwardians could lay down a rate of fire that would not embarrass an Apache helicopter. Anita Leslie, of Irish aristocratic birth, records in *Edwardians in Love*: 'I remember at one stand over 1500 head of pheasants were killed. Lord Howe, Lord Ripon, Harry Stonor, Bertie Willoughby and Bertie Tempest were at this stand and it really was most tiring work to shoot them; but with four guns apiece they brought down this enormous bag.' Prince Victor Duleep Singh reputedly had a party trick with low birds, placing his pattern so carefully that he took their heads clean off, leaving the remainder of the bodies unmarked. Birds have to be very close to pull off that stunt. Richard Purdey, chairman of the illustrious company bearing his moniker, has further proof that high pheasants were not the usual fare. His company records show that the vast majority of guns were ordered with 'plain' barrels; in other words they were bored true cylinder, devoid of any choke.

Today, the British shooting scene is very different. Bags are much smaller, with three hundred head considered a big day. The presentation of the birds has also changed. High-bird shoots are the fashion, and there are at least fifty shoots that can regularly show pheasants above forty yards. Our Edwardians could now encounter their bogey birds with dis-arming regularity. So, do modern shots share their forebears' view that the high, curling pheasant is the trickiest one in the book?

Well, I certainly do. At high-bird places like Stanage Park and Conholt I've been left standing on a carpet of empty cartridge cases with only a few lone birds to reward their expenditure. But the high-bird professors seem to manage them with ease. Wielding hefty over-and-unders, full choke in each barrel and spitting 34 gm of No 4s, these boys can nail those archangels with unnerving regularity. Yet place them in another situation and their frailty can be exposed.

Walked-up birds can be their undoing. The cock pheasant clattering from your feet and sailing low and fast across stubbles and scrub does not present many Americans with a problem. In the UK, gamekeepers and farmers can shoot them in their sleep. But they can reduce some of our driven-game specialists to a hissing fit. One of our very top shots was so shamed by a succession of six clean misses that he bolted home early, even forgoing his post-shoot cup of tea.

But if I were to put money on a bird beating the guns it would be a late-October grouse with a decent rain-laden gale behind it. Grouse butts are sensibly concealed in the folds of the moor, hiding the guns from grousey inspection. Which is brilliant until you climb into one that gives you a maximum of thirty yards visibility in front, the rest of the moor hidden behind a peaty hummock. A big, black pack of grouse then comes storm-ing over at 80 mph, giving you a couple of seconds at most. The results take some bravery to commit to paper. In one downwind drive last season, my host and I drew the hot spots and had wave after wave of grouse mate-rialise out of a sleeting rain and pour themselves between us. At the end of the drive he'd fired thirty-six cartridges, I'd loosed off thirty-three and we had exactly five birds down between us.

At the end of the drive and this ignominy, we both raised our caps to the birds and started laughing. We were still grinning like schoolboys when the head keeper drew up with a brace of springer spaniels, remarked that our end of the line had 'sounded like the opening day on the Somme' and asked where he should start gathering the slain.

When we confessed our appalling score, he grinned widely and told his employer, 'Well, sir, it's your job to beat the birds – and my job to get them to beat you!'

Some of my friends, who are numbered among the fifty best shots in Britain, would not have been beaten. In exactly the same situation, they would have shot at least one grouse for every three cartridges. But these lads shoot a minimum of a hundred days per season, starting on 12 August and finishing on 1 February. For them, nothing really counts as a difficult shot, which is why we curse them at every opportunity, sometimes to their face.

Of course we envy them both their ability and the number of occasions on which they have opportunity to prove it. Yet sitting in the bath, whisky-and-water to hand, would you really wish to change places with them? For us lesser mortals, it's the sporadic glimmering of form, the 'impossible bird' cleanly despatched, which make shooting the finest of sports. If the difficult shot no longer existed, wouldn't the appeal begin to pale?

That perhaps is too philosophical for us simple souls in tweeds. So let me propose an answer to the question, 'what is the most difficult shot?' that's more suited to late nights in pubs and emptied bottles of malt whisky.

It is, quite simply, the bird you have just missed, inexcusably and inescapably, with both barrels. And which every single one of your friends has seen.

Grousing About the Weather

JAMES MARCHINGTON

IT IS MIDDAY. That's three hours since we set off, filled with bacon, eggs and hope, for a day at driven grouse on Dufton Moor and two-and-a-half hours since we arrived at the stone shooting hut high on the Pennines above Appleby-in-Westmorland.

We are still in the hut, huddled against the chill wind and the haar it drives down your collar and up your sleeves. It's neither fog nor drizzle exactly, but something in-between – like being inside a cloud. That's because we are inside a cloud. At 2500 ft, Dufton is said to be the highest grouse moor in England. Unfortunately the cloudbase today is at 2100 ft.

We left the road at the picture-postcard Lakeland village of Dufton and battled the 4 x 4s four miles up the steep valley, bumping over football-sized boulders and slipping sideways in the mud. At the hut the guns jump out eager as Labradors, filling their pockets with cartridges. There is much excited chatter about the sport to come. 'How fast do they fly?' asks one gun who has never seen a grouse before. Estimates range from 50 to 100 mph and more, with the wind in their tails. Everyone agrees you should start mounting the gun when they appear, or they'll be past before you can fire.

Not today though. Visibility is down to forty yards. That's far enough to shoot, although probably not enough to see a grouse in time to mount and swing.

The guns are up for it. Some of them have driven three hundred miles for this. They've been looking forward to it for months. But the big worry is the beaters' safety. In this weather it would be all too easy for one of them to stray from the line. Being lost up here, in these conditions, isn't funny. So we wait, turning up our collars against the chill, cracking jokes and listening to tales of lions and buffalo.

At 11 o'clock Nigel Milsom breaks open the huge wicker lunch hamper and hands round hot soup and rolls. That and a couple of bottles of Merlot help lift flagging spirits. Nigel runs the very comfortable Tufton Arms Hotel down in Appleby, where we all stayed last night. He is our host up on the moor today too. His expression shows the pain he feels at not being able to provide the sport he'd planned for his guests. Normally he would be confident of a forty or fifty brace day, with good, sporting birds spread well across the line of butts. 'You feel uplifted just being here,' he says. 'The landscape is so high and majestic. The grouse are a bonus.'

Charlie Bull, *Sporting Shooter*'s cartridge expert, is one of the guns. He's been shooting here for years. He waves his hand towards the south. 'The view across here is fantastic.' We try to picture it.

Word goes round: Nigel has a cunning plan. We'll abandon the driven shoot, and try walking up instead. We pile into the vehicles and set off back down the hill. Graham, another gun, is nervous of scraping his shiny Range Rover on a rock, but also excited by the chance to try the Hill Descent feature. At 2000 ft we break through the cloud and gasp at the view – a glorious Lakeland landscape stretches before us, lit by golden winter sunshine. So that's what we've been missing.

Four hours have passed and we're back where we started, at the foot of the hill. It will be dark in three hours – and we still haven't seen a grouse.

Still, Nigel has his cunning plan. We follow him up an even steeper track with even larger boulders. 'People pay good money for off-roading like this,' someone quips. 'Am I too close to that rock?' asks Graham. We drive up into the cloud again. At the top, the guns line out at fifty-yard intervals and stride out across the tundra-like plain. You can barely see beyond the next gun. It's disorientating, but you keep walking and hope you're still in line. Suddenly a grouse calls. Silence, then a distant 'Pop, pop-pop'. Funny how the mist muffles the sound. Did they get one? 'Hold the line,' comes the call. No need, we'd already stopped.

'Walk on!' Yes, but did they get one? Talk about the fog of war.

Back at the vehicles we take stock. Three grouse and a woodcock. Not quite the day Nigel had been hoping for but the guns agree he's made the best of an impossible situation. No matter how well you plan, the weather has the last word. And there's always next year.

Bird of the Tops

MIKE BARNES

I WAS IN THE company of seven others – three keepers, four fellow guns – but slipping in and out of a lonely reverie of cross-examination and silent defence over the previous evening's intake. After nearly two hours of walking skywards out of a glen in deepest Aberdeenshire, bouts of doubt about my fitness punctuated the wonder of all that stood about me, moody and imperious, covered in heather whose bloom had long since passed its sell-by date. It was a grey day of damp and lifting wind. Yet truly magical. We were in the heart of the 40,000 acre Home beat of Invercauld estate.

Early conversation had dried as we moved in single file, head keeper John Cruickshanks leading the way at an apparently slower pace than the rest of us yet mysteriously fronting an ever-widening gap.

In the summer Andrew Dingwall-Fordyce had asked me if I fancied clambering up a mountain in pursuit of ptarmigan. For more years than I care to remember I have failed to keep a promise with myself to add ptarmigan to my ragbag of sporting exploits and this was the opportunity to put the matter right. The last Wednesday in September was the appointed day.

The travel arrangements however were not a success. Suffice to say that having made a previous glitch-free visit to Edinburgh by GNER I thought a repeat of the same with a hire car bolt-on would be a piece of cake. It wasn't. The call centre person (probably in a darkened room somewhere in the Punjab) said that the Avis car hire depot was near Waverley Station. Wrong. I then hit rush hour which was a complete nightmare.

However, I eventually broke free to emerge onto the M90 on the other side of the Forth Bridge, with Ballater in my sights. I would be late, but I could phone Hotel Glen Lui at Ballater with a revised schedule. Once clear of Blairgowrie the night descended but the traffic disappeared almost entirely. A string of glistening eyes moved out of my way as I crossed into Aberdeenshire, deer leaving the warmth of the tarmac to let me through.

On to Braemar and eventually the twinkling lights of Ballater beckoned and very soon I was parking my car at precisely the revised time of 9 p.m. So I was back on track – a good omen for what was to follow. Andrew was there waiting to meet me. Upstairs for a quick scrub and back down to a glass or two and then to the restaurant. Life was good.

At breakfast we were joined by fellow guns David and Jayne James-Duff, and Jamie Watson – and at around 9 o'clock we were parking our cars at Invercauld, where keepers John Cruickshank, John Fraser and Alistair Clark were waiting. As always, 'would it be cold on the tops?' I had forgotten my gaiters, but I had everything else and suffering the irritation of a few heather seeds would not be a new experience. Us guns all packed into Jamie's Discovery to follow the estate LWB Land Rover and its trailered Argo. Our bumpy ride coming to a halt in a small flat grassy area surrounded by steep rock. It could have been a car park created by nature – it was in fact the scene of alleged trysts of the old Laird, long since departed.

For us, this was the beginning, the start of our walk to eternity. We followed a path that shadowed a stream. There were steep bits, flatter bits, and everywhere rocks of every shape. Eventually the landscape opened out and we paused to look at the 'hill' which our guide explained held the ptarmigan.

We continued. The setting could not have been more breathtaking, the Highlands in all their moody glory. Absolute silence, but for the rushing streams and the occasional 'kow-ok-ok' of grouse taking to the air, some swinging majestically across the glen. It was stirring stuff.

An Argo appeared with our guns, and now we were armed for the remainder of the walk. As John explained our manoeuvre and moved us into formation, it gave us a chance for a breather, and the opportunity to steel ourselves for the serious bit. From here the gradual climb would get a little less gradual, and decidedly tricky underfoot. But we would be bagging the odd grouse on the way. The wind became stiffer, and we were walking into it.

The early discomfort from a heavy breakfast had long since gone, but was now replaced by a tightness in my chest (why did I have that cigar?), while my legs were being brutally honest about my age. But then 'kow-ok-ok' and a grouse swung round in front of the line from the right. I was in the middle and it hit the wind to curl back across me at a reasonable height, but at great velocity. I had jumped an earlier chance – this time I was more deliberate, collected the bird, and pushed well out in front. Its wings closed shut and it fell from the sky like a rock, drifting with the wind to the foot of the hill which dropped away steeply to my left. Aches and wheezes miraculously disappeared.

Moments like these are precious – John's lean black Lab hurtled across the heather to complete the retrieve. If only Jess had been there – but at nearly twelve, I explained to her, it would have been too much. She had not been impressed.

But now it was onwards and upwards. My fellow guns all had a shot or two, but there were absolutely no gifts. We were now getting higher and the wind was stronger. A combination of fatigue and concentration on footwork meant that quick, decisive gun mounting was all but impossible. The surroundings had changed. We were nearing the tops, all 2500 feet of them. The rock was now quite bare but for lichen as ptarmigan came into view. But more importantly we saw at least three big packs of them. Their bullfrog-like elongated croak eerily ringing out through the valley, cutting and carrying on the wind.

I had been told that the hardest part of ptarmigan shooting is getting there, that the birds actually sit tight and offer an easy walked-up shot. If that's the case then these boys were not playing game. Andrew, at the top of the hill, opened our account with just such an opportunity, efficiently despatched. But thereafter, with occasional exceptions, we just couldn't get near them.

John gathered us together to tell us that he had not seen them as wild, but, encouragingly, nor in such profusion. There were packs of twenty, thirty and more congregating, shifting in front of us. Our best opportunity, he explained, was to attempt to drive them.

We were by now standing on the side of the end of an elongated bowl, practically volcanic in structure. Incredible, grey, bare – just how did these birds inhabit such an inhospitable place?

The other more immediate wonder was seeing the three keepers practically dance down the side of the steep incline on which we have been allotted a spot for standing (departing at our peril!). They then all but skipped across the bowl floor, to skirt round the other side.

I stood, like my fellow guns I suspect, in a very precarious position, partly concealed by a huge boulder, but taking all of my weight on my left leg. There was a lengthy, welcome wait, but then it started.

Ptarmigan, and lots of them, coming on like little white missiles at Jayne and David, positioned to my left down the hill, the birds clinging to the contours in front of them. I watched as they were practically knocked flat by a pack that rushed at them, head height, dispersing behind them to melt into what was a truly spectacular setting.

More birds came – they were almost impossible, truly mesmerising. I tried a couple of shots and failed. They were very low and very fast – apart from their difficulty, there was the danger of falling, or shooting one another. I followed another pack over Jayne, one bird was closer to me and then as it passed between us it flared. I swung my gun instinctively through it, and as if by magic effected the cleanest of shots. But the very special bit of it all was the moment just prior to pulling the trigger. In a flash the picture of the ptarmigan banking across that backdrop was so perfect it purred. It was the very stuff that has so inspired sporting artists over the years. My day was complete when I collected the bird – it was well advanced into its coat of winter white.

More came. The later ones were high up the tops where Andrew took a spectacular shot. Soon the keepers were back with us. We could now gather and stand normally, retrieve our modest bag, and let the adrenalin subside. It was time for food and drink on the rocks, mission accomplished in a manner that none of us could have envisaged.

Presently we gathered ourselves for our downhill return to base. After crossing the floor of the bowl we were lined out on the other side. The unmistakable croak of ptarmigan was all about us, and as we picked our way over the rocks, my next gun right, Jamie, bagged three more with impressive economy, this time in conventional walk-up fashion.

I had another shot. Snatched and missed. It didn't matter. Then we were back in the heather, no more ptarmigan but the odd grouse. By now the light was weak and the air was wet. But 'go-back, go-back' and I had another grouse. My last shot of the day. A brace of grouse and a ptarmigan – I have never travelled so far to shoot so little and enjoy myself so much. We all enjoyed a similar return.

The walk back was no shorter than it had been in morning, but was largely downhill and we were fuelled by the remnants of the sheer exhilaration of what we had seen and enjoyed. There was the odd flypast from a distant grouse, and still the constant gurgle of the busy streams.

We returned to base and then down to the Inver Inn to relive it all over a 'small' one before bidding our farewell to the keepers and each other. Definitely accomplices in an unforgettable experience.

Have Guns, Will Travel

WILL GARFIT

As AUGUST GIVES way to September, we head north to the Highlands of Scotland. Our sporting motto is 'have guns, will travel' and for me this is easy. For my friend Barry, an Anglo-American globetrotter, it means another transatlantic flight. I have to acknowledge this as the essence of good delegation.

On Sunday evening we meet in the bar of the Muckrach Lodge Hotel in Morayshire, a convenient central location for our two-man disturbance of the peace on estates that have keepers who can put up with us and game that can't.

The exciting thing is that all sport at this time in the Highlands involves wild game. However, one of the many difficulties in organising a week of shooting is that wild game is seasonal in its success. This year we were to have started with two days of driven grouse but due to poor spring weather only one driven day was to take place. Our contact, Hugh, is a retired estate factor who has helped greatly in organising our grouse shooting and had kindly invited us to join his party of chums on the driven grouse day. The moor we shot was just as one dreams: great plateaux of heather in bloom, broken by steep gullies with burns of sparkling water, tinged gold with peat, racing over boulders and stones as if late for an appointment with the sea. All is surrounded by hills and with views of the Cairngorm mountains away to the east.

A flick of the skilled flanker's flag and a covey was turned towards the butts followed by a rattle of shots. A single old bird came like a bullet on the wind, a tilt of the wing and it jinked around a peat hag and through the butts unscathed. What was interesting was that there were either single old birds or good coveys of tens and twelves indicating that those that had hatched early had lost their broods but later hatches had got away well. A day of sixty brace had left us exhilarated and the adrenalin glands exhausted. We were late off the hill but the evening sun cast a wonderful glow on the glen below and our only regret of the day was not to stop and enjoy a dram as we inhaled that view.

Back at the Muckrach we were soon at the bar and ready for dinner. It is a hotel ideal for a sporting trip, being comfortable but not chintzy, and hospitable without pretence: good food, well cooked and served with friendly humour. At the end of the day there is a comfortable bed that one can roll into having tripped over your gun case – which once again is a reminder of the wonderful day.

Tuesday was again fine and we met Alan, the keeper, soon after 9 a.m. to walk grouse on the same estate. We drove miles up into the hills and the plan was to walk an area of the moor where on an earlier driving day they saw disappointingly few grouse. Alan and his young underkeeper went between us with their dogs and game bags. Conon, my golden retriever, and I took the left flank and Barry the right. Optimistically, it was arranged as a twenty brace day but that would normally have been for four or five walking guns. However, we soon started seeing grouse and in the thick heather they sat well enough for us to get within shot of rising birds. We soon had a few in the bag and, in fact, came across more good coveys than when the ground was driven earlier. By lunch time we had twelve brace laid out on the track as our game bags were emptied. A dram of McCallans all round and stories and banter flourished as we each ate our piece. Conon lay contented in the sun with his tail wagging. With Barry it was his tongue.

The sun was a joy, the breeze was stimulating and the air exhilarating. Barry was in very accurate form. He's not the fastest gun in the West but his over-under is heavily choked and he kills birds at great ranges. My style is more spontaneous as I am better at reaction shots than premeditated ones. It was a perfect day and our respective techniques again filled our bags in the afternoon. By 3 p.m. we ended back on the track and counted twenty-four and a half brace of grouse and a snipe. A truly wonderful day for two musketeers. We thanked Alan and his mate and bumped our way down the track from the moor. On the crest of the hill, before we dropped down into the glen below, we stopped and put right our failure of the previous day. The late afternoon sun and view across the Spey valley to the mountains in the east was even more special than before. Barry had a bottle of port. The view just got better and better!

Wednesday could have been a problem as it was the day our second driven grouse party was cancelled. However, Hugh had phoned a few of his factor friends and found another walking day was possible provided we were happy for a Canadian doctor to join us. Indeed we were and found that Alec was staying at our hotel so we had made friends before the day dawned.

Barry and I had been to this moor before and had a great day out with Ron the underkeeper. Ron had the long shaggy tweeds of any traditional highland keeper but the earring and hairstyle more commonly associated with New Age fans at the Glastonbury Festival. This year he had obviously come into contact with an Aussie contract sheep shearer, his long locks were away with the summer fleeces. He was still the warm character we remembered. Luckily Brian, his head keeper, was with us, so Ron's sense of humour that had walked us straight up a sheer mountain face last year was tempered and we set out across the flats.

Alec had not shot a grouse before and as his first bird was retrieved his camera was ready to record the moment. 'Click' went his camera and up from around his feet rose a large covey which disappeared over the skyline unchallenged. He shot well but the surprise element of walked-up grouse saved the stock being threatened. Twenty-two brace was our bag after another happy day. We had had a great variety of shots and felt we had earned each bird we had taken.

My Perfect Driven Day

LAURENCE CATLOW

IN DESCRIBING MY perfect driven day to you I shall start at the wrong end of it by considering first of all the perfect bag. I am well aware that every shooter, if asked his opinion on this subject, will come up with a different answer. Just a few men think that as many as possible is always best. The guns on the North Yorkshire shoot (where we shot 184 pheasants, one woodcock and one jay) were most certainly of this persuasion, but most of us, I fancy, believe that a day can bring too many birds. The biggest day in which I ever took part finished with 250 of them; they were very demanding birds and I relished making my modest contribution to so huge a total; but I do not want an enormous number of dead birds at the end of my perfect driven day: it seems to me that we can pull our triggers too often, and it is good, when looking back on a day's sport, to be able to remember every bird that fell to your gun. My perfect driven day would not see the death of two hundred pheasants; it would put more birds in the sky than I am used to seeing, and it would bring just over a hundred of them falling to the earth.

It will take place in early January, when birds are strong on the wing and flush less predictably. The pheasants, of course, will be fast and they will fly at a good height, but I do not want them all at the limit of range because, in that case, I shall hit very few of them and go home feeling miserable. Good, fast, hittable birds are what I want for my perfect day, with just a few of them heading for heaven and so offering the chance of a really memorable shot.

Pheasants fly best with a wind to help them on their way, and so my perfect day will have a stiff breeze blowing through it, with pale sunshine between broken cloud and no fear of rain. There will be frost on the fields, but the air will soften in the sun and by noon the ground, except under the trees and in the shadow of steep banks, will be yielding to my boot. I like a frost that grips and refuses to let go, but such weather is for rough shooting; it is weather for following an eager spaniel along the hedges rather than for shivering on the edge of a covert. My perfect day will be a day of little drives, nine or ten of them, and each drive will offer most of the eight guns three or four chances. We shall walk between stands and we shall be walking through a northern valley and through familiar countryside. Once or twice I shall find myself standing on the edge of a river that I fish during the trout season, so that, while waiting for the pheasants, I can light my pipe and think of trouting. In this way I shall see my shooting landscape in a deeper and a richer context, and I shall love it more.

Most of my fellow guns will already be friends, though it is always good to meet someone you do not know and to discover that your shooting thoughts are broadly similar. I shall be the only schoolmaster in the party, which will make tedious talk about education less likely to interfere with my pleasure. None of the guns, by the way, will have a beard. There will be ten minutes for comforts half-way through the morning, which will consist of damson or sloe gin rather than buckshot. We shall eat in the middle of the day, for, although on short winter days I appreciate the reason for shooting straight through, I prefer my lunch when there is still the prospect of more sport to follow. Let it be a simple meal, let it be a pie and a sandwich eaten in a barn with a generous dram to chase away the cold (I have, incidentally, just poured myself one). Whatever form lunch takes, it should not last much longer than three-quarters of an hour.

You will not be surprised to learn that my perfect driven day will find me on form, though I may shoot badly on the first drive and be doubly delighted thereafter to realise that I have rediscovered the knack of hitting pheasants. But, even if I shoot well throughout the day, a bird here and there will catch me unprepared, or be just too high or too fast for me since, in order to enjoy killing birds, I need to experience the disappointment of missing just a few of them. I shall shoot fifteen or sixteen pheasants on my perfect day, firing something like twenty-five cartridges. My last bird of the day will also be my best bird of the day; it will be a long way up in the sky where it will throw back its head and then descend to the earth like a feathered stone.

I am enjoying my perfect day so much that I am feeling tempted to pour myself another whisky and prolong the pleasure by adding on another drive or two, or perhaps an evening flight. On my perfect day, anyway, I shall have a dog sitting at my peg and it will not be Digby. Old Merlin will be there with me and, though most of the birds I shoot will be dead before they hit the ground, there will be a runner or two, so that Merlin can make light of his stiff joints, hunting my runners down and bringing them in to me.

I have forgotten woodcock, but there will certainly be a few of them. I shall be happy with just one to my gun, although I should be delighted to be given a couple to take home. At the end of the day we shall all declare that things could not have gone better; we shall stand round talking to the beaters about the day's drives and how well they managed them; we shall praise the keeper for the quality of the birds and for his expertise in showing them at their best. Deciding that it is time to go we shall slip him an appropriate tip; but then, unwilling to admit that it is all over, we shall linger by the vehicles and talk about shooting a little longer. One by one we shall drive off and, when at last I climb into the Land Rover, home will be no more than an hour away.

During the journey I shall realise that at last I have experienced the perfect driven day and that perfection demands my best claret. I shall ask myself whether there is still a bottle of Pichon Lalande '83 in my cellar and, when I get home, I shall discover that there is. I shall decant half of it into a half-bottle and cork it up, leaving the other half to settle and breathe while I lie in the bath and then faff around and write up the game book and then bring out the fillet steak. And the ending of this perfect day will itself be perfect if I can tell myself, while drinking a glass of Glenmorangie before going to bed, that tomorrow is another shooting day: not a driven day this time, but a day for bad Digby, a rough day along hedges and ditches, among rushes and brambles in search of snipe and woodcock and rabbits and the odd pheasant. And perhaps this day, too, will in its own way come close to perfection. And if it does excel itself and turn into a red-letter day of the rough-shooting sort, then there will be the second half of the Pichon Lalande waiting to honour it in the evening. I shall, of course, drink it whatever happens.

From Laurence Catlow's *Private Thoughts from a Small Shoot*

Dog Days

ROB HARDY

I HAVE ALWAYS felt there was something missing when shooting without a dog. It seems a less than whole experience. I miss the companionship during the day and feel short-changed after a successful shot if it is not rounded off with the bird being delivered back to hand. For me a gun, cartridges, boots and a dog are integral parts of the shooting day. I'd feel rather bare if I didn't have a dog at heel when walking to my peg or sitting in a hide.

I understand that not everyone gets as much pleasure from watching a dog work as they do from their shooting, but I can't help feeling that they are missing out on a large aspect of the sport. In some cases it may well be that they don't have the room or lifestyle to own a dog but talking to guns often reveals other reasons for the reluctance to use a dog.

By far the most common is that they have either owned or seen others with unruly dogs and this has soured their view. But life would be dull indeed if we gave up every pleasure after an initial poor performance! As with most things in life the effort put in directly equates to the results you will get out; it is for the individual to find the balance that is acceptable to them. Practice makes perfect.

One person will derive great joy from training a dog that will find and retrieve what they shoot, albeit in less than perfect style. Another will accept nothing but textbook handling. Neither is right or wrong as long as their approach does not affect the enjoyment of others. This point is worth more consideration because what is acceptable of your charge when you are shooting alone may not be the order of the day when in company.

Many rough shooters and wildfowlers do not mind if their dog runs in to shot, indeed they claim it is necessary to find all their birds. I have always considered this something of a cop-out. It's fine while they are shooting alone but the same dog is an infernal pest when they are shooting with others who are trying to keep their dogs steady and reward them with a retrieve.

You will gain no favour with the keeper if you are invited to a shoot and your dog takes off from the peg at the first shot and runs amok through the rest of the drive. So try to give a little thought to what you will be using your dog for – or may use it for in the future – when deciding on the level of its training. That said, even the best of dogs will always embarrass you at some point and it is as well to have a trick or two up your sleeve. I remember getting one such tip early in my dog training days. A particularly headstrong springer bitch of mine had just taken off in hot pursuit of a bird, and I was blowing my whistle and shouting fit to burst, none of which had the slightest effect. Just then the large, crimson-faced farmer next in line sidled over and said: 'You don't wanna be shouting like that, they'll all know yer dog's gone wrong. When yer dog does that, just shout "Get on, get on". Then they'll all think it's doing as yer told it.' I'd like to be able to say I've never needed to take his tip!

More vivid, though, are all the memories of the great retrieves of birds I thought I'd lose: the teal drifting out on a tidal river under the moon, or a goose that fell over the flood banking and the dog crossing two drains and a potato field to get to it, or the woodcock wedged halfway up a rhododendron bush with the dog sitting underneath waiting for me. These moments are what makes shooting with a dog really special and adds a whole new dimension to your sport. They also bring into stark contrast the need to shoot with a dog. Up to now I have concentrated on the pure pleasures of working a dog, that little extra they can add to the day. I have not touched on the ethics of shooting without one.

It largely depends on what type of shooting you do. If your shooting is largely on driven days where beaters and pickers-up are employed to gather shot and wounded game, then it is acceptable to shoot without a dog. Even on less formal days where you may stand and walk alternate drives you could get away without a dog if other guns have them. Even then you will not flush as much game from cover without a dog and other guns will soon tire of finding and retrieving all the game while you are getting all the shooting.

For any other type of shooting a dog is not just an aid, it is a necessity. To think about going wildfowling, roost shooting or rough shooting alone without having a dog is a downright disgrace, as you will simply not be able to retrieve all you shoot and that is unforgivable. You owe it to your quarry and to the good reputation of your sport to make every effort to retrieve what you shoot. If you cannot pick it up, then you should not be shooting. It's as simple as that.

Having extolled the virtues and the need to shoot with a dog I must redress the balance by saying you can also have too much of a good thing. Becoming 'over dogged' is an easy trap to fall into, especially if you enjoy the training and start to pick up and beat in preference to shooting. The problem is that unless you have unlimited time on your hands, having more dogs does not mean having better dogs. If you have a couple of well trained dogs, with time to lavish on them, they may well become the talk of the local shooting community. The same amount of training hours spread over four dogs will mean that corners are often cut, commands get less precise and the dog work becomes 'pack like' where birds are hoovered up rather than picked individually. You often see this on big commercial days when it is about numbers in the bag rather than the enjoyment of any particular shot or retrieve. At its worst it can degenerate to a level I witnessed a few years ago. I was shooting with Robin Scott, editor, friend and fellow contributor to this book. We had been invited on a day's rough shooting with a keeper on our way back from Wales. We just did not know how rough it would get!

We met the keeper at the designated spot and he took us to the bottom of a valley bordered by large beech woods. It all looked great. He explained that we would walk the lower slopes of the valley while he walked above with the dogs hoping to flush birds over us and provide some good shots. That sounded better still.

He then opened the back of his Land Rover and out poured a motley assortment of dogs: a couple of Labradors, one definite springer, a Chesapeake and several others that I can best describe as mixtures of them all. The dogs shot off up the valley and fanned out up through the trees in random fashion as we followed.

There was soon a clatter of wings and a hen pheasant curled over Robin which he folded stone dead. The hen had not even hit the valley floor below us when the 'wild bunch' as we christened them passed us on the track and hurtled off down hill after it. A Labrador was first to find the bird and did start to retrieve it before it was scragged by the

Chesapeake, which began to bring it back but swallowed it on the way. By the time it got back to the keeper all you could see of the hen pheasant was a foot sticking out of the side of the dog's mouth. The keeper didn't seem to notice the incident, while Robin and I exchanged unbelieving glances.

The 'wild bunch' took off back up the valley side, whooping like an Apache raiding party and soon produced another pheasant that soared overhead and fell to a Winchester Western cartridge. Very apt for this shoot, I felt.

Again the chase was on. Unbelievably a couple of the dogs had actually marked this bird, but neither wanted to give it up. The brief tug-of-war allowed the rest of the bunch to descend, and the bird was dismembered as we stood open-mouthed in disbelief. Not so much as a tail feather made it back from the next cock pheasant, so we decided we were not shooting to feed the dogs and made our excuses and left. It was an extreme case indeed, but does demonstrate that competition in the field can quickly ruin the best of dogs. The answer is not to let your dog get into such situations. Far better to put it on the lead or back in the car rather than allowing it to get dragged into a fight for every bird.

I've noticed over the seasons that the level of steadiness and general behaviour of a dog is more often than not directly linked to the character of the handler. Some guns always have a steady dog, and they are also the gun that always seems to have time to spare on every shot, sweeping bird after bird from the sky with unhurried ease. In contrast, the wild-eyed beast straining at a leash the size of a ship's rope is invariably partnered by the chap dancing between pegs, twisting himself into knots trying to shoot birds behind and fumbling cartridges from his cluttered pockets.

Unquestionably the best handlers are cool, calm operators that make every command crystal clear and have an unhurried knack of being in the right position to defuse a dangerous situation before it happens.

I hope I have at least gone some way towards encouraging those who have been teetering on the edge of gundog ownership to take the leap and discover the many joys that shooting with a gundog brings. There will be frustrations, and the odd harsh word, but I will guarantee that if you stick at it your time and energy will be repaid tenfold by the added fun, pride, loyalty and companionship that working your dog adds to a day's shooting. Just have your excuses at the ready!

The Island of Woodcock

BARRINGTON BARNES

THERE IS A LONG tradition of travelling to the Scottish islands for sporting shooting. One of its adherents was the late B.B., whose pseudonym initials my father, son and I all happen to share. This morning, though, I have little time for tradition as my son – known in our family as 'the General' – and I are to shoot the island's north shore and in my mind's eye I already see the braes and burns which we will hunt with our spaniels.

My springer spaniel, Brandy, has suspect stamina in the cold and wet so I feed him a warm milk and porridge breakfast, the remnants of which the little cocker, Lark, scoffs with gusto. For sure, the work of these two foot soldiers will underpin the success of our sport today.

A short drive to our starting point takes us round the north coast with the sea just a stone's throw from the track and several diminutive Hebridean islands in the distance. Time enough to admire the view when we have made some height. For now, we negotiate the stock fence and head up the hill. Almost at once we are climbing through a mature wood with magnificent beech, oak and other trees. I soon come to a burn, the banks of which become increasingly steep as we ascend.

The two spaniels meanwhile are raring to hunt but I keep Brandy at heel for now. The wood floor is mainly bare of cover and there is no need for him to waste his energy here.

Twenty minutes later I emerge out of the woodland at the second stock fence, beyond which is the prospect of the open hill. I wait until the General shows on my left and waves his intention of following an old dyke studded with stunted bushes and patches of bracken.

My own frontage features the upper reaches of the stream I have already mentioned, which now has a nice huntable bank on its east side and a grassy flat to the west. I elect to walk this side and set Brandy to hunt the bank.

If ever there was one, this is a place that speaks of woodcock; here in the discreet braes above the burn are numberless places for woodcock to rest. Out on the illimitable hill, where the wild black cattle roam, there is feeding aplenty. I carry my gun ready for instant action now, and I am already mounting it as the woodcock rises and flies low and directly away from me. A snap shot and it's down in a clump of reeds. I send Brandy at once and in seconds he is at the fall. My expectation reaches fever pitch as he feathers to the scent, and brings the mottled brown bird to hand in fine style.

I take a minute or two to admire this beautiful bird, my quarry, and smooth the ruffled feathers before stowing it carefully in my old game bag. Then with a wave to the General, who is now flanking way out on the higher ground, on some foray of his own, I push on up the burn.

Quite soon Brandy owns to another scent and returns several times to the bole of a stunted tree, but no bird rises. I hear a double report from my son's gun and then feel I am through the prime ground, being now too far out on the hill and too high for 'cock. Although I persist for another two hundred yards, there is no flush, and, leaving the burn, I work round the shoulder of the hill towards a patch of whins which look more promising. The General has spotted this too and signals that he will take a line downhill of the bushes.

I enter Brandy who goes in with relish and soon flushes a pair of 'cock. One slips out unsaluted but the other springs high like a teal and falls to a stylish shot from the General's gun. That's one each and a brace of woodcock by 11 o'clock.

Taking an impromptu break we enjoy the distinctive Hebridean sea view from 750 feet and I point out Mora Island where, it is said, two guns once accounted for over one hundred woodcock in a day. Enough said! For us ten would be a dream day.

Setting off again, we plan a rough route that will take us downhill through what looks like a snipe bog and then into some interesting scrub woodland which we can see on the rising ground the other side. The bog produces a single snipe which falls to my gun. As so often with snipe there are agonising moments of uncertainty before Brandy brings the morsel to me almost hidden in his mouth. This bird joins the woodcock in my bag.

In spite of the success with the snipe I am not sorry when I have completed the crossing of the bog as the walking is treacherous and the higher ground is altogether easier. Here there is much bracken, brown and half down now after the attentions of the winter frost and snow. This cover enables Brandy and Lark to demonstrate their best work and they turn out three or four 'cock, two of which go into the game bag, but in more than two shots.

With two couple of 'cock and the snipe we stop for our piece, with the General carefully selecting a sheltered spot on the hillside which gives a spectacular sea view. We have had a first rate morning and are well pleased with both our dogs and our shooting and there is sure to be more sport ahead.

As it happens, the afternoon disappoints. We tackle the expanses on the lower west end of the hill and find the cover on it to be too widespread for just the two of us. We try cherry-picking the most likely looking spots without any luck. Then the dogs, visibly tiring now, put up two woodcock in quick succession, when they are ranging out further than they should be. Our combined efforts result in one more cock. As we come off the hill, we look forward to a cup of tea before the flight.

This foray entails us climbing up the slopes yet again from sea level, and then taking up station on open rough grassland outside a forest block. I choose the lower position and, as the light fades, note that whilst I can see well enough on the downhill side, a woodcock uphill of my stand would soon be lost against the hillside background.

Meanwhile Brandy (shivering from a mixture of cold, fatigue and excitement) and I await the coming of the 'cock. If they flight tonight then they will flit out at last light. There, high on the hill, the night slowly strangles the dying day and it is good to wait, eyes straining to see the first woodcock. Time stands still on the timeless hillside and no birds are seen.

Then, like a ghost bird, a woodcock passes close by my left-hand (uphill) side and I snap a shot at it into the murk behind, and have no idea whether I have hit or missed. A minute later another flights high, wide and silently to my right. I stretch out over the void with a deliberate lead and shoot it. Stricken, it sets its wings and glides down into the rushes one hundred yards below me. That will be the devil to pick! A lull follows and then one more, a crosser this time which I kill cleanly in front, and then (as suddenly as it began) the flight is over and the pick-up begins.

Brandy picks the crosser quickly and then at my bidding hunts above and behind me for the first bird. It's dark now and I slip on a headlamp and encourage Brandy until, to my delight, he returns with my woodcock.

This leaves just the downhill bird and my son joins me – having completed his own pick-up with Lark – for this final search. Brandy is all in now but the younger bitch is still game for a search and, after working the reeds, pulls uphill several yards and makes a clever retrieve. Bless her!

Back by the seashore, we turn out our game bags and count the total for the day: eleven woodcock and the snipe. Five woodcock and one snipe are mine so Brandy and I have shot our share today. More important, the General and I are now two tired, happy men, with exhausted dogs, who have all enjoyed a red letter day in superlative surroundings.

Later, with the dogs long since fed and abed, we review the incidents of the day's sport over fireside drinks. We can recall each woodcock flushed, and sketch for each other cameos of our spaniels quartering the bracken and the whin. We hear again that thrilling rasp made by the 'cocks wings as they rise from cover. We dwell a while longer on our flight time, when the winter pale colours seeped out of the hill face and we took our last light chances with a mystic bird in a wild place.

Time enough for tradition now, and we remember B.B., that great lover of Scottish sporting shooting, and the good dogs with whom he and we share our triumphs and disappointments.

This most memorable day of ours has, we think, been in the tradition of the great man and glorious spaniels. And today, just like him during days gone by, we have enjoyed a secret island, entire unto ourselves; a winter place so beautiful that even torture would not compel us to say its name. Sleepily now, we raise our glasses to old B.B., champion of the spaniel and the rough shooter's friend.

Lovable Rogue

CHRIS CATLIN

THE WIFE OF ONE of the guns on my local syndicate kindly provides us with a midday snack. It's almost a shoot tradition for her to catch up with us in her van after the third or fourth drive, and her arrival is eagerly awaited. The couple have a farm near Melton Mowbray, so there's always a pork pie aboard – and usually plenty of freshly baked sausage rolls.

Usually, but not always. On one famous occasion the couple's chocolate Labrador, Fudge, intercepted the goodies while they were still cooling on the kitchen table. The way the good lady tells it, Fudge accounted for no fewer than fifteen of them before she could stop him.

'After that he just capsized and couldn't seem to get comfortable,' she recalls. 'It was the only satisfaction I had.'

Just about every Labrador owner has a similar tale to tell. It makes you wonder how this galumphing glutton, alias the Labrador retriever, has managed to weedle and wangle its way into so many dog owners' hearts. But there's no arguing with the statistics: some 36,000 Labs are registered with the Kennel Club each year, more than twice the numbers for the German shepherd, its nearest rival.

Maybe one of the reasons is the Lab's versatility. It's fair to say that since it first appeared in Britain as a ship's dog from Newfoundland, the Canadian province of which Labrador is part, the Lab has added more roles to its repertoire than the late Sir Laurence Olivier.

Guide dog for the blind, hearing dog for the deaf, drug detection dog, fetch-and-carry dog for the disabled, explosive-sniffing dog, search-and-rescue dog, the list goes on and on. And then, of course, as the Labrador Retriever Club reminds us all, there's the Lab's role as a 'loving and trustworthy companion'.

Now, Lab owners shouldn't get too sentimental about all this, but the Club may just have a point. Were those original ship's dogs selected for their ability to retrieve fish or ship's ropes from icy waters – or was it for their companionship?

After all, if you were stuck on a sailing ship from Newfoundland for weeks or months on end, would you take along a French poodle for company? Come to think of it, maybe that's why the French came adrift at Trafalgar.

Funnily enough, it was around the time of Nelson's victory that the Lab started to establish itself in a new British role, as a retriever of wildfowl and game.

In his 1814 book, *Advice to Young Sportsmen*, the celebrated wildfowler, Colonel Hawker, described the Labrador as by far the best dog for every kind of shooting. He went on: 'Their sense of smell is hardly to be credited (and) in finding wounded game there is not a living equal in the canine race.'

It was left to two other shooting enthusiasts of the time, the 2nd Earl of Malmesbury and the 5th Duke of Buccleuch, to pioneer the breed as a gundog.

Thereafter the Labrador gained enormously in strength and popularity. Early Kennel Club records show that in 1912, just 281 Labradors were registered. The total rose to 916 by 1922 and to 26,392 registrations by 1989. That made the Labrador Britain's most popular breed, a position it has held ever since.

Field trial success went hand in hand with the Labrador's growing popularity. Labradors secured their first field trial win in 1906 and gradually took over from curly coats and flatcoats, a breed that included golden retrievers until 1913. Since World War II a golden retriever has won the International Gundog League's Retriever Championship only three times; otherwise the honours have gone to Labradors.

Robin Wise, who chairs the Labrador Retriever Club (founded in 1916), is a field trial judge and enjoys taking her own Labs picking up. She and her husband, Douglas, a keen shot, live on a small farm on the upper reaches of the river Cam, where they keep horses and – no surprise – breed Labradors. If anyone does, Robin ought to know what makes the Labrador so special.

'I think the answer is that they have a wonderful temperament that allows you to use them for anything from family pet to working them in all kinds of roles,' she says. 'They fit in with your way of life.'

Indeed they do. To illustrate her claim, Robin singles out the role played by Canine Partners for Independence, which trains Labradors to help anyone in a wheelchair. They'll pick up their owner's mobile, fetch their coat or do anything they need to do.

'Labradors are very therapeutic for people who can't talk or who have had strokes. People get enormous pleasure from just stroking them.'

But wait a minute, aren't we forgetting the roguish Labrador we all know and love? Sure enough, the Wises have had one or two of those.

'Trouble was a wonderful dog and my husband's shadow,' Robin recalls. 'Her favourite trick was to jump up full-length and remove his cap.'

One day, on the eve of Douglas Wise's fortieth birthday, Trouble was left at home alone. People were coming to dinner next day and Robin was getting herself organised to go picking up. She had bought the biggest joint of beef of her life and left it thawing on top of the deep freeze. Big mistake.

'When I got back at five o'clock I found a large piece of butcher's brown paper – and one very fat Trouble who had thrown up on the floor. I can't say she was my best friend at that moment,' she says.

Not at that moment, perhaps – but again later, surely. With Labradors, that's usually the way it is ...

The Artful Dodger

RICHARD BRIGHAM

THE DRIVE IS almost over, the bulk of the pheasants have been flushed. As beaters tap out the last few yards of cover, an autumn-coloured bird bursts from amongst the dense brambles and fallen leaves. Like a flickering shadow it weaves among the twisted branches with a skill that bears testimony to its nickname of Timberdoodle.

'Woodcock!' Waiting guns tense as the cry echoes through the trees, eyes straining for the slightest movement from the edge of the wood. Wary beaters mentally note the stoutest tree trunk, nearest ditch or thickest patch of cover. Which way will the woodcock go? Where will it break out?

No bird is so shrouded in mystery, so unpredictable or so prized for its elusiveness. Nor, indeed, is there any bird more likely to test the etiquette and safety of the waiting guns. Able to provide the easiest or the most testing of shots, the woodcock can flit calmly over a line of guns like a giant autumn moth – or gyrate dizzily along the wood's edge to create mayhem amongst them.

On that rare occasion when a shooter has the chance of a left and right, a moment's lack of concentration can easily spell disaster: a cool head is every bit as important as good marksmanship.

A surprisingly fast mover on the ground, this subtly plumaged bird is seldom seen – even by the most ardent naturalist – unless it is actually put to flight. As a result, the woodcock's lifestyle and habits remain something of a mystery.

Migrant woodcock arrive mainly at night along our eastern shores from mid-October. Sometimes they come in huge numbers from across the North Sea, generally preferring the nights of a full moon in late October and November. This annual 'fall' of woodcock supplements the small resident breeding population.

The birds disperse widely to spend the short winter daylight hours lying unseen amongst damp areas of cover, moving to pastures and soft open ground at twilight to feed. Woodcocks gorge themselves before returning to roost at the first hint of dawn.

Apart from an odd insect or other invertebrate, they feed almost exclusively on earthworms. Whether of the long or short-billed variety, a thin woodcock is a rarity – even in severe weather conditions. Those that are underfed are almost certainly sick or injured.

Much prized as a trophy, the woodcock presents a difficult, at times virtually impossible, task for the taxidermist. The removal of a stubborn layer of fat combined with delicate skin and loosely rooted feathers will sometimes defeat even the most patient craftsman. In my opinion it is far better to eat such a delicacy, saving only the pin feathers for your hat band or for use as paintbrushes.

Mounted in a suitable handle, the stiff feather with flexible tip compares to a fine sable. It can prove invaluable for intricate watercolour work or scale tipping a mounted fish.

While most migrants head for pastures new by early spring, a handful of breeding birds will remain in favourable woodland. Very early on gentle spring mornings a strange frog-like croaking may be heard as the male, quartering his territory in confident, stiff-winged flight, carries out the 'roding' display to a normally unseen mate.

The sound carries quite a distance and resembles the creaking of an unoiled gate hinge. Returning from one or other of my local hostelries in the wee small hours, time and again I have been guided through the woods by that sound. As the treetops begin to reveal themselves against a brightening sky, and with some way to go to my bed, I always envy the woodcock's powers of flight!

You Can't Beat a Wet Patch

EDWIN OXLADE

JOKES ARE ALWAYS made about the rain in Ireland, where drizzle and showers are laughed off as just another 'soft day'. It's true that the country gets more of the stuff, on average, than most parts of Britain. Even in the north-east of the island, at the fringe of the rain belt, we get our fair share. And that can be good news for the shooting man: it means plenty of wet places and plenty of snipe.

A group of us took to meeting up each weekend throughout the season for a day's rough shooting. Mostly it was rabbits and, at that time, they were thick on the ground. Every patch of rushes held a rabbit or three and every bit of whin would produce a bolter as the dogs worked through it.

A day comes and someone – it is never me because this is not my patch and I consider myself a guest – decides that, for a change, we'll do the snipe spots. This means piling into one or two cars; then it's stop, all out and line up across a field that looks no different from all the others. But the ground soon becomes noticeably wet underfoot as it drops down towards a low spot.

Another few paces and the first snipe takes to the air with that unique alarm call that never fails to make me jump. It happens so quickly. More birds spring from cover. Shots are fired. In a moment it's all over. Retrieve the bag, back to the car and off to the next snipe hole.

We might make seven or eight stops, places where every year snipe gather, places that defy the best efforts of landowners and their deep ditches, gravel-filled trenches and clay pipes to dry them out.

These areas may be no bigger than someone's back room or they may be the size of a football pitch. Sometimes they are obvious bogs, fenced off to stop cattle straying into them and getting stuck: once we had to help rescue a bullock immersed up to within a few inches of its backbone in glutinous peat.

Bogs are best surrounded rather than walked through – the nearest we ever get to driven snipe, with the dogs splashing their way through the reed stems and willows. Occasionally there are whole fields, the ground so poorly drained that any part of them can hold snipe. The best spots usually have an inch or two of permanent surface water. If they didn't dry out in the summer they'd be called ponds.

There is no point lingering at any one spot. The snipe – there may be just one or two, sometimes none, or there could be two or three dozen – are usually away before you can reload. If we get one each we're doing well. A left and right is a feat to remember and recount in conversation for a good time after.

I am not a particularly good snipe shot but I've improved over the years to the point that snipe hold no fears for me. I don't rate them a particularly difficult shot compared to some I can think of. And I'm sure the problems attributed to the snipe's much proclaimed zig-zag flight are exaggerated.

Birds do usually bank sharply to right or left as they rise and they often change direction again before they really gain height. But it's more like a car on a winding road than a bouncing ball. Treat them like any other bird, remembering that their small size and the suddenness with which they appear gives them an illusion of being super-quick.

If there is a secret to shooting snipe consistently it's in firing at the most effective range, which for most guns is about twenty-five to thirty-five yards. If the snipe get up at that distance from you – and sometimes they can be very wild – then hit them as soon as they leave the ground. Or, if they sit tight and rise when you're almost on top of them, let them get well away from you. At forty yards a snipe may seem a mile distant but it's still very vulnerable to an ounce load of seven-and-a-halfs.

Watch a good snipe shot and what strikes you is the speed of their reactions. In a split second the gun is up and the bird is down. Ask him how he does it and he'll say: 'I just point the gun and shoot.' At least that's what my friend Nigel says and he's about the best snipe shot I've ever come across. Put him in a pigeon-hide, however, and he goes to pieces.

At the end of the day the bag is usually passed to me – I'm the only one who'll eat them. The Irish (and I don't include myself here, since I'm Irish by adoption only) are not adventurous in their eating habits for all their physical closeness to nature. But anyone who's ever lined up a row of fat plucked snipe on a baking tray in preparation for a real gastronomic treat will know what the others are missing. And they'll also understand why I'm always happy when someone suggests we 'do the snipe spots'.

CHAPTER TWO

·

Wildfowling

First Flight

LAURENCE CATLOW

JUST BEFORE THE end of the month I finally ran two boxes of bismuth cartridges to earth in Penrith. It cost me twenty-five pounds to get my hands on them, but I should have been willing to part with twice as much; for they meant that at last I could pay my first predatory visit of the season to the little flight pond that lies in the hollow of a field just over my boundary at High Park. I drove back to Sedbergh singing at the wheel of the Land Rover, singing and dreaming of mallard-shapes circling overhead in the deepening light, circling above me and then dropping down towards the water where I love to wait for them as the light fades. This singing and dreaming was on a Saturday afternoon; in the course of it I decided that, if things went to plan, the coming Tuesday would be the evening of my first flight.

Tuesday did not bring ideal conditions for flighting duck; it brought weather of a sort I much prefer, especially early in the season when duck are less wary and the wind is less important. Tuesday brought a very quiet evening, with grey light gathered beneath a ridged and furrowed cover of cloud. It was a soft, still evening with damp air, and the colours were gentle impressions of green and brown and yellow and grey; there were no sharp outlines. It was the sort of evening when the darkness comes as an almost imperceptible blurring and thickening of the light, seeping out of the moist earth and spreading itself very slowly round me, as I sit on an up-ended plastic bucket beneath a gnarled crab apple tree, sitting and smoking and waiting patiently for the first sound of wings.

Almost always I arrive far too early at my flight pond; it is a planned rather than an impatient sort of earliness, because the waiting is half the pleasure of it all: sitting there on my black bucket as the light fails, as pheasants disturb the mood of the evening and clatter noisily up to roost, as crows flock past on lazy wings towards their dormitories in the trees. On warm September evenings there are still midges dancing in the last light. Sometimes a young buzzard comes flapping into the pines behind me – temptation, if it comes to me, is virtuously resisted – and always there is a robin whistling very quietly somewhere along the line of the hedge. Now and then a pigeon passes overhead, and very slowly the sounds turn almost to silence, with only a faint stirring of the leaves above me and the ceaseless murmur of the sike behind. Somewhere a cow bellows; a roe deer barks in the wood, and all the time shapes grow dimmer and sink slowly into the rising darkness while, sitting there on my bucket beneath the leaves, sitting there with fallen crab apples all round my feet, I am absorbed into the hushed peace of the night.

It is this peace that draws me to flight ponds: the peace and the strangely complementary expectancy that fills it as I sit there waiting for the sound of wings. And the mood tightens to excitement as soon as that pulsing rhythm is heard beating invisibly in the darkening sky; and when sound turns into seeing, when those long-necked silhouettes are suddenly before me on their cupped wings, dropping purposefully towards the water, then for a second the excitement explodes and one or two shots ring out. There is to flighting a wider range of feeling than comes to any other form of shooting; to experience the full richness of it you must be there early. I was late on Tuesday and it was still wonderful.

The evening was already far gone when I came to Low Park Pond. I had been delayed at school and already there were duck, perhaps a dozen of them, feeding along the edges of the water. They flew off quacking and I settled down hurriedly on my bucket, settling Merlin beside me and comforting myself with the thought that he should still be able to come flighting with me when grown too old and too stiff for steep banks and thick stands of gorse. Pheasants were at roost and there was no sound from them. The air rustled faintly as the last black shapes of crows moved overhead. Duck should come only when the crows have found shelter in the trees; they should come only when the shooter begins to wonder whether they will come at all. Wild weather brings them sooner; they are often earlier at the beginning of the season and, if disturbed while feeding, they will often attempt a prompt return.

On Tuesday there was no time for quiet thoughts and tobacco among the fallen fruit. Suddenly, somewhere above the lazy flapping of the crows, I heard a more urgent and wheeling rhythm of wings, and mixed in with it was the nervous mutter of duck talk. They were certainly wary birds; they were surely the same birds that I had put off the pond only a few minutes ago; but the wide high circles became lower and narrower, while the sound of wings grew nearer and louder, until suddenly two shapes were planing down through the greyness, shapes with wide wings and broad bills and long necks; and then there were two shots and both shapes fell; and then Merlin bounded off to bring them both back to me.

I was in love with bismuth, for my first two shots with it had given me a right and left; very soon a dim shape crossed the far side of the pond; a third shot rang out; the shape folded and fell and Merlin had soon found it for me. By now I felt that I should never miss a duck again, until this delusion was blown away by a foolish shot at a high shape right above me, a shape that, if I had waited, would soon have turned into a much nearer though still sporting shape; it was a wild swipe through the sky, with over-hanging branches preventing a proper swing or a second barrel. It was a foolish shot and it persuaded me that three duck were enough for one evening; for, if I crept away while the mallard were still coming in, I should be able to think of another flight in as little as three weeks; and then, I promised myself, I should not arrive on the edge of darkness but at the first deepening of the light, ready to sit on my bucket and smoke my pipe while the shadows rose, while the pheasants shouted and the crows flapped to roost, ready to drink in the peace that is the prelude of the excitement to come.

So ended the season's first flight. The mallard have been plucked and stored in the freezer; they are plump birds and they will be honoured, at their eating, with a bottle of Clos l'Arlot '91. I shall drink a toast in their honour – you will have realised by now that I am addicted to little rituals of this sort – thanking them for the sweetness of their flesh, for the wonderful sound of their wings and for the sudden shape of them against a grey and darkening sky. I may announce to my guests that the way they reached my table was full of beauty, inspiring in the man who shot them a deep sense of gratitude for his presence and his place in the created world, and a deep thankfulness that he could find flesh for his belly in a manner that filled him with both peace and praise.

From Laurence Catlow's *Private Thoughts from a Small Shoot*

A Day in the Life of a Goose Guide

ALAN MURRAY

As a goose guide you meet people from all walks of life. They all have one common aim, to chase wild geese. I take a party of five per week. The week starts on Sunday evening when the 'fowlers' arrive. I go for a meeting at the hotel to welcome old friends, get to know new ones and introduce the uninitiated to my rules and regulations.

The discussions always revolve around guns, cartridges, how many geese are about, the bag the week before, the species and the weather. This lasts all evening until, weary from the journey and a few drams, my party heads for bed with my instructions for the morning. Usually they are showing the early symptoms of goose fever.

As I pass through the gates and up the drive leading to the hotel around half past five the following morning, I can see the dark shapes milling about at the back of cars, the red lights flickering amongst exhaust fumes, an odd dog trotting around. The week has begun. The convoy sets off, following me into the unknown.

The farm I have chosen for this first morning is high up in the Lomond Hills overlooking Loch Leven, a beautiful view of a major goose roost. When the cars are parked and the boys are ready, we carry out a final check. Have you got everything? Right, away we go.

On arrival at the chosen field I decide where to set up. I never commit myself to any particular place until I have seen the weather, wind and cover on that morning. Granted I know all my ground and I have a general idea or plan, but I like to leave this decision until the last minute. The geese taught me that.

The party has a cup of coffee and a chat whilst I set out the decoys. Some come and watch, trying to learn a bit and ask questions. I particularly like it when the young boys ask because if you cast them in the right mould then the geese and fowling will have a good future.

Next on the agenda is setting out the boys. I prefer ditches or walls whenever possible as I'm not a real believer in artificial hides. Natural cover is the best, the geese know these familiar sights.

This morning it's a ditch we're in. The guns are spread out at twenty-five-yard intervals. If there are any novices or young boys I like them nearest to me on the first couple of mornings. I don't allow the boys to shoot until I give the word, for two reasons: I know when the geese are in range; and we are shooting as a party and I want everybody to get a chance if possible.

Dawn is breaking now so the geese will be moving shortly and the first little parties in the half light are what I'm looking for. The wind is a fresh south-westerly and it's going to be a clear morning. Not my favourite conditions, but we have to make the best of what we get. For decoying we want a very still, hard frosty morning. Goose fever is running high.

We could hear the first geese – pinkfeet. Before they could be seen I started to call. This is the cue to keep your head down and lose yourself in the ditch side. The pinkfeet answered briefly and then all went quiet. I called again, nothing. Next a whoosh of wings and they were above us, four pinks not ten feet up, crossing the ditch. They came so suddenly none of the guns saw them.

'Get ready, boys!' The geese were going to bank round and do a wide arc right into the deeks. Sure enough they crossed the ditch a hundred yards up from us, swung to the left and came in across the front of the boys.

'Take them!' Six shots knocked out three and the last one started a panic climb but one solitary shot brought him down. Excellent, I thought, the geese came well, the guns kept their cool and shot straight. What a start to the week! It wasn't to last.

The geese were leaving the Loch in full force by the time we had picked up and got back to the ditch. Big skeins were stitching the morning sky in all directions, a beautiful sight from our vantage point on the side of the hill.

What happened next I can only put down to whiffling and the guns' reaction to the incredible sight of more than a thousand geese doing their aerobatics.

The big skein was heading up the hill towards us. I started to call and they come straight at us, saw the decoys, and began circling. The noise was deafening. Two geese landed in amongst the deeks. That was the signal for the guns to get ready. The boy next to me was shaking to such an extent I thought he was on his way out.

Geese fell from the sky, upside down, side slipping, the noise of air rushing through feathers, the calling and chattering was tremendous.

'Take 'em!'

How the boys heard me I don't know. Eight shots rang out, the geese put on their brakes, pinions creaking as they climbed away in seconds up to safety and back towards the loch, the clamouring fading as they went.

I saw two geese fall in amongst it all so I checked with the guns. They didn't really know how many had fallen, the two I had seen were amongst the decoys. A walk into the field, a search about, but no more were to be found. After much discussion between me and the rest of the party we were all of the same mind.

'How the hell did we miss?' Nobody was sure who had shot the two geese. As for the boy who didn't shoot, it was him by my side. His gun barrels were wafting about like an aerial in a gale – he just didn't know which bird to take – so he didn't bother and just watched. A good decision under the circumstances.

Six geese in the bag and the flight over, the sun was well up by now.

Back at the hotel it was a hearty breakfast while the flight was relived again and again. We went over all the details, right down to the mouse that ran over one of the gun's arms whilst he lay waiting. As for me, I was attacking my brace of kippers and thinking about evening flight.

Evening flight is just that. We flight the geese as they go back to the loch to roost. I try to position the guns a field away from where the geese are feeding and await their departure. One of the secrets to doing this is to be far enough away not to disturb a feed, yet close enough to have the geese over in range. I always tell the boys to leave the first lots as you will get a number of small groups leaving before the main lots. This is so you let some through unscathed and everyone gets a shot or two when the big skein leaves.

Tonight it wasn't to be. It was mild and still, the fresh south-westerly from morning had died away and the geese jumped and climbed and were well up before they got to us. It happens many times, so it's no good bleating. That's the magic of wild geese – the uncertainty.

The first day is over and was a good one. The party is in good spirits. No doubt we shall stop on the way home for a dram or two and a chinwag about the day's shooting, which is, after all, part of a goose-shooting holiday.

In Praise of Big Bores

RICHARD SHELTON

My LATE FATHER's career as a wildfowler began in the 1930s, flighting grey geese, duck and waders along the north coast of Norfolk. There he came in contact with some of the most experienced East Anglian fowlers of their day, including Alan Savory, Henry Aldridge and Sam Bone. Alan Savory is the best known nowadays, principally because of his skills as a writer of 'fowling articles and of the classic, *Norfolk Fowler*. Squadron Leader Aldridge was a close friend of Savory's and lives on in the latter's vivid writings. In his lifetime, 'Hoppy' Aldridge was best known for the fact that he had lost a leg in a flying accident before the war and after it for calling his fellow members of the Wells-next-the-Sea Town Council 'a bunch of lily-livered rats'. Old Sam was my father's favourite, a professional guide of the old school and a gentleman to his broad Norfolk fingertips. Long after the 'fowling careers of both were over, they would meet in the summer to relive the good old days before the grey geese left Wells (I am glad to say that the pinkfeet are now back in unprecedented numbers). One of Sam's last clients was a Catholic priest, well respected by his Bishop but something of an unknown quantity on the shore. A thick fog hung over the dawn foreshore as Sam placed his 'gun' and withdrew to the safety of the dunes. 'Bang, bang ... bang, bang' echoed repeatedly through the murk. The good Father was 'shooting strong', rather a surprise to Sam who had heard only one party of geese and those only Canadas from Holkham lake. Eventually the barrage died away and Sam, making use of the unconscious sense of direction for which he was famous, sought out the priest. He found him soon enough, surrounded by dead and dying gulls, and addressed him with the memorable words, 'Well Your Reverence, I daresay if your owld grannie 'ad a' 'ad feathers on you'd 'a' shot har as well.' There is no record of 'His Reverence's' reply but I do know that old Sam did not take him out again.

What united Sam and the other experienced Norfolk hands was that, when flighting wary geese on the foreshore, a good big gun would, in the right hands, easily outperform a smaller bore incapable of putting enough large shot into the air to kill geese cleanly at sixty yards or so. For many years, my father's favourite gun was a double hammer, bar action 10-bore (in reality a 9-bore) by the Scottish maker, Julius Coster. It was chambered for $3\frac{1}{4}$ inch cases made of thin brass and had all the power of an 8-bore. He shot his first grey goose with it (a whitefront) and many another afterwards. I never really knew that lovely old gun but I did know its sublime successor. It was an 8-bore by James Purdey. Only in its size and lack of ejectors did it differ from the elegant back-action hammer game guns favoured by celebrated guns like the Marquess of Ripon and King George V to make their great bags in the true heyday of formal shooting when 'corporate days' were unheard of and all game shot was valued as food. For the first time in my life I was aware of the indefinable 'presence' of a really large gun by a 'best' maker. The late Geoffrey Boothroyd compared the experience to standing at Paddington station in front of the gleaming King class locomotive at the head of *The Cornish Riviera Limited* express. Certainly the great Purdey was softly agleam on that dread day in the early 1950s when my father, only too aware that the grey geese had abandoned Wells and that brent were now protected, sold it to a fellow fowler for forty-five pounds! My last contact with the gun was its coloured photograph on the cover of the catalogue of a great auction house. It had a guide price of many thousands.

It was to be many years before I found myself on the foreshore, awaiting the 'fowl with a double 8-bore of my own. Anything more unlike the late lamented Purdey could not have been imagined. It had been made, probably at some time in the late 1860s or early 1870s, for or by H. Holland, the firm that would later achieve world renown as 'Holland & Holland'. That was the good news. The bad news was that both the barrels and the stock had been crudely shortened in the interests of conferring a degree of handiness on the old cannon, which still weighed well over fifteen pounds. A scruffy box of long green reloaded cartridges, loaded with black powder and God knows what shot, came with the gun. Sadly, the barrels were by now far too short for the slow-burning black powder to complete its combustion within the gun itself which, even in broad daylight, emitted a gout of orange flame over a foot long every time the trigger was pulled. Weak shooting was the inevitable result which, combined with the barn door patterns from the stubby true cylinder barrels, destroyed its capacity to hit hard at long range. However, its capacity to assault its owner would have done credit to Lennox Lewis, thanks to the fact that the sear of the left lock was so badly worn that firing the right barrel tended to jar off the second, a most disconcerting experience to one not expecting it and one that knocked me clean off my feet the first time it happened on the foreshore. Its one moment of glory was accounting for two cock wigeon with one shot during the hard winter of 1963. Not long afterwards my ever indulgent father passed on to me his hammerless 3¼ inch 10-bore by that renowned maker of large bore guns, J. & W. Tolley. Its spotless, thirty-two-inch Damascus barrels were choked full and full. It shot excellent even patterns and the following season I killed my first goose (a pinkfoot) with it. Needless to say, I had

no further use for the cruelly shortened Holland 8-bore. My dear wife who, being a child of Fife, has a far better head for business than I have, sold it for me while I was away on duty at sea. So great had been the fall in the value of the pound sterling that it fetched forty-five pounds, exactly the same sum as my father obtained for his incomparable Purdey.

One of the problems with the Tolley 10-bore was that it was no longer possible to buy the 3¼ inch cartridges for which it was built. I carried on reloading my tattered old paper cases for as long as I could but eventually was reduced to using shorter commercial cartridges which contained no more than a 3 inch 12-bore case. The Tolley shot well enough with them but it was frustrating to know that the splendid old gun was no longer able to develop its full power. Soon, the production of even these inferior loads was ended by Eley Kynoch and, for a time, the 10-bore saw little daylight. I was sorely tempted to have the chambers lengthened to take the 3½ inch American case but feared that, even if the altered gun passed proof, putting such a quart into a pint pot would one day crack the rather lightly built Anson & Deeley action. Fortunately the problem was solved for me by that great friend of the home loader, Mr. Ian Charlton, proprietor of Clay & Game Shotshell Reloaders. He was able to supply me with enough empty 3½ inch plastic cases to feed the 10-bore's appetite for many more seasons. All I had to do then was to cut the cases to size with an antique tool drawn from my small collection of shooting bygones, load up the cases with the right cocktail of primer, progressive powder, wads and shot (all kindly supplied by Ian) and look for the geese, secure in the knowledge that, for the first time for many years, the Tolley 10-bore at morning flight now had a sledgehammer in each chamber. Fruit was duly borne but not on the lavish scale first principles might have predicted.

The fact was that the 10-bore had by then been relegated to my 'fowling second division by the chance acquisition of a magnificent 8-bore by the same maker. It had led an active early life on the estuary of the Tay but for many years it had done no more than gather dust in a gun room replete with lighter game-shooting aristocrats. Unlike the 10-bore, it was a back-action hammer gun built not long after the application of choke boring to large bore guns had given J. & W. Tolley something of an edge over its competitors. It was also a little older than the 10-bore (Bill Harriman, Geoffrey Boothroyd and I estimated a likely build date around 1878) and not in such pristine condition – but its ability to pole-axe high geese and other distant 'fowl was impressive.

Hoodwinking the Pinks

IAN MASON

WE'D BEEN TOLD to keep our heads well down, so we did. Five of us, crouched still as statues behind a long camo blind, all resisting a powerful urge to sneak a look at the approaching skein of pink-footed geese.

Our patience was rewarded. Above the clamour of the pinks, the signal 'right lads' barked out and up we popped, guns slipping into shoulder. I momentarily froze; nothing, but nothing, had prepared me for this.

The sight and sound of pinks piling into the decoys, furiously back-pedalling, wings cupped, with a rate of descent that would put a skydiver to shame was a treat to witness. As the leaders flared, I picked a bird at the edge and swung. I missed behind but connected with the top barrel. My first pink thudded to earth thirty yards out.

Mind you – as with all wildfowling – the day had not been plain sailing. We were in twenty acres of stubble near Mintlaw, Aberdeenshire. Our mission was to field-test some new lightweight screen printed, flock coated, foam decoys.

Our decoys had been in place long before a watery dawn broke. A mixture of the new decoys, and older full-bodied or half-shell plastic decoys, had been scattered in two large groups with a gap in front of the guns to tempt in hungry pinks.

Our guide, local goose supremo Scott Cruickshank, was apprehensive: the early omens for the day had not been encouraging.

It was well after 9 a.m. before the first skeins appeared on the horizon. Scott had been drawing them in by blowing winks, honks and gabbles worthy of a Mercury Music Award.

The pinks were interested. They would approach and circle, but would not commit to the pattern. As they moved away, they were drawing following skeins with them.

Scott whipped out of the hide, had a look around, and took decisive action. The rising sun, although weak, was reflecting off the older plastic decoys. These were hurriedly pulled up and heaved over a hedge. Scott also decided that the gap between our camouflaged blind and the gorse to our rear was too wide. The hide poles were repositioned closer to the hedge and angled inwards so that we could tuck ourselves well under the lip and remain invisible to geese drifting beyond the decoys.

Payback was immediate and the next skein behaved as if house-trained. The combination of the decoys and Scott's wonderful rendition of aggravated honking and feeding gabble seemed irresistible.

Over the next hour we had some magnificent sport. Scott called a halt when the bag had reached eighteen, more than adequate for six guns, he told me. 'If people want to shoot big numbers I'm not their man. I think an absolute maximum of five birds per gun is right.'

He's concerned that some guides are tempted by offers from continental guns to shoot larger bags. 'We have to resist this. I have never been a "killing man" and never will be. All the geese we shoot get eaten; I've always been taught to shoot for the pot, and that's how it should be.'

'Some of these groups – especially the Italians – only stop shooting when the geese stop coming in. That's wrong, we should get the right bag, then get out and let the geese feed and feel comfortable. If you don't, they will not come back. If the geese go, there will be a lot of people unemployed – hotels, gunsmiths, shops, petrol stations . . . a lot of businesses up here depend on geese, not just the guides.'

He's right there. Across Scotland, guides accompany about four thousand clients each season bringing millions of pounds into the local economy. What makes Mintlaw a Mecca for goose shooters is The Loch of Strathbeg, nine miles down the coast between Peterhead and Fraserburgh. This RSPB reserve is where the geese roost at night. A quarter of the world's population of pinks visit the loch.

Around the time of our visit in mid-October up to 40,000 geese drop in: more than 24,000 have been sighted at the loch on a single day. About half will fly further south to Lancashire and Norfolk leaving the rest to winter in Aberdeenshire. The pinks arrive from Iceland in mid-September, greylags arrive about eight weeks later.

But, back to our day ... the decoys performed handsomely. For busy guides like Scott, lightweight decoys could be a boon because growing numbers of decoys, often fifty to 150, are needed to attract wary geese – especially later in the season when skeins have been shot a few times. This is where close cell foam decoys come into their own: light as a feather for carting to the stubble, but strong enough to weather the strongest wind once anchored with sturdy fibreglass legs.

Our trip to Scotland finished with an afternoon walking a bog for plover, snipe, duck and pheasant followed by a swift pint and then a moonlit flight pond to drop a wigeon I will never forget – but that's another story. It's a long way to Aberdeenshire for us Southerners, but goodness it's worth it!

Out for a Duck

FRANCES THEOBALD

I'M JUST AN old-fashioned girl, with an old-fashioned view of romance. So when my newly-acquired husband said he was going to show me a good time, my first thought, naturally, was what to wear. I had plumped for my little black number, just right for champagne by candlelight, when he cut me short.

What he actually had in mind was to introduce me to the joys of wild-fowling – and that meant thermal undies, warm jumper and wellies. One of our affectionate little discussions soon found the middle ground between a French bistro and a teal flight: I would accompany the old smoothie to a salt marsh, and on the way back we would pick up a Chinese takeaway and a bottle of Sainsbury's special. I don't come cheap, you know.

As we drove through the country lanes, I thought ahead to the duck. No, not Pete's wild and elusive variety but my crispy, aromatic one – with spring onion, pancakes and plum sauce. Why didn't I marry a chef who could disappear into the kitchen and emerge half an hour later with that kind of delicacy? Instead, I was heading for the back of beyond with a man who would vanish into the mud flats and return, an hour or so later, with just one, uncooked ingredient. Was he barmy, or was I?

We parked near the sea wall, collected our things and made our way to the edge of the creek. The tide was almost out, with just a trickle of sea water running down the middle. Out in the distance, sensible people in nice warm houses were starting to put on their lights. Maybe one or two were even taking out their chopsticks ...

Cold and hungry I might have been, but remarkably I also felt at peace. The wildfowl were making their way along the creek; the distinctive 'curlwee' call of a curlew echoed around the banks; duck wheeled high in the sky.

About twenty yards from where we stood there was a small island. That, said Pete, was the place to be. Looking at the mud we had to cross, I tried to persuade him otherwise. After all, I was just starting to appreciate the tranquillity right where I was. But I knew it was useless. Pete was displaying all the symptoms of MSD (male selective deafness).

Splaying his feet, he whisked up our things and skated effortlessly across the mud. 'Okay, your turn. Just keep going, don't stop.' Well, it all looked easy enough. I positioned my feet with toes out, heels in – and followed suit. I remember the ominous sucking noise as my boots got stuck and I lost my balance. Suddenly there was the taste of mud in my mouth.

I have to hand it to Pete: he mounted a pretty swift rescue operation. There was some muttering about not stopping, but otherwise he was all action. With a yank he pulled me clean out of my boots, and, with my feet flailing, he hoisted me over to the island. Gentleman to a fault, he even went back for my wellies.

Just a few minutes later, the teal started to come in. The big moment for Pete, but for me – a nightmare. This being my first encounter with darting, twilighty duck, I thought they were bats. And bats, I just can't stand them. Spiders in the bath, earwigs, snakes, mice, no problem, send 'em all my way. But bats, I just know they're heading straight for my hair.

This was a women-and-children-first situation, so I made to climb onto Pete's shoulders and across his back. He just had time to put his muddy hand across my mouth (yuck, that taste again). Quiet, he whispered: these are ducks, not bats.

Crouching back down, I watched as wigeon and teal suddenly materialised out of the dusk. It was like following a Battle of Britain dogfight. Pete was taking his shots calmly, reloading and shooting again, and again, and ... silence. It was as if a switch had been flicked on for a few moments, then off once more.

Pete retrieved the duck and carried them to the bank. As he steered me across, I just had time to glance back at our island: it probably hadn't changed in centuries, it was beyond technology. Now, in the darkness, I began to understand why Pete had headed there.

Despite our new-found rapport, I still had to remind the intrepid wildfowler to stop on the way home for our takeaway. He suggested tossing a coin to see who would go in and collect. As usual, I lost.

I sploshed over to the counter, avoiding eye contact as I placed our order. Yep, number twenty-eight, that's the one! Fortunately there was a free corner where I could be alone with my own, very special smell of the salt marsh. Other customers shrank away. But I could still smile, as I waited for our carrier bag, at the contrast between duck in a tinfoil box – and teal flickering in and out of the sunset.

Next time Pete said he wanted to show me a good time, I was ready for him in full battle dress and war paint: little black number, high heels, the works. And, right on cue, out he walked in boots and camo gear. So whose duck was it going to be this time?

Rainbow's End

MIKE SWAN

FEBRUARY ON the foreshore is a funny month. Given a cold snap, it can be vintage stuff, with lots of duck on the shore, and all of them in their very best breeding plumage. Usually it is just a damp squib. However, our representatives at BASC and in the other shooting organisations have rightly fought to retain the right for us to follow the wildfowl below high water mark in February. At least one pilgrimage to the coast is therefore essential, even if conditions are hopeless.

So it was that I set off to the Medway on 7 February a few years ago with my shooting friend and photographer, Paul Quagliana, on a trip that I had failed to deliver for far too long. Ever the professional, Paul brought his cameras, and I had to force him to bring a gun too.

My plan was a double one; a tide flight, and then back to the little dock at high tide, to tow the boat home for the summer and its annual clean up. To start, we would set a few decoys on a big creek, and hide in small side creeks, but the rising waters would wash us out of here about an hour and a half before high tide, when we would retreat to higher ground.

The tide reached the boat mooring about four hours before high water, and we set off down the creek to the main channel and then on out to the marsh, moving enough teal and wigeon to arouse cautious optimism on the way. When we arrived, I set Paul to work to build his hide, while I strung a dozen decoys across the creek.

We hardly saw a duck move in the next hour, and nothing came near us, despite a useful north-westerly breeze. With the tide now round our feet, it was time to make a move. So, we moved and I quickly set a few decoys for Paul, before setting up for myself about a hundred and twenty yards away. Back in my hide, with the boat stashed in the marsh grasses, I opened a beer, and settled to my bacon butty, while keeping a watch out across the main tideway. A shadow behind my right shoulder led me to look round in time to see a pair of mallard bearing down across the wind and out of the sun. Spinning round, I grabbed the gun and snatched a shot as they rocketed away behind my left side. The duck fell almost at my feet, but I wobbled rather and missed the drake.

In the commotion that followed several hundred duck lifted from the main channel, and a few headed our way. Keeping a low and careful watch, I concluded that a single cock wigeon would be our only offer, and shot it, regretting that there was nothing for Paul. But no, a high hen pintail that was coming between us turned over him, and he knocked it down in fine style. Yes! I punched the sky. Even if nothing more came, our trip was a success, and there were enough birds to send Paul home with the makings of a dinner party. As a bonus Paul's bird was a good blind retrieve for my young bitch, Lizzy. She took a little encouraging, but succeeded eventually, watched carefully by her mum from Paul's hide.

We had hardly settled back down when I spotted a few more birds approaching from across the main channel. This time it was Paul's turn from the start, as a fine cock pintail fell to his shot. Unfortunately, this one was a diver, and it fell far enough out into the tide that I decided to set off after it with the boat rather than give either of the dogs a long tail chase. By the time I had run the hundred yards to the boat, started the engine, and driven out there, the bird was about three hundred yards offshore.

With the pintail gathered, I motored back towards Paul to show him his prize. 'My first ever pintail!' he called as I bobbed about just offshore. Well actually no, it was his second, but I think he can be forgiven for not realising. Coming head-on wigeon and pintail hens are pretty similar, and not like any of the protected species that we expect on the shore.

For the next hour we had a steady trickle of birds, and as expected, there was a flurry of teal activity at around high water when the bulk of the marsh flooded. One particularly memorable moment came when two teal came past Paul low, from the north. They swung out over the main channel, then saw our decoys, and began to circle back, collecting up a third bird from out to the east. In a rare moment of straight shooting, I managed a right and left, leaving Paul with a rocketing third bird which he felled perfectly.

A little later, just as a squally shower came rolling in from the north-west, Paul dropped a teal in the marsh between us, which Crumble seemed to make no sense of. Fearing that it may have made the tide, I set off to join Paul in the search, running the dogs along the water's edge, and watching the tideway for any glimpse of a beak above the waves. Teal in particular seem to have an amazing ability to remain largely submerged, and snatch a breath when you cannot see. Just as I was about to give up, the dogs nailed it from under a clump of vegetation within a yard or so of where we had marked its fall. As I took the bird from Crumble, the sun broke through, and we were treated to a wonderful rainbow. By now the tide had turned too, and we enjoyed that wonderful moment when the newly washed marsh vegetation shines and glistens in the sun.

There was not much time left now, and we settled back in our hides for the last ten minutes, gathering another teal each, before I started to wind in first my decoys and then Paul's. Just as I got to his I spotted a low teal heading for him over the waves, and made myself as small as possible on the open marsh. I still don't know why he failed to get onto it, and then suddenly realised that it was coming in range of me. There was only one thing to do: shoot it and rub salt into the wound by saying, 'That's how it's done you know!' Here came another good lesson for Lizzy, who was watching the whole event from my hide. I left her there, and called Crumble, who was sitting much closer in Paul's hide and sent her to pick the bird. She showed exactly what she felt about being abandoned to the *Shooting Times* photographer, by delivering my teal and then going straight back to Paul. Maybe he was a bit freer in sharing his sandwiches than she has come to expect of me!

A few moments later we were in the boat and on our way home watching the avocets, that have become a winter feature of our marsh over the last few years, wheeling over their high tide roost and gleaming in the sun. Our final bag, of fifteen duck was way above my expectations of such a late season day and only goes to show that you can strike lucky if you stick with it.

Sport for All Seasons

WILL GARFIT

ONE EVENING NOT long ago my son, Henry, and I were fishing together on the Horseshoe Lake on my small reserve, shoot and fishery near home. It had been one of those rare and special evenings when the trout rose well and took the fly confidently. They fought like marlin in the cool, clear water, giving wonderful sport.

At the end of the day, as we admired the sparkling rainbows and a butter-flanked brownie, we recalled the evening just a few weeks earlier at the end of January when we had stood on the same spot and each shot a duck. I had put some friends in the hides on another nearby lake, which we feed in order to attract a few mallard for a shot or two at the end of a late season shooting day.

A group of five Canadas circled high as we watched and then flew lower over the lake where the guns were still awaiting the last of the duck. There was a barrage of shots and we were amazed to see four drop, then even more surprised to watch the fifth lone bird turn and fly straight towards us. We fired simultaneously and I could clearly see the double shudder of impact. Its head fell back and it landed with a big splash and was soon retrieved by Conon.

We continued to muse and realised that in little more than an acre we had a full season of sporting recollections. In summer we had so often fished into golden evenings until the swallows had had their fill and the bats arrived for their feast.

Henry learned to swim in the lake as a child and now dives from the fishing platform he helped me build. On hot balmy August days the water is warm enough for me to strip off and go for a swim. Any day of the year suits Conon but he enjoys those swims together when we do synchronised doggy paddle!

On Wednesdays the fishery is closed and in the light evenings Brian, my right-hand man of all things whether keepering, tree production or as bailiff of the fisheries, will come with me and Henry, if he is at home, and enjoy shooting rabbits.

They need to be controlled and it makes a good sporting safari with one acting as driver, the second as spotter and the third, with silenced .22 rifle, shooting from the vantage point with head and shoulders through the sunroof and a cushion as armrest on the roof. Usually a sure place for a shot is again on the bank of the Horseshoe Lake.

As summer turns to autumn we have had evenings when my old friend, John Humphreys, comes with rod and gun. We fish for end of season trout but, if the geese are heard approaching, we lay down the rods, load our guns and kneel in the rushes for a shot.

When things have gone well we return home with both a brace of trout and a goose – fish and fowl make a hearty meal from sport beside the same tuft of sedge. Last autumn two ospreys – one adult, one juvenile – visited on their migration south. They too showed how to catch the end of season trout.

Then, after all the rods and fishing gear have been hung up for the winter, the same stage makes a quick change and is set for the last drive of the shooting day. Numbered pegs have been placed on the outer grass curve of the Horseshoe Lake and guns await the pheasants which fly across the water having been driven from game crops grown way beyond the lake.

Those pheasants see the guns and climb to top the poplars which were planted soon after I made the lake in 1979. My vision was for them to grow to over a hundred feet tall and make pheasants to test even the most accurate of my friends.

These poplars are already sixty or seventy feet high, and even now, the pheasants make very acceptable sport. At the same time the duck fly from lake to lake and the guns need to keep a 360-degree watch, as while pheasants come from the front, the mallard may come from behind.

We do not get the hard winters now but it is the same lake on which the children learned to skate and we will again, I am sure, if Jack Frost returns one winter and the leather of my old skating boots has not become too hard.

February and March can also come up sporting trumps as the willows on the corner of the lake are a favourite pigeon roosting spot. Henry had a good flight there and some great shots in January and I went there in early March and tried setting out a dozen decoys on the grass beside the lake, in front of the willows. This worked surprisingly well and attracted other pigeons to fly over the willows where I waited. Conon retrieved from amongst the trees or from the lake itself and by dusk we had a bag of thirty.

As Henry and I made our way back to the hut to weigh our fish we agreed it was our favourite sporting spot in the world. All in all, this magic acre produces sport in every season and beauty on every day.

Geese

PHIL GRAY

Large, unploughed wheat stubbles had attracted a number of Canada geese to the farms around that of my friend H. On a very windy evening I hid among high rushes in a dyke at one end of a stubble. Some duck began to flight, lower than usual, into the southwest wind. Just before dusk, thirty geese came in high, over me. Turning back into the wind, they re-crossed the dyke half a mile back and pitched on the stubble.

I crept along the bottom of the dyke, now in water, now not, the vegetation catching at my ankles, causing me to stumble. At last I got within a hundred and fifty yards of the feeding geese and stayed at an angle so that if they jumped, they might fly my way. Also, any more coming to join them would have to come into the wind and so, somewhere near to my hiding place.

One skein came in from the southeast to pitch in with the main gaggle. Should I move? No, stay put. Then a faint call from the northeast caused me to turn – a dozen geese, in line abreast, approaching fast. I got right down in the cover. At first I thought they were going to pass wide, but for a change, when they drifted it was to bring them closer. Huge silhouettes – unmissable. I fired twice at the same bird and could not believe that it flew on. Then, as I watched through the glasses, it left the skein. All at once it towered straight up, up, up, then folded and plummeted to earth. I knew it was dead but it would soon be dark and I wanted to find it in the last light. As I began to climb out of the dyke, I spotted another skein approaching, almost on the same line. Down again and they were on me. This time I swung the gun faster as I fired. The goose I had selected flung back its neck, shut its great wings and thumped down onto the stubble.

I climbed out of the dyke to assist the dog and was amazed to find all the original geese still there. The wind had hidden the sound of my shots from them. Of course they jumped now, but I had to search for the other goose. Mij brought in a heavy Canada and then we set off on the line taken by the towered bird. We were a little off the line, but I spotted a grey and white shape a hundred yards away. Sure enough it lay there – neck under its body, wings half open, but it was not the Canada I had assumed it would be. I was delighted to find that it was the first greylag I had ever shot. I had had most other species of goose, so this was especially pleasing. Back at the dyke, I stayed until dark. The geese did not return, but I added a drake mallard to the bag in the very last of the light.

Towards the end of the month, I had gone to the Low Wash to wait for teal along the tidal river. The moon was almost full and at such times, there is often a movement of duck during the day. It was dead calm on a lovely autumn afternoon, as I settled into a butt I had created out of living willow. John Overend turned up to take up position near one of the ponds behind me. During the next couple of hours I shot three teal and missed another and a mallard.

In the late afternoon sun, two short-eared owls came hunting along the riverbank. I was standing in cover so tall that only my head showed above it. I was watching the owls, when a sparrowhawk came streaking along, skimming 'my' cover. It was within three feet before it saw me and flared off, giving a momentary glimpse of every feather. A close encounter indeed.

Dusk was a fiery, blood-red affair – the river looking like liquid gold. Twenty curlew with bubbling calls came over our ponds and then across the sunset – sharply defined silhouettes. A burst of wigeon whistles heralded the approach of a dozen or more of the 'fowler's favourite duck. They came high, straight along the river, falling like a shower of arrows to the ponds. Too high for me but John got a shot after their rapid descent.

One unexpected privilege resulting from the publication of my book, *The Washlanders*, is the new friends it has brought me. One such was Patrick Kearney. He called on me one September day and we fell so naturally into an entertaining afternoon of 'fowling talk, it was as if we had been friends for years. He invited me to shoot on the Cley marshes.

The first opportunity had arisen so I drove to Cley, arriving mid-morning. I had no trouble in finding the house, right on the coast road, a lovely rambling old Victorian place, with three dormer windows that looked out over the marshes. A wildfowler's dream home in fact. Indoors was just as good – books filling shelves in every room, stuffed wildfowl in most rooms and paintings by Patrick up the stairs – magnificent water-colours of old sailing and steam ships that ran into Cley in the days when it was still a small port.

About three quarters of an hour before dusk, we went out of the front door, straight onto the beach road which runs between the Cley fresh marshes, famous for its birds, on the right and the saltmarshes and channel into Blakeney Harbour on the left. At the end of the road is a car park just under a great shingle bank, which runs on for a mile or so in a long peninsular ending at Blakeney Point and which on its far side is pounded by the North Sea.

A lower sea bank protects the road from high tides from the saltmarsh side. We went over and walked along its base. Two companies of several hundred wigeon had flown over us to drop in to the sanctuary of the flooded fresh marshes. Patrick said, 'Oh. I'd better just say that guests aren't allowed to shoot until we get onto the marsh proper.' I saw some geese approaching and Patrick said, 'Looks like some brent coming.' Then, as the skein changed course on a line that would bring them over our heads, they called. 'Not brent, greylag!' said Patrick. 'Are *you* allowed to shoot along here?' I asked. With the reply in the affirmative, I added, 'Well, I should get loaded up, they're almost on us!' Too late to hide, we just stayed still. The skein began to climb, but still came over within forty yards. Patrick swung up his 16-bore and fired, but the geese flew on.

We crossed onto the marsh and followed the base of the shingle bank. Duck flighted over at intervals, but were very high.

One party of twenty pintail seemed lower – I missed them though and so did another gunner, who was hidden not far ahead. To keep out of the other chap's way, we waded across the hard sandy bottom of the main channel to the saltings on the other side and followed the channel out; halfway to a large humped dune that Patrick called 'The Hood'. There we split up, hiding in creeks a quarter of a mile apart.

The sun was gone and clouds were hurrying across the sky. Companies of wigeon could be seen passing overhead, but miles high. From all points of the compass came the occasional 'thud' of a shot, so some fowl must have been flying lower. Bang! – a shot from Patrick. Seconds later a duck came from his direction. It flew fast, low and swerving and proved much too good for me.

In the very last light, an arc of wigeon swung into the wind right over-head. This time my shot connected and the bird, obviously dead, was blown by the wind onto the far side of the channel. The water here was too deep to wade, so I waited for Patrick, whose footsteps I could hear splashing towards me. He led the way to the crossing point and once over, we worked our way back through the saltings with his torch. We never did find that duck, it could have been in any one of the creeks and gutters, which my friend clambered in and out of with remarkable agility for his seventy-two years.

After a sausage and mash supper, we sat drinking in front of a roaring fire of driftwood until one o'clock in the morning, during which time it transpired that Patrick had shot with my great uncle, Jack Cowling. I was shown some lovely old shooting books, letters from Peter Scott, concern-ing an occasion when Patrick shot with him from the East Lighthouse, at Sutton Bridge, and my host's own diaries from which I extracted records regarding Whittlesey Wash.

After breakfast the following morning, we took a walk along the shore to see the duck and brent geese on the Norfolk Naturalists' Trust's marshes and on the privately shot Pope's Marsh.

Over a last cup of coffee before I left, Patrick told me that for success-ful shooting here, a really strong east wind is almost a necessity ... he promised to telephone me when conditions were favourable.

Teal Appeal

CHRIS CATLIN

Some shooting memories stay with you for life.

It could be that first cock pheasant downed in full flight by an excited youngster armed only with a hand-me-down .410. Or the second barrel of a tricky right and left as the last two partridges of the season flare past you on different sides of your peg. Or it could be. . . .

Close your eyes and, if you have ever enjoyed so much as a day's shooting, you'll almost certainly be able to replay at least one unforgettable video clip from your personal archive.

Mine has a small party of teal materialising as if by magic out of the twilight to my right. They had to clear a belt of low trees before dipping down abruptly to land on one of the fish farm's ponds. I had time for only one shot and, more by good luck than good judgment, brought down the tail-ender.

Beyond the pond and trees, I could make out the twinkling lights of Tulkarm, a Palestinian town just across the border from Israel inside the occupied West Bank.

I was shooting with another newsman, an American-born Israeli, who had been telling me how his father used to take him duck shooting in Dakota. As we retrieved the teal, the chanting of the muezzin drifted across to us from the minaret of a Tulkarm mosque.

It was the first time I had had the chance of a teal, and yet it was the setting as much as the shot that has lodged in memory.

That was more than twenty years ago. The Israelis were pulling out of Lebanon – shades of the more recent past – and the whole country seemed to be breathing a sigh of relief.

At the shooting ground we used to frequent, near Caesaria, Jews and Arabs together enjoyed the challenge of breaking a few clays. Expatriates like me felt welcome there, as sportsmen do among fellow sportsmen. Times change ...

Fast forward to another evening flight, this time on farm ponds in Essex where I have waited for teal quite a few times in recent years.

Here the noises on the evening air come from the heavy traffic and the occasional airliner heading for Stansted. You have to listen hard to catch the characteristic 'tearing paper' sound of teal wings and strain your eyes to pick out the incoming duck against a darkening sky.

On a December evening, as we retrieved the bag by flashlight with the help of a couple of spaniels, we found that one of the teal drakes was carrying a foreign ring. It was stamped 'Gdansk, Poland', telling us the teal had travelled far more widely than the few miles from the local reservoir. Images of Lech Walesa and Poland's Solidarity free trade union sprang to mind. I pocketed the ring as a souvenir.

Later, a shooting friend suggested I could find out more by contacting the British Trust for Ornithology, an independent partnership of bird-watchers and professional ornithologists whose website encourages reporting on ring recoveries. I sent off an e-mail with the details of ring number PA09728 and waited.

It wasn't long before I heard back. It turned out that the teal was ringed as an adult six years earlier on the Slonsk Reserve, near Gorzow Wielkopolski, in western Poland, six hundred miles away from where it was shot. So the little drake was older than I thought, and it must have been a regular winter visitor to Britain.

According to Graham Appleton, the BTO's spokesman, more teal have been ringed than any other wildfowl species except mallard, so there was no shortage of recovery reports like mine. Shooters here and abroad retrieve hundreds of rings each year.

'We've had wildfowlers phoning up with ring details because they want to know how old the bird is and so how best to cook it,' Graham added with a smile.

Among the reports quoted by the Ringing Office was one from closer to home, reporting that a teal ringed in Texel, Holland, had been shot at Poringland, near Norwich.

Another teal ringed six years earlier by the Wildfowl and Wetlands Trust at Slimbridge, Gloucestershire, had been shot near the Finnish port city of Oulu. So these teal certainly get about.

Many thousands of recovery reports – from research organisations, ornithologists and birdwatchers as well as shooting enthusiasts – were pieced together to help compile *The Migration Atlas*, the Trust's encyclopaedic work on the subject published in 2002.

Taking teal as an example, the atlas estimates the resident British and Irish population at between 1900 and 3275 pairs, whereas at least 200,000 individual migrants winter here from breeding grounds that extend from Iceland through Scandinavia to northwest Siberia.

Some ring recoveries of teal and other migratory wildfowl are a story in their own right: like the pochard ringed at Martin Mere, Lancashire, and shot more than three years later, some 1700 miles away, near the Russian city of Orekhovo-Zuyevo, by a local wildfowler.

'The ringed duck (GN34484) was shot on 26 April 2005, one hundred and fifty kilometres from Moscow in a swampy area near the village of Khalturino during the spring hunting season,' he told the BTO by email.

'He died like a hero saving the lives of his comrades. His death was quick and easy. My Beretta is a merciful gun and my bitch Funny, a German short-haired pointer, never leaves trophies for foxes.'

I smiled when I read his message, a reminder that no matter where you shoot you'll find people who speak the same language. And I think I know the story that Russian wildfowler tells when he and his friends revive shooting memories over a bottle of vodka.

Wigeon Wonderland

RICHARD BRIGHAM

I T WAS A COUPLE of days before Christmas, and the weatherman had promised wintry weather: hail, high winds, sleet – and even snow!

For once he was right. During a rather sleepless night, I could hear something unpleasant hitting the window with each gathering gust. At 4 a.m. it was blowing a gale, and though still dark when I peered hopefully out of the bedroom window, the place was lit by a strange brightness – snow. What a day to be setting out after wildfowl on the windswept north Norfolk coast!

After a mug of tea I pulled on several layers of clothing, loaded up the truck, cleared the windscreen of powdery whiteness and set off, slipping and sliding along treacherous roads, with gusts of wind at times rocking the vehicle. The journey, cross-county, took almost an hour, but within a mile or two of the coast road the snow gradually began to peter out, and when I pulled up within a hundred yards of the marsh the ground had been completely cleared by the salty air. The wind showed no sign of abating and cut like a knife, but this was all to the good.

Six a.m., fantastic conditions – and wigeon whistling in the distance! I couldn't wait to get out there. My first taste of the elements always sets off an uncontrollable excitement, on what has become a yearly fowling pilgrimage to one of my favourite places on earth.

When the north wind bites – and bite it does! – it's hard to believe that in gentler mood in spring and summer, this self-same place plays host to nesting avocets, oystercatchers and bearded tits, and the sky is full of the endless and carefree drumming of snipe and 'peewitting' of green plovers. Bitterns skulk ghostlike amongst the growing Norfolk reed and warblers weave their fragile nests in its secret shadows, filling the air with a veritable orchestra of trilling and churring from dawn to dusk.

But then – comes winter! Balmy summer breezes are replaced by chill northerlies whipping straight in from the Arctic! As the summer shift flee southwards, the cries of fishing terns are replaced by the whistles, quacks, honks and growls of a growing army of wildfowl – legions of them – battling daily against the four winds that at times threaten to blow them back out with the tide.

Four hundred yards to go. Laden with gun, cartridges and a bag of decoys, it was not all plain sailing across the flooded marsh. With just the stars and a lazy crescent moon to guide me, I saw reflections in splashes of water that were certainly not there on my last autumn visit. To add to the urgency I could hear wigeon moving, besides the anxious flute-like piping of teal and golden plovers, and the chatter of mallard. Once, barely audible, the wild, far-off cries of pinkfeet rang out above the distant pounding of breakers on the windswept shore. What a place!

Almost there! Just as I spotted the hide marooned in several inches of water a small pack of pinkfeet took to the air, completely unseen, sounding less than a hundred yards. Their calls quickly faded upwind into the distance.

Reaching the hide, it was a relief to find that the sunken barrel, still covered by a sheet of tin, was bone dry inside. The gear was quickly stowed, the decoys set: a few wigeon tethered to half-pound weights to the front, slightly upwind, and a little fleet of teal to one side.

It took ages to get light. Slipping a couple of cartridges into the breech,

I crouched snugly in the tub, scanning the skies for any sign of movement. I could hear duck moving all around – some directly overhead – but apart from brief, tantalising glimpses against stormy clouds, nothing gave time for a shot. Struggling against a strong northerly, little bunches of wigeon came in low, splashing down without offering a chance.

Gradually the light improved. Another pair flickered in across a break in the clouds, hanging briefly against the first light of dawn – a chance! The first shot dropped the leading bird, the second taken as it towered upwards and levelled out, neck stretched forward, almost stationary in the wind. Both splashed heavily and lay belly up in the water.

The surrounding marsh erupted fowl, mainly wigeon and teal, but in the light patch there was barely time to mount the gun before each had passed and was lost in the blackness. Several sizzled over just above head height, some so close that I could hear the wind tearing through their pinions.

After the initial disturbance, duck began streaming back in, approaching at a nice height, but dropping to water level as soon as they arrived – far too low to get a sporting shot from my position. I decided to move.

This was more like it. Crouching beside a screen of reeds just sufficient to break my outline, I got a couple of single wigeon as they banked to come in. I completely missed a teal that whizzed past like a bullet from behind, but recovered by adding a nice double from a small pack of wigeon battling against the wind.

As the sky suddenly flooded with light, wigeon began decoying well, though the decoys bobbed about like corks on the choppy water. Returning to the top hide, I picked the fallen birds en route, and also discovered a deeper channel, well over the top of my boots. Both were brimming with icy water, but I hardly noticed it.

As the sun rose and gained in strength, the skies evolved into the most gorgeous mixture of blues, pinks and pastel greys, and that wonderfully weird brown clarity typical of the place – indescribably beautiful. There was even a brief rainbow as a sudden hail shower pelted the marsh like falling shot, stinging my face and forcing me to cower in the barrel, revelling in and totally bewitched by the wildness of it all.

And then the wigeon went mad! At first, ones and twos and odd half-dozens. Moved by a rising tide from their far-off roosting ground, they blew in from behind, sweeping past, kiting in a wide arc and whiffling down towards the decoys. Approaching with the wind in their tails, the sound of shots was blown away, giving no warning to those behind. Picking my shots, I soon had at least another dozen down, but with conditions weighted so heavily in my favour and birds by now almost suicidal, for a long time I could only watch, completely spellbound, content to just crouch in the barrel as pack after pack threw themselves down to the refuge of the choppy waters.

This non-stop flight lasted at least two hours, the air a constant confusion of birds from every level and direction with hardly a shot fired, until eventually a few teal turned up amongst the mass of wigeon. There's nothing finer than a brace of roast teal, so I tried to pick some out. There are few more testing shots in a gale. In that confusing way teal have, a few sneaked in low and unshootable, but others peeled from the wigeon packs to give a fleeting chance as they soared in and out in moments.

A pintail drake, high above the swirling wigeon, spotted me as I glanced up briefly. As I swivelled around to bring the gun to bear, it saw me first and was quickly wafted out of range on the wind.

My face and hands lost all their feeling as yet another blizzard of wet snow lashed the hide. From the north a skein of dark shapes approached, rising and falling with each gust, silhouetted black as pitch against the sky. Brent geese, wave upon wave, seemingly as endless as the breakers on the shore. Arriving from breeding grounds in the now frozen north, brent are a fully protected species. Skein after skein followed the path of the first over the next hour, passing from one horizon to the other.

Suddenly the marsh was bathed in bright sunlight, transforming the landscape. Lapwings tumbled like blown scraps of paper in the distance, ragged strings of curlew swept past and several tightly packed flocks of golden plover appeared from nowhere, swishing right over the hide. A couple of times I half-raised the gun, but a shot would have downed several, possibly wounding others. Instead, I waited until a thin string were passing, only just quick enough to take a loner off the rear.

The teal were quite tricky, jinking snipe-like in the gale. I kept getting one and missing one, but managed half a dozen besides picking out a few more wigeon and making up my brace of golden plover as a single came piping high overhead.

The morning had flown. Far too soon it was time to go. I gathered my soggy gear together and left the birds in peace, the long slog with a heavy load leaving me puffing and panting long before I reached the truck. I felt totally drained – both physically and mentally – but looking back, was delighted to see little flocks of wigeon still pouring in to an ever-growing black raft on the flightpond.

I'd been rained on, snowed on, pelted by hail and sleet, besides being blown inside out and completely soaked through. I'd also been very lucky.

If there is a heaven, then for me, this must be it! A spectacle that fulfils every emotion, besides the hunting instinct that is as old as man himself. What a hell of a morning – a flight in a million!

See it – hear it – feel it – revel in it – but most of all, respect and be a part of it.

CHAPTER THREE

·

Decoying and Various

Doing it the Leisurely Way

FREDERICK FORSYTH

FRIENDS SOMETIMES ask me: what's the matter? Surely you can afford to shoot grouse, pheasant, partridge? Well, it is perfectly true that I can; more to the point, kind friends had asked me to join them on their private shoots as a guest.

Then two winters ago, after knocking expensive parcels of feathers out of the sky for fifty years I took the two pairs of matched and scrolled 12-bores down to Christie's and let them go.

So, I have given up all forms of shooting? Not quite. Hence the surprise of my friends who do not know what they are missing. I now just shoot the humble but challenging wood pigeon.

I have long thought the wild wood pigeon quite wrongly derided – because he is available twelve months out of twelve, is classed as a pest and therefore comes absolutely free. No keepers, no beaters, no pickers; just a patient gun and (if you are lucky) a day of extremely varied and challenging shooting, without sustaining hypothermia.

There are four ways of taking the pigeon. I have indeed been out with the professionals, when four or five guns spread over an intensively reconnoitred twenty acres, will knock down enough birds to fill the rear of both pick-ups. One is in awe of the sheer marksmanship.

Or one can simply sit with a high-powered air rifle in a grove of trees at dusk and wait for them to drift in and perch. But it is a bit like sniping and can only last until the sun sets.

Walked-up birds can be testing, rocketing out of trees and hedges at half a second's notice, skimming the ground, jinking and swerving before climbing like a jet plane as if they know they just passed out of range.

But being a writer (we are known as solitary sods) I like to spend a spring, summer or autumn day quietly perched on a shooting stick in a hide of cammo netting staring out over my display of decoys, waiting for the targets to flight in towards them.

Shooting over decoys has the same characteristics as my other pleasure – fishing. The angler sets out his baits as attractively as he can, arranging his lures so as best to tempt his prey. Then he sits and quietly waits. So does the pigeon-taker over decoys. Those without the gift of silent and motionless patience should stay with the noisy camaraderie of the driven shoot.

Now let me put in a word of defence of the maligned ring dove. Unlike the grouse, pheasant or partridge, he is smart as paint. The pigeon only needs a hint that you are there – a flash of sun on metal, a move of white skin in the undergrowth, and he is gone. They are very shy targets indeed.

And they are tough. Those pads of feather and breast-meat can take a pasting and he'll still keep flying. He may be dying, but if he can make half a mile and drop out of sight, he will.

Finally, he is tasty. I only skin and slice off the two pads of breast to provide a pair of three-ounce steaklets. And yes, the meat is hard and dry. But it is fat-free with zero cholesterol. I have a recipe for Kentish pigeon pie that involves twenty-four hour marinade in olive oil and cheap port, and a long slow simmer in the lower Aga with a fatty sausage and root vegetables. Delicious – a cross between pheasant and venison, but better.

But first, as Mrs Beeton would say, acquire your pigeon. Despite his extreme wariness he has a few weaknesses. One is curiosity to see what it is those fellow pigeons down on the field have found to eat. Another is his insistence on switching diet in unison according to what is available. And a third is his habit of moving around the countryside on regular flight lines. Find out where they are flighting and what they are down on right now, and you can have a splendid day.

All that said, those decoys have got to be damned convincing. Anything unnatural, and he will swerve away while still out of range. To this end an amazing amount of research has gone into the invention of the perfect decoy. Glance at the range in any large catalogue and you will see what I mean.

I have long been of the opinion that utter immobility of the decoys is a giveaway. One or two at least should show a hint of movement and the shooter's natural ally here is the wind. And the most convincing decoy of all is a dead pigeon; just shot but carefully 'dressed' to appear alive and about to land.

For years now I have favoured three or four long graphite wands, jabbed into the field pointing upwind, with the first birds of the day displayed at the end, wings spread, head down as if looking to land, but not lolling at the end of a dead neck. (My own aid is the humble pipe cleaner to create an alert bird bouncing gently on the breeze.) It is the movement that catches that very sharp eye from up to half a mile away and brings him in.

Of course the latest must-have is the pigeon magnet, with the birds whirling round and round on their battery-driven carousel. I saw one some years ago, examined it closely, and decided to make my own. The shop-bought one, I felt, was spinning too fast. A friendly electrician cut the spinning rate by half, so my own now circle much more gently. And I bought two 'blanks' of float rods from my local fishing-tackle shop, and even without the last two feet (too thin and wispy to sustain a dead bird) they are still much longer than the standard version, giving a most seductive sweep to their decoy cargoes.

I have built myself a lightweight frame hide which I can run on the farm trailer to any part of the spread and place where the birds are crossing or feeding. Swathed in cammo netting, up against a hedge it soon becomes invisible. Inside it, I can survey the field through the 180-degree letter-box aperture ... and wait.

Earlier I used the word 'challenging' and I meant it. They come from all angles, and at all speeds. Some whirl in from left or right; some circle high, pass out of vision through the blind spot behind the trees and reappear. Some drift on rigid wings from behind, suddenly appearing heading away in front; others come from the front, rise and turn, planform, for a full deflection shot left or right.

Sometimes one will land unseen in the trees above, or just appear walking among the decoys. These are the lucky ones; they will live to fly another day for at the next shot they are gone.

It is a contemplative way of spending a day. A flask of tea, a snoozing Jack Russell, the near certainty of seeing all sorts of wildlife hopping by – I once had a fox a yard away. No hurry; a dozen birds will do nicely. Cost? Zero. Oh, and if you happen to be writing a novel and have got stuck on the storyline, this is the place to work out what happens next!

Decoyer's Delight

PETER THEOBALD

As I slowly parted the ears of wheat on top of the stook of corn and cautiously peeped through, I could see the wood pigeon was still there, pecking away at the seed. The range was about twenty yards, too far for my clapped-out BSA Meteor, which would barely kill a sparrow beyond fifteen paces. I needed to get closer, much closer. So, ignoring the scratches on my bare arms and legs, I squirmed forwards on my stomach. Reaching the next stook, I took a few moments to regain my breath, before slowly, oh so slowly taking another look. The pigeon, looking much bigger at close range, was completely oblivious to my presence and continued lazily eating its lunch.

Sliding the barrel carefully through the ears of corn, I levelled the open sights on its pink breast and squeezed the trigger. A meaty thwack sent the hapless bird tumbling backwards, and I scrambled excitedly to my feet to collect my prize. My first ever pigeon! I was ten years old and this little episode took place forty-five years ago, and though I have shot many tens of thousands of pigeons since, the details remain etched in my memory. To this day, I have never lost respect or admiration for this most resourceful of birds.

If I had to choose one word that epitomised what I get out of shooting, that word would be 'anticipation'. I never tire of the excitement when there is the chance of a good shoot in the offing. With pigeon shooting, the looking forward to and planning of the day is an essential part of the enjoyment. Will the birds be there tomorrow? Will they decoy? How will the wind direction influence where I set up?

The feeling of anticipation intensifies when you have been watching the birds build up in numbers on a particular field. It is obviously the same in other fieldsports. Have the teal found the bucketful of food you scattered on that tiny splash of floodwater? Will that record pike you just know is lurking on a bend in your favourite river take your lure? Will the cock pheasant that lives in the hedge across the road make the mistake of flushing on your side of the hedge? The list is endless, and no doubt every sportsman could relate a scenario which sets his adrenalin flowing. That, of course, is exactly how it should be. The day when the prospect of some sport fails to excite me will be the day I hang up my gun for good.

Funnily enough, when the challenge of the unknown is removed from the pigeon shooting equation, the outcome of the day's shooting, no matter how large the bag, is somehow diminished. I had such a day recently. With all the rain we had had recently, drilling had come to an abrupt halt on all the local farms, the pigeons soon clearing any loose grain from the fields. Quite by chance, I spotted several pigeons leaving a field of set-aside late one afternoon, so I decided to investigate the next day. The field was full of self-sown wheat from the previous year, and had been recently flailed so that the entire ground was covered in loose grain. It was also covered in a grey carpet of feeding pigeons, at least three thousand of them. It was the classic situation most pigeon shooters dream about, every bird in the district feeding on the only source of food for miles around. When I phoned a friend to join me the next day, I was so sure of a good bag that I stuck my neck out and told him, 'We should get at least two hundred.'

Having set up two hides overlooking one set of decoys, we started shooting at 10.15 a.m., only leaving our position to collect more car-tridges. We simply had no time to tidy up or pick any dead birds, as the pigeons poured non-stop into the decoys. We ran out again at 3 p.m., and though we still had some more back in the car, we decided to call it a day having simply shot enough. It took us the best part of an hour to pick up, and stow the bag of 351 into the car. So why no sense of elation at such an outstanding day's decoying? After all, we had both taken some fantastic shots, high driven birds, and some really long crossers. For me, the reason was that it had all been too easy and predictable, and the outcome was never really in any doubt. In other words, there had been no anticipation.

Sometimes we dream of a day when the pigeons come in a never-ending stream, or pheasants head unerringly towards your peg, or the biggest trout throws itself onto your line. But these days should remain a dream, because as soon as they are realised, the mystique vanishes.

Even though I can take advantage of most pigeon shooting situations, I still try to look at decoying through the eyes of a beginner. If I were to list, in order, the ten most important things to make a decent bag of pigeons, number one would undoubtedly be finding a field with enough birds feeding on it. But how on earth do you find the field that is attract-ing the most birds at any given time? No amount of decoys, set in what-ever shape pattern, or perfectly built hide, will make any difference if the birds are simply not using your chosen field in sufficient numbers.

So how do I go about finding a situation which might yield a good bag, when, to the untrained eye, just about every field of oilseed rape (for example) will look the same? I have to say that after forty years of chasing wood pigeons, you do tend to develop a kind of sixth sense as to when or where to look. This may sound a little trite, but pigeons are creatures of habit, so if a certain field takes their fancy when it is sown with, say, peas, then there is every chance that the field will attract them again the next time peas come round in the farmer's crop rotation.

The next hurdle to clear is judging when to shoot the field. Too soon, and the full potential may not be realised. Too late, and the birds may have simply exhausted the food and moved on. This is a tricky one, as so many factors can influence your decision, not least of which is having an idea of how many pigeons are in the area. They can appear almost overnight if a suitable food supply is discovered.

The weather on the day can also play a significant role in determining the day's outcome. Ideally, you want low pressure on the barometer, which usually means an overcast sky, and a good wind to channel the birds on their flightline, and keep them low. What time of day should one set up? Most beginners believe you have to be out at the crack of dawn, because that is when the hungry woodie leaves the roosting woods. On the face of it this is true, but most successful pigeon shooters prefer to let them have their first meal in peace, knowing that when they return for the all important second feed, they will do so in much smaller flocks and decoy better if they have not already been banged at at dawn. Indeed, you run the risk of them not returning at all if you bash into the big early bunches.

As you can see from the foregoing, a lot of positive elements need to come together if the day is to succeed, but this is precisely what makes pigeon shooting so addictive. I never tire of that adrenalin rush of anticipation when a good day is in the offing. There is no better sight than watching a busy flightline heading towards the field where you know a thousand pigeons have been feeding all week.

I firmly believe that once you have reached this happy state of affairs, the rest is comparatively easy. It should not be rocket science to discover what part of said field the pigeons prefer today, or to erect a hide in such a way that you remain hidden from the bird's incredibly sharp eyes, and at the same time are comfortable enough to swing your gun freely. Positioning the decoys is a matter of personal preference, as long as you remember the main criterion is to get the birds fairly and squarely in range in front of your hide. All sorts of electronic gadgetry will help you do this, but ultimately, if you are on the field the birds really want, a pattern of ordinary decoys will do the trick. To see a pigeon utterly deceived by your set-up is a fulfilling experience. However, there are occasions when not only pigeons are suckered in.

I had just finished setting up on a field of drilled peas some years ago, and was putting the finishing touches to the inside of my hide, when a farmhand on a quad came trundling along the headland. He stopped his machine to admire my set-up – or so I thought.

But no, he had a more serious mission. He was going to give these damned pigeons the fright of their lives! Pulling his cap firmly down and revving the engine, he accelerated frantically through the gears as he hurtled towards my decoys. He must have been doing 40 mph and was only thirty feet from the pattern when realisation set in. These pigeons were not going to fly! He pulled hard left, sending the quad into a broad-side slide. A cloud of dust flew from the tyres as he expertly corrected the spin by lurching violently to the right, incredibly still avoiding my precious decoys. It was all over in a matter of seconds, and the driver sped off into the distance still blissfully unaware of my presence.

He probably wouldn't have been fooled by some of the latest electronic gadgetry that many people insist is essential for decoying. Whilst I use rotary decoys and other contraptions on occasion, I have no illusions that they will ever replace good fieldcraft and shrewd observation. Despite the latest technology and the efforts of decoyers like me, pigeon populations continue to grow. And, assuming that we in this country can legally pursue wood pigeon for the foreseeable future, they will remain, for me, the ultimate quarry.

Fieldcraft

JOHN BATLEY

IF FIELDCRAFT could be bought it would be worth, as the perfume adverts say, at least two hundred pounds an ounce. But it can't be bought; it is acquired only through many hours of patient study, dedication and a feeling for being at one with nature.

Perhaps the best way to describe fieldcraft in action is to go out pigeon decoying with someone who, on arrival at a chosen field, will give the field what appears to be a quick glance and then point to a spot in the hedge on the other side of the field and say, categorically: 'That's where the hide goes.' Needless to say, when you do build your hide in the chosen spot, pigeons flock in to your decoys.

Another good example of fieldcraft is to go woodland stalking with a real expert and watch how, when walking cautiously through a wood, your companion will, for no apparent reason, suddenly signal you to stop and, as you wait motionless, a deer will break cover thirty yards upwind of you and then casually wander off down a ride without a care in the world.

There is a tendency for poor hunters to invest good, experienced hunters with mystical qualities and luck; but neither of the two examples could be called luck. On both occasions the person who made the decisions was someone who knew his fieldcraft and had studied his environment and his quarry.

On the educational courses which I run as an introduction to pigeon decoying I take the participants out into the field on the second day of the course (the first day is dedicated to theory), and try to teach them to find flight lines. I often stop on the edge of a barren forty-acre field and ask the would-be decoyers to suggest a flight line. The usual comment is that as there are no pigeons flying it is impossible to find a line of flight. This is just not so; with the application of just a little fieldcraft the task is quite straightforward.

Firstly, as the prevailing wind in this country is from the southwest, the majority of really productive flight lines in the UK run east to west. Secondly, pigeons will fly along the contours of the land in preference to flying over them. Thirdly, pigeons, because of their inherent fear of winged predators which patrol hedgerows, will fly through gaps in hedges and trees rather than fly over them. So, suddenly, with the application of a little fieldcraft the forty-acre field can be reduced to a way into the field through a gap in the hedge or trees (probably on the eastern side of the field), a way across the field by following the contours and an exit on the western side of the field through another convenient gap or gateway. Of course, this is slightly oversimplifying the issue but, as a starting point for finding a flight line on an unknown field, it is a great help.

Some people seem to have an inbuilt sense of direction whereas others never seem to know their north from south. Again, the application of fieldcraft can point you in the right direction. Never mind if there is no sunshine, in the days before electric light and heat most houses in the countryside were built facing south to take full advantage of daylight. Most hay and straw barns with one open side have the open side towards the east (the rain mainly comes from the west in the UK). Most churches are built facing east to west (with the altar facing east towards Jerusalem). And of course, those two old chestnuts, moss grows on the north side of trees and all rivers eventually flow into the sea.

Fieldcraft, as applied to pigeon shooting, can make all the difference. Imagine that you have been invited to a roost shoot at an unknown venue. Your host drops you off at the edge of a wood and casually says: 'This should be about right, tuck yourself in there somewhere and wait for the birds.' You blunder off into the wood without making a plan and spend the next hour and a half dodging around from tree to tree, listening to pigeons dropping into trees just out of range and sight whilst other guns are giving a good impression of World War III in the distance.

It would have been much better to have worked out what to do before even going into the wood. Which way was the wind blowing? Was this the prevailing wind for the area? Once you know the wind direction you know which way the pigeons will approach the wood. Head into wind (if there is no wind on that day assume that the birds will come to roost into the direction of the prevailing wind). Next, look at the trees. Are they deciduous or conifer? Pigeons like to settle in high bare branches of hardwoods to digest their last feed of the day before dropping into conifers where they will spend the night warm and safe from winged predators which cannot get at them in the dense foliage.

Now, venture into the wood and try to find a clearing between the hardwoods and the conifers and look on the ground under an ash, beech or oak for fresh pigeon droppings. You should stand with your back to such a tree and wait for the birds to come into the branches, and when they do come try to look up at them from under the brim of your hat or cap, rather than lifting up your pale face to the sky. Now you should get some shooting. Standing with your back to a tree camouflages your silhouette and is a much better option than hiding behind a tree and popping your head out every time a pigeon appears. Pigeons are frightened of sudden movement by man rather than by man himself.

When you are out decoying remember that the

most basic rule of fieldcraft is observation, and observation in pigeon shooting is reconnaissance. Do your reconnaissance and establish your flight line before you even venture onto the field. Once you are certain of where you are going to build your hide (directly under the flight line), walk the birds off the field and build your hide with as little disturbance to nature as possible. Wildlife takes about twenty minutes to settle back into its normal pattern so if you have been in your hide for half an hour after setting up and have seen nothing flying to your decoys, the chances are that you will see nothing for the rest of the day either. Archie Coats would move if nothing happened for half an hour after setting up.

A few tips on hide discipline: don't let the dog (or yourself, if you have no dog), go out for every bird that you kill. It only disturbs nature and providing that the pigeon keep coming to your decoys, leave well alone for as long as you can. If you do go out into the field, walk – don't run. Pigeons see men (in particular, farm workers), every day of their lives and generally they are not scared of them, mainly, I believe, because the average farm worker goes about his business without running. In your hide, arrange the netting, or natural cover, so that you can see out without having to stand or show your face over the top of the hide. Cover up white or shiny objects in the hide and try to sit still when you are not shooting. And one more thing, don't blame everything on the pigeons, if the birds don't come to the decoys it is probably your fault, not theirs.

Many of us set up our decoys, return to our hides and sit waiting patiently staring at the decoys from the hide and congratulating ourselves on our good-looking pattern without thinking that we have only looked at them from our point of view and not the pigeon's. What we should do, once we have set up the pattern, is to walk a couple of hundred yards out into the field and look at the pattern from the pigeon's point of view as he will approach the decoys. Archie Coats always said that 'you should think like a pigeon', in order to be successful at decoying and I see absolutely no reason to contradict him.

I am reminded of the story of a famous golfer who, when it was suggested to him that he had been very lucky to win a particularly difficult match, said: 'You know, the funny thing is, the older I get and the more that I practise, the luckier I seem to be.' So it is with fieldcraft, the more you practise, the more you learn and the more you will understand about your quarry in its own environment.

Rabbiting

IAN VALENTINE

CHARLIE GIBSON watched the guns loose off both barrels at the bolting rabbits and shook his head. 'Pair of muppets,' he growled, both thumbs pointing to the ground. 'Their heads are scrambled, these two. If we'd brought our nets along we'd have been home by now.'

For the cost of just two driven pheasants on Home Counties' parkland, a sportsman can get a full day's rabbit shooting with Charlie and his old friend Barry Moore on the hills above Kelso. The cost includes breathtaking views, your lunch and five hours of merciless leg-pulling from two rabbiters who know what they are talking about. Those of a sensitive disposition need not apply.

Dressed in matching army surplus jackets, hard-wearing boots and skin-tight gloves, Charlie and Barry were well equipped to deal with the worst Scotland in February could throw at them. Their waterproof trousers had an extra layer of insulating mud and a cocktail of grime that would take weeks for a forensics team to identify. Charlie's grey hair hid under a fleecy bonnet in the compulsory green camouflage, while Barry bared his smooth scalp to the elements. From the contours of their faces, they had spent many contented years outdoors, laughing in the wind and rain. Yet today only a few rippling clouds broke up the expanse of pale blue and it was almost warm.

'That's Cumbria you can see in the distance,' said Charlie in his warm Geordie accent, scooping the albino ferret from the hole where the bunnies had emerged. 'Those rabbits are probably halfway there by now. But you're not the first two to miss rabbits on this hill, as they can take some hitting,' he continued, pushing the reluctant pink-eye into a home-made wooden carrier. 'Going that quickly down the slope you've got to lift the gun as you shoot to give them some lead. It has to be instinct. As soon as you aim at them, you've missed.'

'Aye, they say you should go for a head shot,' added Barry, with the same colloquial lilt. 'But that's not easy. You'll notice that most of them, to start off with at least, will be shot up the bum.'

We worked our way slowly up the incline, traversing to each set of burrows that showed signs of occupancy. 'You always move up the slope,' said Charlie, pointing out a well-worn rabbit run, linking two sets. 'The last thing you want to do is go chasing after rabbits that have already been bolted higher up the hill. They won't come out and neither will your ferret once she gets hold of one. You'll spend your whole day digging.'

On reaching each set, Charlie would select one or two of his ferrets from the eight in the box and drop it by a likely hole, before retreating at speed to see what would happen. Often the ferret would disappear immediately and a rabbit would scoot out of another hole. Like two opening batsmen, the guns soon began reading the speed of the pitch and each would earn a thumbs-up from Charlie when they bowled over a bunny cleanly.

But sometimes, despite the best laid plans, nothing would happen. At certain sets, where Charlie swore blind there would be a good showing, the ferret would reappear immediately from the hole and lope about in a disinterested manner, blinking at the sunshine, before wandering away from the site altogether.

'Well, I suppose they know better than we do,' Charlie would grumble. At one point the ferret scampered right back to her wooden box, unimpressed by her handler's choice of warren. 'I think she's trying to tell you something,' Barry smirked, putting her back in the box.

'But that's what you want from a ferret,' snorted Charlie. 'If there's nothing there she comes out immediately and it's on to the next set. There's no shame in having a blank.'

Every warren had a story to tell, with Charlie and Barry reading signs that would have gone unnoticed by the untrained eye. A piece of fluff told of a courtship tussle between a buck and doe. 'At the bottom of the hill, they'll already be breeding,' the master rabbiter said, 'but the colonies at the top won't come into season for a few weeks yet, until the vegetation has grown up some more.'

Barry showed us the small piles of grass and moss, neatly spread out beneath a hole that the inhabitants were drying out for a warm nest. 'And do you see this black ground around the mouth of the holes?' asked

Charlie. 'That's why the farmers don't like rabbits. Eventually the ground goes sour with all the built-up excrement and it's no use to anyone. That keeps us in business. And here's a tip for free,' he added, tapping his nose and dropping to a whisper, 'if a farmer ever asks you to clear a field of rabbits, make sure the first one you get is the one he sees from his Land Rover every day. He then thinks you're doing a good job. But you're not going to print that, are you ... ?'

Charlie and Barry are well into their sixties, yet both retain the same boyish enthusiasm for the sport that attracted them so many years ago. But while the spirit is as keen as ever, neither can sprint up and down the inclines like they once did. Indeed, only last year, Charlie received a gentle reminder that time marcheth on. He was out on the hill alone after rabbits, when he tripped on a hole, went over an ankle and ripped his calf muscle.

'I was truly crocked and totally deserted. I could have fired as many distress shots as I wanted, but no one would have come. They'd just think I was having a good day. I knew also that there'd be no stockmen in the area – there are so few of them nowadays as it is – so I had to crawl down the hill to the nearest road. From that day I've carried a mobile phone – switched off, mind – just in case. My wife, bless her, doesn't like me going out on my own anymore, though I'd like to think I'm a bit wiser than I once was. Experience teaches you when to chicken out.'

More often than not Barry will be with him, as he nearly always has been for the last thirty-five years. They worked together at Nestlé and Charlie taught his colleague the dark arts of ferreting, taking off to the hills at the weekends to hunt rabbits. But despite Barry's wealth of experience, he is still the junior partner in a master/apprentice relationship, filled with non-stop bickering and goading.

'I used to batter Barry's lugs at work and I batter them still,' said Charlie, unable to hide the affection in his voice. 'Thirty-five years he's been rabbiting and he still doesn't have the first clue what he's doing. All he does is talk. I swear he was vaccinated with a gramophone needle as a baby.'

Barry quickly came back at his old chum. 'He's the one like a scratched record. Always was at Nestlé and now that we're retired, he's even worse. But I tell you, there's only one thing I miss about work and that's the holidays.'

'What's that, pet? You yabbering on again?'

'I'll "pet" you!'

'You don't say that when we're alone!'

'Oh.... Shut your cake hole!'

It needed one of the guns to intervene or they would have been at it all day. 'For goodness sake, lads, will you stop your squabbling. I thought we were here to shoot some rabbits!"

The ferrets were the true stars of the show, although they were not in it for the glory. They wanted a rabbit so they could gorge on its blood and sometimes they got what they wanted. A faint squeaking noise would reverberate around the subterranean maze telling fellow rabbits, and those above, that a ferret had chased a bunny down a one-way alley. Like the thirsty vampire, a ferret cares not a jot whether its victim lives or perishes, just so long as it gets its fill of claret.

Likewise, he is an expert sleeper, capable of dozing in a cosy earth for the rest of the day when his belly is full, so Charlie and Barry needed to act swiftly if they were to keep their charges hungry for work. Each scamp wore a transmitter round its neck that would emit a signal to a hand-held locator. Charlie barked orders and Barry began to pace about the set, swinging the locator above the grass like an orang-utan with a Geiger counter. The gizmo pipped louder and faster as it approached the transmitter below and Barry soon had his mark. Once content that the ferret was still – most likely feeding – a seasoned spade removed the top layer of turf before a long metal graft excavated deep into the web of tunnels below. All the while Charlie offered advice as though Barry was digging out a ferret for the first time.

'Slowly Barry, you're about on him, pet. Careful of my ferret, now, do ye hear!'

Once the hole yawned wide enough, Barry turned from ape to ostrich, pushing his head under the surface to return with a grubby, bloody-nosed, disgruntled ferret, which he stowed away in the wooden box. Charlie then reached into the hole to retrieve and dispatch the unfortunate coney.

'You always want to grab the rabbit by its back legs if you can,' Charlie advised, holding the rabbit aloft for examination like a midwife with a new born baby. 'Rabbits can give you a nasty nip otherwise.' After the soil and turf had been replaced, the old rabbiter took out his trusty pocket knife and sliced the ends off the creature's soft ears for later identification. 'No shot in this one, you see, so I'll keep it for my supper. When I was a kid, if you didn't catch a rabbit, you didn't eat meat. This youngster will be beautiful!'

Charlie's preferred recipe for rabbit involves pressure-cooking the jointed back legs and saddle for an hour, before casseroling the meat in gravy with tins of potatoes and vegetables. 'And the only thing better than that, is to eat the leftovers cold in a sandwich.'

'I'm also quite traditional,' added Barry, pleased to get a word in. 'I'm not keen on those curries or kebabs or what not. My wife makes the best rabbit hotpot with black pudding, sliced potatoes and thick crusty pastry. When I eventually snuff it and go upstairs, I hope He is not a rabbit!'

Three hours later, with the shadows lengthening, Charlie put two of his angels into the last set at the top of the slope. The excitement had stayed with the party throughout the day and fifty rabbits were now in the bunny bag with the guns out-killing the ferrets at a ratio of four to one. Seconds after the two polecat fitches were dropped into the warren, a pair of rabbits bundled out of an adjacent hole. We all rocked forward in anticipation, only for them to disappear into another orifice. Yet still they were not safe and the chase continued, with the noise echoing up to the surface. Suddenly, two bunnies erupted from the underworld and bolted across the field towards the safety of a hedge. Both guns fired a single barrel and the two fugitives somersaulted to a standstill. The ferrets quickly emerged to see what the fuss was about, before trotting back to Barry.

'That's good shooting!' cried Charlie, his hands held high in celebration. 'And here's the ferrets to tell us the warren is empty. Now, I do like that!'

Doing It My Way

GEORGE WALLACE

THERE IS, so they say, more than one way to skin a cat and doubtless that also applies to controlling foxes. So, although my personal preference is a 90-grain hollow-point bullet leaving the muzzle of my .270 at 3400 ft/sec, there are occasions when some less robust measure may be appropriate and just as effective.

'Everyone,' said Max Bygraves, 'loves a story.' This is mine.

In the early hours of Sunday morning 24 May 2003, Miss Money-penny became a chicken take-away.

The little house where our free-range hens spend the night is only six or seven yards from the bedroom window. The blasted hens wake up at about 4.30 a.m. at the end of May and complain loudly if they find them-selves confined to barracks. At that hour of the morning I can do without moaning chickens just outside the window and we anticipated no danger so their door was open, as it had been for a month or so.

I went out at about 7.30 a.m. because there was a meeting of the Express Rifle Association that Sunday and I had to do the chores before leaving home. I topped up the hens' water and food and collected the eggs and, as I did so, noticed a few feathers on the grass. A quick roll-call revealed that Miss Moneypenny, our best layer, was missing.

The spoor led across the lawn, under the fence, over the field and under another fence before disappearing on the farm road. The culprit was clearly a vixen with cubs to feed and, because of those cubs, she would certainly be back to the fox equivalent of KFC the following night. Plans were therefore laid and countermeasures put in hand.

We consulted Brendan, one of the 'keepers on the Wynnstay Estate where we live, and he produced a dead pheasant poult for bait. This was attached firmly to the trunk of the crab-apple tree beside the hen house with a length of green training wire. The tug-of-war between fox and tree would, I hoped, wake me in time to deal with the intruder.

That night the door of the hen house was firmly bolted and the .270 with its sound moderator stood ready beside the window. I slept, I like to think, with one eye and one ear open. I felt a little, just a little, like Jim Corbett up his tree waiting for a man-eating tiger.

We heard no sound but at dawn the pheasant was gone, leaving behind a leg, neatly bitten through above the wire and still attached to the tree.

There was a meeting of the war cabinet over breakfast. This was getting serious.

Another pheasant was provided by the long-suffering Brendan and this we attached to the handle of a tin bucket with the same length of wire. The bucket was then placed on a tree stump so it would fall when the fox grabbed the pheasant and the resulting clatter would, hopefully, wake up the guard. Once again the .270, quiet and deadly, lurked menacingly by the window. And this time the plan worked.

Well, when I say it worked, it sort of worked. Up to a point.

At 3.45 a.m. there was a rattling crash like an armoured knight falling off his horse and Mrs Wallace, younger and more nimble than I, was at the window in an instant. A series of excited squeaks (her version of the *view halloo*) informed me the fox was on the town-oh.

I took a little longer to get legs and brain connected but then grabbed the rifle and sought out the shadowy shape of the chicken thief. The range was only about ten yards and the vixen, a blurred shadow in the pre-dawn gloaming, was weaving drunkenly about the field having apparently been clobbered by the descending bucket. Easy-peasy! Game, set and match to Wallace.

But beware of over-confidence. Murphy is out there and, since his Law and Writ are absolute, it was at this point that the wheels came off.

The available light was no problem for the Swarovski 'scope on the rifle but it was certainly a problem for the poor old bugger holding it because, in the excitement, I had forgotten to put on my glasses. I was therefore trying to use a 'scoped rifle at very short range – never an easy matter anyway – in poor light and without the glasses I wore when adjusting the focus. Even Swarovski can't allow for complete idiots and by the time I'd got my act together so had the vixen, which cleared off pursued by maledictions rather than the intended bullet.

But maybe there's a lesson in all this foolishness for, although I did not get the fox, she never returned and the remaining chickens have been able to pursue their apparently important daily routine without further harassment. As we say in Wales, 'There's environmentally friendly for you, isn't it?'

Do foxes communicate? I think they do – and not just because of this incident. We have not, touch wood, had a fox in the garden in the three years since that day. An occasional feral cat (*requiescat in pacem*), a few rats (*ditto*), and a hedgehog or three (safe because they eat slugs and snails) have triggered the security light, but not a single fox have we seen.

Interesting, don't you think?

Roost Shooting

DARREN CRUSH

THE SUN WAS starting to set as I made my way out to the wood. A Mars Bar was stuffed into my jacket pocket, an AYA side-by-side was tucked under my arm and I was wearing a camouflage outfit that would have done justice to those mysterious men in Hereford.

It was only a short walk from my parents' cottage and, as I left our excitable cocker spaniels panting and leaping about their run, thoughts of what might be encountered on that breezy winter's evening swam through my mind.

I'd been roost shooting only once before and that was under the guidance of one of the local gamekeepers, an old countryman who knew more about the countryside than anyone I'd ever met. The memories of that first foray had stayed with me, but now I was venturing out solo, calling on all that I'd been taught, to try and bag myself what many regard as the ultimate sporting quarry. I was after a bagful of wood pigeon.

There were a number of options open to me, and in the end I settled for an elderly lime tree, its uppermost branches swaying lightly in the wind and aged limbs creaking as if telling tales of yore. Dusk was closing in as I positioned myself at the base of this great tree, blending in as much as I could to my natural surroundings – watching, waiting. It wouldn't be long now.

Gradually the wood took on a completely new character. No sunlight broke through the branches, no pheasants crunched through the undergrowth – by now they were roosting, high up away from predatory eyes – no songbird bird called, just quiet. It was the kingdom of the nocturnal hunter.

My senses took on an acuteness rarely experienced in daylight hours. Every noise was strangely amplified. My eyes grew accustomed to the failing light but were still fooled into seeing things as the shadows grew longer. My sense of smell was overcome by the musty aroma of rotting bark. Surely not long to wait.

As I looked down for a moment a branch snapped to the left, away behind me. I turned, slowly. And there, trotting nose to the ground, was old Charley doing his rounds. It was his turf now. He drifted to within ten yards of me, scarcely noticing me – the cammo must have been good – as he glided amongst the shadows in search of a meal.

I returned to scanning the skies. In the distance a cock pheasant called.

A car's headlights hovered over the road two miles or so away. I tightened my grip on the gun. Finally it happened.

Bending its wings to land, a solitary pigeon drifted in on the wind to pitch down on one of the top branches of my tree. 'I'll let him be,' I remember thinking. 'He'll attract others in.' And that's just what he did.

Soon a small flock were bending their wings in similar fashion and homing in on my tree. 'Don't rush,' I thought, 'pick your bird.' I took the shot and ... Yes! No time to think, onto the second bird ... and down spiralled my second pigeon. The others vanished as I ejected the spent cartridges. Two shots, two pigeons – not bad for starters.

The evening wore on and I missed some, hit some, until another three were added to the bag. The light faded. I knew it was time to head home.

On that short walk I felt like the luckiest person alive. Next day I presented my mentor with the pigeons he had taught me to shoot. That night we enjoyed pigeon breasts, a dash of home-made wine and his speciality – apple pie. All natural, all gained by our own hand. Just the way it should be.

Thieving Magpies

ANTHONY BAKER

MAN AND BOY, I have probably spent more time than most people pitting my wits against the wily magpie. It's nothing personal, mind you. I'd be the first to admit the countryside would be a poorer place without this decorative bird, decked out in one of Nature's dinner jackets like a gentleman thief. But that's my point: magpies are not just fond of bright things, like trinkets and rings. They are voracious nest raiders whose numbers must be controlled if other species – denizens of garden and hedgerow as well as game birds – are to be given half a chance.

The growth of the motorway network has for some reason led to a vast increase in the magpie population. Probably it's all that carrion available from road kills of rabbits and the like. If you have a shoot near a motorway, it doesn't seem to matter how many magpies you exterminate – there are always more to take their place. On the small South Yorkshire shoot which I help to run, a good eighty or so are culled each season. A maggot farm on one of the beats attracts them like iron filings round a magnet.

For his own reasons, my father pursued a lifelong vendetta against this garrulous member of the crow family. As boys we learned that downing magpies on a drive was just as important as shooting game. The best part of a lifetime later, I still follow his example – even at my own home, which looks out over an orchard.

Not wanting to cause trouble, I make sure a neighbour with a nest on a boundary hedge is out of the house before the nest is blown. Sometimes I decoy with food on the orchard lawn before taking a quick shot through the kitchen window with a 12-bore. And, as an engineer, I've designed and built my own version of a Larsen Trap using counterweights instead of coil springs. It has been sensitive enough to catch blackbirds, starlings and a rook as well as magpies. It has even caught the biggest moggy I've ever seen, nearly the size of a tiger kitten. Along with the other non-magpies, I let him escape. After all, you have to live with other people in a small village.

Sometimes, of course, people ask me to tackle a magpie problem for them. Like the time when, on a skiing holiday in Norway, I ended up in a log cabin with a magpie's nest in the nearby forest. The Norwegians did not care for our black-and-white neighbours, whose early morning chattering disturbed their lie-in.

Thanks to my reputation as a magpie hunter, I was asked to destroy the dome-shaped nest. The silver birch was an easy climb, but I had quite a struggle pulling away the twigs from the nest itself. The lining, usually made of mud, was particularly unpleasant. Only later did I notice that the tree was close to the tipping site for the cabin's earth closet. It must have been the magpie's revenge.

Of all people, I should have known that trouble with those birds runs in the Baker family – as my father found out on one of our regular anti-magpie sorties from our home outside Leeds. Often we marked the nests before the leaves were on the trees, like this one in a sycamore which we had spotted from the car. As second gun, I was to take the bird as it flew off when father blew the nest.

Sure enough, he gave it both barrels, the usual debris fell, and … an ominous silence. Suddenly the bedroom window of a nearby house flew open and a man shouted: 'I know what you're doing. I've sent for the police. You've woken the children.' We beat a hasty retreat.

Fortunately father used to go trout fishing with the local police inspector and, in the shooting season, he would occasionally deliver a brace of partridges at the station (you can tell how long ago this was).

Anyway, after a day's fishing that June, he was dropping the inspector off at his home. 'Been doing any magpie shooting lately?' the policeman

asked with a grin. We took his enquiry as a friendly warning.

Of course, the police inspector knew that father always had it in for magpies and used to organise a campaign against them by a group of shooting friends. Together with his pal, Ned Wade, he even plotted the magpie nests in their part of suburbia on an Ordnance Survey map.

One year there was a prominent nest on some land just off the Leeds ring road which caught their eye. They duly arrived one afternoon and Ned explained to the lady of the house about the damage done to songbirds by magpies raiding their nests.

The lady agreed completely, and said she could not stand them. The trouble was that her husband, Fred, would never allow my father and his friends to get at the nest. 'He just loves to see those colourful birds strutting about the lawn,' she explained.

By coincidence John Pickard, another member of the group, said he knew Fred and would 'have a word' with him. He arranged to meet Fred for a drink at a pub in Horsforth the following Wednesday at seven o'clock.

By a strange coincidence that was exactly the time when Fred's missis allowed in the team to shoot up the nest. There was just enough time for John Pickard to arrive at the pub at a quarter past seven – and apologise to Fred for being late!

Rat-a-tat-tat!

JAMES MARCHINGTON

IF THE SAS WENT rat shooting, this is how they'd do it. It's dark. So dark you can pass your hand across your face and not see it. Your ears tune in to every little sound – the shuffling of dozens of pigs, the occasional grunt, the dripping of water, the soft splosh of your feet on wet concrete.

A sharp red beam snaps on and the little light dances across sleeping pigs, feed troughs and drinkers. It sweeps back and forwards before it trips over a rat, hesitates and locks on. Instantly a red dot glows on the rat's body. There is a sharp crack and the rat rolls over – but you can't see it because the lights are gone. In the blackness you hear the muffled click of a bolt opening but there is no rattle of the empty shell hitting the floor. Just the double click of a new round being chambered.

Another rat has fallen prey to Charles Furda and Ken Smith, South Yorkshire's vermin control equivalent of the Counter Revolutionary Warfare wing. With ruthless efficiency they work through the building of forty pig pens, moving like ghosts and only flicking their lights on for a second at a time.

The smell is beyond description. The air is thick with the stench of pigmuck and ammonia. In the darkness you can hear things scuttling near your face. Your head snaps round instinctively.

It's probably a good thing you can't see what made the sound. There are some big, powerful rats in this corner of South Yorkshire. They grow fat and sleek on the pigfeed.

Charles and Ken have finished the first building, but the night's work is only just beginning. There are several more buildings to do. Then they'll come back to the start and do it all again. After an hour and a half the rats have grown confident and they're back.

The rats are left where they fall. At the end of the night's shooting, Charles and Ken go round with thick rubber gloves and collect what's left. There aren't many. The rats collect their own dead and drag them away. The pigs chomp up any that fall in the pens. Charles throws the rest on the farm muckheap. They aren't there in the morning.

It's taken Charles and Ken years to perfect their technique and their equipment. They're fanatical about their kit. Charles has something of the eccentric inventor about him. A printer by trade, he drives a model steam engine at weekends, adapts the guns himself and loads his own .410 cartridges. If there isn't a suitable tool for the job, he'll make his own – like a powder measure made from an old brass cartridge case.

Charles and Ken took on the rat control contract at this pig farm four years ago. Since then they've killed more than six thousand rats, each one noted down in the meticulous records that Charles keeps.

The buildings weren't designed with rat control in mind, and Charles soon found that standard .410 cartridges are too powerful for the job. 'We had a lot of busted water pipes to begin with,' he says. With a lot of trial and error, he has developed his ideal rat load. It fires 100 grains ($\frac{1}{4}$ oz) of dust-shot, riddled to be between size 9 and $10\frac{1}{2}$. The pellets are made of pure lead so they're extra soft. Shot is loaded into cut-down .410 cases, with a pinch of powder.

Charles re-uses the cases over and over – most of them are fired more than a hundred times. That's why you won't hear them hit the floor. He has removed the ejector lugs from his bolt-action Webley & Scott so he can slip the fired cases into his pocket.

That's not all he's done to the gun. First he removed the original stock and stored it carefully out of harm's way. Then he set about designing his own stock of plywood, with built-in laser pointer and lamp. The wiring is all concealed in the stock, so it doesn't get tangled. Power comes from a rechargeable battery in a belt pack. It plugs into a DIN socket at the base of the pistol grip.

There are two switches set into the fore-end, where they fall just under Charles's thumb. There's a flip switch for the lamp and a push-button for the laser. The laser is adjusted so that the red dot falls exactly in the centre of the pattern. All Charles needs to do is flip on the red-filtered lamp and scan for a rat. Then he presses the button to put a red dot on the target – and pulls the trigger. The rat doesn't stand a chance.

You don't even need to bring the gun to your shoulder. If the red dot is on a rat, it's a dead rat. That's a big help when you're shooting over, under and around obstacles – and there are plenty of those on the pig farm.

Ken's gun is adapted too. Like Charles, he's fitted a laser pointer and red lamp on his O/U Manuarm .410. His home-brewed lighting unit fits in place of the gun's fore-end, and it's powered by a belt battery with a DIN plug like Charles's. Charles and Ken have standardised the wiring so they can swap kit if need be.

It ain't pretty but it works. Six thousand rats can't be wrong!

CHAPTER FOUR

·

The Gun Cupboard

The Gun Cupboard

DAVID FROST

It started life as an Edwardian bookcase but some former owner had seen a new use for it and converted it to a gun cupboard. Until security paranoia took hold it contained three guns. The first is a 20-bore non-ejector by Watson. I bought it at the Game Fair for my son, then aged three! It seemed a pity to leave it gathering dust so I had the stock lengthened to my own measurements. It proved ideal for summer pigeon shooting where the light recoil was easy on a shoulder protected only by a shirt. I liked it so much that when Nick became old enough to use it I had to buy myself a Webley & Scott 20-bore to replace it.

Next comes a Midland Gun Co 12-bore with the barrels marked 'for 3-inch paper cases'. I still have a few of those in various shot sizes, but a more common load nowadays is $1\frac{1}{4}$ oz of No 4 or 5 for duck, non toxic of course. Half the fun of wildfowling is deciding on the best combination of shot and cartridge size. My own preference is for a Grand Prix No 6 load in the right barrel while in the left I use a Hymax or more rarely $2\frac{3}{4}$-inch magnum.

The battery is completed by the 12-bore Webley & Scott I was given for my twenty-first birthday. It has served me faithfully for over forty years as game, wildfowling and clay pigeon gun. I normally feed it paper case No 6s and then do not have to worry unduly if the ejectors throw the empties beyond recall. With the wisdom of hindsight I would have had twenty-eight-inch barrels rather than thirty-inch, however the overall effect is pleasing since the stock is $17\frac{1}{4}$ inches and well balanced by the longer barrels. I shall stick my neck out and claim this as the longest one-piece stock in the country.

The cupboard holds much more than just a few guns. Binoculars are a *sine qua non* for any wildfowler. The choice is as baffling as the choice of guns. I now use a pair of 7.5 x 42 having tried assorted combinations over a period of years. Smaller and lighter binoculars such as 8 x 40 or 7 x 35 have poor light gathering characteristics.

Books and back issues of *Shooting Times* take up much space but give proportional pleasure. I enjoy browsing through bookshops. Second-hand books can be very good value compared to the cost of buying new and there are many old books which give entertainment for modest outlays. It is interesting to trace the changes in the shooting scene so faithfully recorded in successive editions of the Badminton and Lonsdale libraries.

I am surprised at the number of sportsmen who fail to keep a game book. Apart from bringing back memories of a good day's sport, it's an invaluable record of what happened in a particular place under certain conditions. The recording of these details helps to build up the knowledge needed to be a good 'fowler, pigeon shooter or organiser of a day's formal shooting.

Skipping the cleaning kit, hand warmers and hip flask we come to the drawers. One contains the dogs' paraphernalia. A rabbit skin dummy and an assortment of Turner Richards canvas affairs fill the bill here. Summer walks are much enhanced for both owner and dog if a dummy is carried in the pocket.

The lower cupboards hold the bulky equipment. Some ammunition lives in a splendid cartridge magazine I picked up cheaply and when filled to its four hundred round capacity, I realise why. The original owner must have had a solidly built loader. The upper shelf holds waterproofs – leggings for game shooting and shorts with a reinforced seat to go over waders on the marsh. Then there are the all important ear protectors and an assortment of cartridge belts. One holds cartridges for wildfowling. Ready to hand it helps in the last minute rush which usually accompanies my dash to the foreshore. Another holds 20-bore cartridges, carefully segregated from the 12-bore.

For a forgetful fellow there are many advantages in having all the shooting equipment in one place. Every time I pass the cupboard it acts as a constant reminder of pleasant seasons past and to come. All in all it is a good use for an old bookcase that might otherwise have been discarded.

Second-Hand Buy

LEWIS POTTER

IT'S ALWAYS A thrill to examine a used gun and potential purchase, admiring the lines and trying the handling. Before long you are captivated by the intricate engraving, the elegant barrels and Nature's swirling patterns in the walnut stock. Money changes hands and hopefully you can look forward to many happy hours in the shooting field with your new gun.

Sometimes that pride of ownership evaporates as you gradually realise that the old gun is more than a little shaky. Under close scrutiny it exhibits wear and damage or, worse still, repair work you overlooked in your excitement to become its new owner. To avoid that horrible sinking feeling, and recriminations with the previous owner, you need a clear idea of what you want before you embark on a purchase. Back this up with a series of simple checks and you are far less likely to purchase a 'dud'.

A few years ago a friend of mine would often be seen with a newly purchased gun. It was invariably in sound condition and usually bought for a fair price. Associates on the shooting field regarded him as the luckiest man in the county – but in fact it had little to do with luck. As a practising cynic he approached any purchase with the view that the gun was quite possibly rubbish – until, that is, he had satisfied himself that it was otherwise. Indeed, he might have examined and rejected fifty guns before purchasing his latest.

You do not have to go to quite this extreme, but it is always worth assuming that any second-hand gun may have faults, or at least wear. Always remember that with the passage of time a famous name is no longer a guarantee of soundness. If it is bodged and worn out, it could be the most expensive piece of scrap you ever purchased.

To start with have a good look at the general condition. Is much of the barrel blacking missing, the chequering worn, the engraving rubbed or the head of the stock against the action black with oil? Any of these tell-tale signs can indicate a prolonged period of use and subsequent wear.

When it comes to the woodwork, look for splits in the fore end or cracks in the stock, particularly in the chequering, and make sure the stock is tight to the action. You will also need to check that the stock length is right for your build and, provided you have on a similar thickness of clothing to what you wear in the shooting field, you can test this by offering the gun up to your shoulder. The cast of the stock is very important. Holding the gun in front of you, if the butt goes to the right it is for a right-handed shooter and the opposite for a left-hander.

With the gun closed, hold it up to a good light source and look for any glimmers of light between the barrels and breech face; ideally there should be none. And, when you take off the fore end, check that the barrels are still tight against the action. If not, there is unacceptable wear on the cross pin and hook and sometimes on the locking mechanism.

Look down the barrels for pitting and check the outside for dents. Do not forget to look down the muzzle end; pits and dents that are barely discernible from the breech end can be glaringly obvious when viewed from the muzzles.

Ribs should not be loose. Check by hanging the barrels by the hook from the finger of one hand and flicking the barrels with a fingernail of your free hand. Good barrels will ring, in some cases almost like a tubular door chime; any dullness usually indicates a loose rib. If a rib has been loose for some time and the barrels are rusting unseen under the ribs, the gun is simply a time bomb waiting to go off.

With the gun reassembled and snap caps in place, check that the triggers cannot be pulled with the safety in the 'on' position. With safety off, try the triggers – they should be crisp, without being dangerously light or excessively heavy. If it is an ejector gun, open slowly and watch: both snap caps should clear the action face and leave the gun at the same time.

Ideally some checks will need to be done by a gunsmith: gauging the barrels and comparing the result with the proof marks, checking barrel thickness (particularly just before the choke section) and also measuring the actual chokes.

No reputable dealer will object to this. Alternatively, if you are buying privately, agree with the vendor that these checks (especially gauging the barrels) are part of the deal. After all, if the barrels are out of proof it is illegal to offer the gun for sale.

Barrel sleeving, where a pair of new tubes are spigoted into the breech ends, is an acceptable method of replacing the barrels. Indeed, most new over-and-unders are produced using this system. Bear in mind, however, that if replacements are not original it does reduce the marketable value of any gun.

While early sleeving jobs are marked 'sleeved' on the barrel, later ones are not. In some cases the joint line will be visible about three and a quarter inches from the breech ends but with a really good job it is almost undetectable. With laser welding now often used for sleeving it makes an invisible joint but in all cases there will be a Proof House stamp in front of the joint area on the new tube.

Barrel lining is another method of restoration where the original barrels are opened out and full length tubes are inserted. This has the particular advantage with Damascus barrels that they retain their original appearance. The process is identified at reproof with the words 'lined barrel'.

So much for the simple checks, now what about deciding beforehand on the type of gun you intend to buy? Will it be an ejector or non-ejector, a boxlock or sidelock, an over-and-under or a side-by-side? Indeed, you may even be one of those rare individuals whose taste runs to a fine old English hammer gun. Whatever you decide, price will usually be the deciding factor.

As a guide, a boxlock side-by-side ejector can be nearly twice the price of a similar non-ejector gun. A sidelock ejector can easily be twice as much as a boxlock ejector, and much more than that if it bears a famous name.

The bore size also has an influence on price. The ubiquitous 12-bore is always a safe bet and prices reflect this. The fashionable 20-bore commands high prices, sometimes silly ones, while the 16-bore tends to be neglected and thus a very good buy.

The 16-bore has a lot to recommend it. Slimmer and lighter than most 12-bores, the standard load of 15/16 oz is for all practical purposes as useful as the 1 oz load of growing popularity for 12-bores. The 28-bore is a rare find but makes a super gun for a beginner and a much more useful tool than a .410.

Good quality .410s are scarce and expensive while those at the bottom end of the market are cheaply built and can be disappointing to use.

Those wonderful big bore wildfowling guns have a romanticism that adds pounds to the price. They also seem to suffer extremes of use, having had either a hard and salty life or being virtually unused. A good quality wildfowling gun is the vintage Bentley of the shotgun world, big, heavy, immensely satisfying to use, expensive to run and very much an acquired taste.

Suppose you are going to buy a side-by-side boxlock. It is often assumed that any boxlock is an Anson & Deeley type, that famous and remarkably simple design with a minimum of parts to wear or break.

If it is an English gun that assumption will usually prove correct, but some early breech loaders, often of continental origin, will prove to have quite different mechanisms even though they look like 'conventional' boxlocks. These range from the ingenious to the unnecessarily complicated, negating the usual reason for buying a boxlock, namely its relative simplicity and ruggedness.

Whether you opt for a side-by-side ejector or non-ejector is a personal choice. If you buy an ejector gun you are paying extra for the mechanism and usually fancier engraving and better walnut. However, it is possible to find non-ejector guns with fine engraving and attractive woodwork.

If you do not really need ejectors then such a gun can give good service and great pleasure. I find a non-ejector sweeter to open when fired. Some ejector systems stiffen this action considerably and, when worn, some of the more unusual designs can be horribly expensive to repair properly.

Given a free choice, most sportsmen's votes would be for a sidelock ejector bearing a famous name. The comparative scarcity of such desirable items – and many shooters' limited budget – usually mean they look for a less expensive alternative. Probably the most affordable of these is the boxlock with sideplates that resembles a sidelock. This is a handsome if purely decorative arrangement and gives the owner a certain 'field credibility' – until his companions find out it is not a real sidelock!

Financially the next step up is the sidelock non-ejector. These are really hammer guns, with hammers inside the lock coupled to a self-cocking mechanism. Such non-ejectors are normally encountered at the cheaper end of the market but there will be some made by even the best makers. However, many shooters regard sidelocks without ejectors as 'something and nothing', so prices tend to lag well behind those for ejector guns. It is possible to convert many non-ejectors to ejector guns, but conversions are not cheap and also require reproof.

Finally, a word on side-by-sides and over-and-unders. As far as I'm concerned it's a matter of personal preference – provided you are clear about the uses to which you will be putting your gun.

If you spend most Saturdays at a clay ground I don't need to tell you what most of your fellow sportsmen have already decided; but if you expect to be walking long distances out rough shooting, there's a lot to be said for the weight advantage and quick handling of a side-by-side. Whatever you choose, enjoy your shooting!

A Century of Shotguns

MIKE GEORGE

DURING THE PAST one hundred years not much has changed in the ways in which the guns we shoot operate. Rather, it has been a century of gradual refinement in which designs have been fine-tuned quite a lot, but nobody has thrown away the book and started again completely from scratch. A shotgun still looks like a shotgun – and thank goodness for that!

Of course, 'best' shotguns, whether made in London or elsewhere, are still largely made and finished by hand in pretty much the same way as they always were, but what has changed – and changed hugely – is the way in which the guns that most of us shoot are manufactured. The most significant changes have come during the last thirty years. Put briefly, high-precision machine tools have taken over from the handworking skills of craftsmen. Craftsmen still play a huge part in gunmaking, but their skills are different; more in tune with modern engineering practices.

In the old days it used to take a lot of people to make a gun. Barrels were often bored from solid forgings, so there were barrel borers and barrel filers, and somebody to solder their finished work together into what we nowadays know as the barrel set. Actions were laboriously hand-cut and filed from solid steel forgings, then another craftsman made the joint between barrels, action and fore end. Lockmakers filed the lock parts from solid steel, and springmakers made the springs. The preparation and fitting of the gun's woodwork was equally labour intensive and time consuming.

It was a very good system while labour was cheap, but it did have one drawback. With every part hand-fitted, every gun tended to be something of a one-off. There was not really such a thing as a spare part that would fit straight out of the box. Pretty well every spare had to be hand-fitted by an expert gunsmith.

Before World War II Britain had been the finest, and possibly also the most prolific, of the world's producers of sporting shotguns in all price classes. They ranged from London-made 'best' to everyday, knockabout guns, most of which were made in the factories and workshops of Birmingham. In the 'middle range' were some excellent provincial gunsmiths, plus a number of dealers – right down to small-town ironmongers – who had their own names engraved on the ribs of Birmingham products.

Although there were some foreign-built guns about, mainly from Belgium, these, with the possible exception of the Browning B25, were thought of as inferior. The British trade had got on its feet during the Industrial Revolution and, with a few glitches here and there, had largely flourished until after World War II.

Fortunately, the 'bespoke' gun trade still flourishes in London and elsewhere in Britain, and nothing in this world handles and shoots like a British-built 'best' gun. Others may look as good, and cost as much, but they lack that certain 'feel' that spells perfection. Fine if you can afford one, but what happened to all of those guns which would, at today's monetary values, sell new from around five hundred up to, say, five thousand pounds?

Most are now built in either Italy or Japan, and even countries like Russia and Turkey are making their mark. Nowadays there is not a British-made gun in what we might term the 'affordable' price range for the average working man or woman, so what went wrong?

The fact is that after European engineering industries had recovered from World War II a malaise settled on the majority of British manufacturing, and not just on the gun trade. In the 'affordable' range we built some pretty dreadful cars and motorcycles. We failed to invest in new designs and tooling, and continued with some hugely labour-intensive practices, with the long-term result that all affordable cars available today are either built abroad, or in the UK by foreign-owned companies. As in the gun trade, only the quality specialists have survived.

The 'affordable' gun trade's problem was that it was under-financed, unimaginative, and had totally failed to invest in modern machine tools. To cover the discrepancy the trade perpetuated the myth that handmade, or at least hand-fitted and finished, was good, and machine-made was bad.

I recall visiting a British workshop which built reasonably up-market but well priced side-by-side game guns in the very early 1980s. They had actually invested in a then modern computer-controlled machining centre. Despite its capabilities for superbly accurate work, which I knew well, it was far from being their pride and joy. They reluctantly allowed me to photograph it, but I was asked to stress in my report for a magazine that it was only used for rough metal removal, and that all the main work was done by hand. Their real pride was in a line of blokes standing at benches and laboriously hand-filing and polishing components from rough-cut lumps of steel. Having visited the Italian manufacturing plant of a world leader in machine tool design and been allowed to 'drive' one of their new products only a few weeks previously, I was hard pressed not to laugh out loud. It seemed to be like a great opportunity missed.

That gun manufacturer's products didn't last much longer. The guns handled and shot nicely and were as good as any of comparable cost, but didn't command anywhere near 'best gun' prices. The problem was in the labour-intensive way they chose to make them.

Another workshop I visited in the same era was still churning out rifle parts on hand-controlled lathes and milling machines provided by the Cincinnati Machine Tool Co as part of the American Lend-Lease programme to aid British industry relatively early in World War II. They had been in service for over thirty years!

During this time the Italians were seriously tooling up for the future with modern equipment. The Spanish, whose economy was far from brilliant after years of virtual dictatorship under Franco, maybe hung on to handworking in small workshops longer than most, but they were quickly catching on. So were the Japanese.

In all British manufacturing industries in the era there were excuses powered by myths. Glib phrases abounded, like 'foreign-engineered goods are cheaper because labour costs are lower' and 'how can we compete when the Japanese will work for the price of a bowl of rice a day?' In the immediate post-war world the attitude may have been based on fact, but it certainly wasn't true as the European Union got into gear and Japan's economic miracle took off. European and Japanese wages were on a par with our own, or even better. The difference was that they had foreseen the changes and invested in the tooling.

Nowadays, if you choose to visit the website of any of the major gun manufacturers, you will find they are actually proud of the state-of-the-art machine tools and the other cutting-edge industrial processes they use. Gun spares, when they are needed, increasingly fit straight out of the box, with no hand fettling. As just one example, at least one manufacturer now offers a 20-bore barrel set which will fit their 12-bore action. You can buy the 20-bore barrels, attach them to your gun, and shoot, with no hand-fitting. That same manufacturer boasts that every other spare part fits 'as supplied', with no hand fettling.

That's the glory of using modern computer-controlled machine tools to build guns, and using them properly. The machines will turn out hundreds, thousands, or even millions of parts, all of which are absolutely identical in dimensions and with an identical quality of finish. It is the way in which all modern engineered goods are produced, and modern factory-made guns just get better and better.

Modern guns are also much tougher than their pre-war counterparts. A present-day clay shooter may fire five hundred or more shots a week, every week of the year. He expects his gun to last – and it does. An increasing number of modern guns also go through superior steel-shot proof – the toughest proof test in the world.

Much of this anthology is about nostalgia, and British shooting has many things to be proud of in its long and honourable past. However, the manufacturing side of our shotgun trade in post-war years is not one of them. It is, sadly, a saga of lost opportunity.

Gun Safety

ROB HARDY

READERS MAY wonder what special knowledge someone needs to write on the subject of safety in shooting. Well, in my case the answer is no more than the experience of participating in the sport. I worked as a shooting journalist for ten years and have the dubious honour of being a statistic on one of the mercifully short lists of shooting accidents that happen each year. I bear the scars from twenty-eight shotgun pellets, a dozen of which I still carry around with me. My main reason for writing this is that I would not want a single one of you to join me.

It happened like this. Towards the end of the season I was standing in a line of guns facing the beating team, who were slowly working their way through some cover. Suddenly a fox darted out and raced between me and the neighbouring gun. Several of us shouted 'Fox!' and as I did so I lifted my barrels skywards with the intention of turning and shooting behind the line.

My neighbour was quicker on the trigger – but he was swinging through the line as he fired. At first it felt as if someone had thrown a handful of pebbles at my legs. Then there was relief that my spaniel, sitting a couple of feet in front of me, had not been hit. Then came the pain.

My neighbour was mortified and, to his credit, did everything he could to help . . . and later to make amends. I was rushed to hospital, where eventually an operation was needed to remove those pellets the surgeon could easily reach. The rest were best left where they were. I was examined by one doctor after another, all keen to gain experience in treating gunshot injuries. A couple of months later I was more or less back to normal. End of story.

Despite what happened, it still reassures me that so few accidents happen each season even though hundreds of thousands of sportsmen take to the field, firing millions of cartridges – every shot potentially lethal. This reflects great credit on the shooting community, although with some of the rushes of blood we all witness, once or twice a season, I can't help thinking there is also a fair slice of good fortune helping the figures.

On the whole, shooters are safety-conscious individuals. They have to be these days, the tenuous hold on our right to keep a gun and enjoy our sport is under ever closer scrutiny from both inside and outside the sport.

The merest whiff of 'unsuitability' and you could find the blues and twos at your driveway to whisk away your prized collection.

It should be the responsibility of anyone who picks up a gun to make sure they can handle it safely and make the shooting experience a pleasurable one, not just for themselves but for all those around them.

I consider myself fortunate. Like many people raised in the countryside, I had family and friends around me who were willing – even from an early age – to spend time with me, teaching me the rules, many unwritten, that go hand in hand with a day's shooting in the field.

I served my apprenticeship in the beating line, watching from a grandstand view how the experienced guns dealt with birds. The ones they would shoot, the ones they would leave. How walking guns took difficult birds in cover and how their swing would be checked the moment safety might become an issue. I was drilled with shooting lore, ever to be burned on my soul.

The rules for using a gun safely could be summed up very simply:

- Treat every gun as if it were loaded.

- Never let your gun point at anyone.

- Never shoot where you cannot see.

- No bird that flies or beast that runs is worth a man's life.

I learnt all this and more before ever being let anywhere near a gun, empty or loaded. My first foray with a gun 'alone' came after several seasons of beating, sitting in duck or pigeon hides and gun-cleaning duty.

It was with an ancient Relum Tornado under lever air rifle. We were spending Christmas at my uncle's in Buckinghamshire, and as it always was when you were a kid, the snow was deep in December. He had an allotment, squeezed between a large wood on one side and a thick blackthorn hedgerow on the other, and the only show of green for miles were his Brussels sprouts.

Needless to say, the wood pigeons were taking full advantage and I was allowed to take the gun (a great lump of pale yellowish wood) make a rough hide in the hedge and act as a human scarecrow, keeping the marauding hordes off the festive greens. I shot a handful of pigeons that week, although the pellet tin seemed strangely empty by the end.

Thinking about my winter woodie forays now, it must have been absolutely freezing tucked in that hedgerow for hours, but I was never aware of feeling the slightest bit cold. The one thing I was fully aware of was that, even though I was alone, I was constantly being assessed from the house. Had I broken one of the rules above or showed the slightest disrespect to my surroundings, the gun would have been withdrawn until the lesson was relearned.

I'm not saying that you need to shoot for a lifetime to be a safe shot. I have seen many an experienced gun pull off a shot that they knew better than to take. Similarly, I shoot regularly with latecomers to shooting who are as safe as houses.

Now that shooting has developed into a sport for the masses, rather than the pastime of landowners, more and more people have taken up shooting, rather than being born into it. The majority of these are now introduced to the sport via clay pigeon shooting, and at all but the most primitive of grounds there is a strong emphasis placed on safety.

All registered grounds must have a designated safety officer and most also have coaches who have been through training programmes with organisations such as the CPSA or BASC, where safe gun handling is paramount. Learning the sport with such a coach is the modern day equivalent to the parental nurturing that was once given to emerging shots and is an excellent way to learn the basics.

Difficulties arise when the shooter decides they want to make the transition to shooting live quarry. Many clay shots make this transition and are some of the safest of shots around, but new lessons must be learnt. With the best will in the world, clay pigeon shooting cannot teach people to deal with many situations they will face in the field.

On a clay ground the shooting positions have been chosen for their safe angles and good backgrounds. You do not need to deal with roads, footpaths, people or livestock, all of which will be potential hazards from a pigeon hide or game peg.

Targets on a clay shoot are generally seen clearly for most of their flight and even if you do have to take a shot into cover, you can do so secure in the knowledge that the shooting area is kept clear.

To take the same shot at a woodcock flitting low through the trees or pheasant flying down the edge of a wood has lethal potential. So it is the all important decision-making process – whether to take the shot or not – that will be a new experience to the clay-only shot. The ability to let a bird fly on, or ground game pass, is one which all safe shots have. A simple act, you may think, but cool consideration is needed to come to such a decision, and all in a split second. This can only come with experience; some never achieve it.

No clay ground can properly recreate the mixture of excitement, confusion and mild panic which is experienced when faced with live game. A good clay flush is fun to shoot, exciting even, but most people would be hard pressed to say that it sends the adrenalin soaring like a covey of partridges exploding from cover, or sets your heart pounding in your chest as a skein of geese approach.

This is the X factor in shooting live quarry, the reason we venture out in all weathers, but it is also a deadly ingredient. It clouds the judgment and makes otherwise sensible people do things they would never do – more importantly things they think they could never do.

This is because by their very nature accidents are not planned, they happen because people get things wrong. Some people just never learn, or seem incapable of dealing with these 'pressure' situations and just have to take that shot. We all know one, but how do we deal with them?

The first reaction is, don't let them shoot. But the trouble is, they are often experienced shots. Game shooting tradition says they should be clearly told during the briefing before shooting starts, and so should be asked to put their gun away and leave the field for such transgressions. But how many shoots do this? In my experience, very few. In fact, I cannot ever remember being on a shoot where someone got the Red Card.

The usual approach is a warning, or even a few candid comments from the other guns.

'I see you are using No 6s, here have one of mine for the one you just gave me.' Or, 'I didn't know we would need Kate Adie to beat for us today.'

The perpetrator is then eased out during the season if things fail to improve and not invited back the following season. But is this the right way to deal with them? Have we become soft on safety?

After all, we are not talking about a bad tackle or foul stroke here, you may not get a second chance. So should we all become a lot less tolerant of such incidents and not just moan about them in the pub after the gun has left?

Maybe we should be making it very clear that no one is going to put up with such behaviour. The problem is that shooters are generally good, decent people – and this doesn't just apply to the safe shots.

The Lure of the Vintage Gun

DAVID BAKER

THE STRANDS THAT twist together to create the allure of the vintage gun are many and variable. This very complexity is, I am sure, part of the fascination.

After a lapse of over forty years, the motives that prompted me to leave a bid on an old hammer gun in a general auction are certainly somewhat clouded. As far as I can recall, it was a recognition of the quality of the Rigby hammer gun and the fact that something like it could be acquired for so little.

In this respect, second-hand guns are no different from all sorts of other manufactured items in that, with careful selection, there are wonderful bargains to be had by the second user. I do remember, most vividly, taking the locks off this gun when I got it home and being amazed at the quality of workmanship. Quite simply, I had not realised that such beautiful craftsmanship was a part of gunmaking. The parts fitted together as they do in a fine watch and everything was polished to a mirror finish. Everywhere I looked on that gun, quality was obvious; the fit of metal to metal, of wood to metal, the absence of any tool marks, even in the most obscure recesses.

The downside was that this experience of quality showed me just how dreadfully crude was the Belgian hammer gun I then used. The problem was that the Rigby's barrels were beyond their safe life. Truly, in the bores, there were more dark pits than polished parts.

My dilemma was solved by the purchase of the wreck of a Purdey hammer gun for five pounds from Gallyons in Cambridge, and after repairs and reproof, I had a gun of quality. The fact that I had only opted for black powder proof was, in retrospect, something of a blessing in disguise, because the boom and smoke of these distinctive cartridges became akin to my trademark. I shot with that gun for years, mostly pigeons and, with its true cylinder boring, it was perfect both for decoying and roost shooting.

A bonus to having all the makings to load my own black powder cartridges was that the move into muzzle loading was but a very short step. Reloading was essential as there were no commercially loaded black powder cartridges, so I used clay-ground pick-ups to make my own. The first muzzle-loader came as the result of another impulse purchase from the antiques stall in Cambridge market. The stall boasted an array of about a dozen muzzle-loading shotguns, most of which were sad, rusty relics, but one caught my eye. Not only was it not rusty, more importantly it looked as if it never had been rusty. More, it had the patina of a cherished gun. So I bought it for twelve pounds and was lucky to the extent that the bore was as good as the outside of the gun. All it took to get me shooting the gun was a trip back to Gallyons to buy a tin of percussion caps.

It has to be admitted that I never became a truly dedicated muzzle-loader. Despite this, I have acquired over the years a very mixed group of such guns. Typical of this casual collection was a 6-bore single barrel, almost certainly built for live pigeon trap shooting.

Another muzzle-loader with a story is a 10-bore weighing nine pounds with a forty-inch barrel I bought in an auction in San Francisco and carried home as part of my luggage, simply trundling through the 'Something to Declare' lane at Heathrow.

The first time I saw my next muzzle-loader in the same auction house, it was one of a bundle of old guns tied together with binder twine. It was so dirty that it was totally black, with no clue as to the material of the barrel or stock, but it had attractive lines and was fitted with the peculiar external mainspring lock that is called a Miquelet.

The first pleasure was to clean the gun and find all sorts of hidden features. A real joy was that this gun derives from a true, artisan tradition of gunmaking somewhere on the Iberian peninsular. The black, featureless barrel proved to be a very fancy multi-pattern type of Belgian damascus. The all-metal ramrod had once been part of a Napoleonic War period French musket, while I am certain that the lock was also on its second incarnation. Now with percussion ignition, I am sure that it had once swung a flint.

Holding all this together was a stock made of reddish-coloured, straight-grained timber, probably cherry, but it could be any member of the plum tribe. Such a stock is typical of the guns of Spain and Portugal. Again it is a 10-bore and again I was able to have it polished out to please the eye of the proof master. It only weighs six pounds and I have shot snipe with it. Not many snipe are shot with single barrel Miquelet lock 10-bores in Pembrokeshire!

For serious shooting, certainly out in company with others carrying breech loaders, I have, for the most part, used a hammer gun. At first it was the Purdey, but then came a rival.

Bought in the now-defunct Knight, Frank & Rutley auctions was a nitro-proof side-lever hammer Horsley. The Horsley had two virtues: it was nitro-proved so cleaning was easy and there was no need to load special cartridges. Even more important was the long straight stock that suited me. There was some choke in the left barrel so, for several seasons, it became my duck gun, while the Purdey remained the game gun.

Shooting with a vintage gun is but one of the strands that make up its fascination and it does not stand in isolation. Rather, it opens the door and leads further.

My path has been the study of the mechanical evolution of the sporting gun, inspired by the writing of the late Gough Thomas. His weekly column in the *Shooting Times* was required reading in the 1970s and it contained sufficient allusions to the history of the sporting gun to prompt further study. Starting with the local reference library, I graduated to the Cambridge University Library, a copyright library which gave me access to a virtually complete set of the nineteenth-century classics. On top of this there was a full set of nineteenth-century British patent specifications so, as my readings and researches took me beyond the published works, I had a new seam to mine.

As I read I became critical of the published magazine articles. I could recognise the classic works rehashed with little or no added original material. With the confidence, or perhaps arrogance, of a young man, I believed I could do better. At the outset I faced the problem that all potential outlets had regular contributors, with no need of an upstart no matter how good his stuff. But magazines come and go and eventually I found a slot. Now I realise that the real rewards of writing have come from contacts made and guns seen. Quite simply it has opened doors like nothing else I know.

In this respect, the highlight of my vintage gun career was the invitation to write a book on the Queen's guns at Sandringham. I wrote up my experiences in an article called *Mine for a Week*, and that's just what it felt like. The cabinets were unlocked and the photographic crew and myself were just left to get on with the project.

I will always treasure the experience of having had in my hands every one of King George V's hammer Purdeys. There are four trios – I have handled all twelve. This includes the special lightweight set built after His Majesty's near fatal illness. Then there were all the other guns and rifles used by a whole list of royals from Prince Albert onwards, and all of this in Sandringham House.

Just as cherished are memories of the less exalted collectors who have trusted me to see and photograph their treasures. Not just in this country but literally all round the world. For while it is true that exposure to as many different examples of all the diverse manifestations of the gunmakers' art is the best way to learn and appreciate the guns, in reality friendship is even more valuable.

Looking back, I have come a long way since I found that hammer gun in an auction of assorted household effects. The path has taken me to some strange places, from overgrown graveyards on cold wet days looking for the last resting place of some hero, to the basement archives of the old *Field* offices. As a direct result of the writing, I have shot bob white quail in Virginia with a 20-bore pinfire Lang and stubble quail in Queensland with the first snap action made by Horsleys. I have been into storerooms of Le Musée d'Armes in Liege and sat and chatted with the curator as he ate his packed lunch. Contrast this with the tour of the huge military museum in St Petersburg, which included a considerable collection of sporting guns and rifles, probably Red Army loot. At the end of the visit we were ushered into the director's office and informed that we were 'free to leave'. The Soviet Union was then still in existence and remarks like that, coupled with the armed border guards swarming all over and under our coach and searching our baggage, were sobering experiences.

The threads and strands running through all these stories are connected by the vintage guns. These survivors of our technical history hold a rare fascination. Every one has individual charisma and charm creating an aura which surrounds me every time I have one in my hands.

Progress Doesn't Always Take Us Forward

GEORGE WALLACE

MY LOVE AFFAIR with rifles started in the Army Cadets – and before any of my so-called friends start, yes, the rifles were breech-loaders. I'm very fond of muzzle-loading rifles but that's another story.

It all began in the days when, even for hunting, open sights were the norm and telescopic sights were still regarded in some circles as disreputable, unsporting and only to be used by cads, bounders, assassins and such.

While progress in the realm of optical sighting equipment has been dramatic and very welcome for most purposes, it is also a fact that too much reliance on technology causes many of the old skills to be lost and forgotten . . . and then regretted and mourned when it's too late to bring them back.

Much of the fierce pleasure of hunting, as opposed to pest control, comes from getting in close and beating your quarry at its own game and in its own environment. The shot itself should, for both ethical and practical reasons, be almost a formality. Under such circumstances there seems little need for high velocity cartridges or high magnification 'scopes.

We often think, perhaps because of advertising 'hype' or perhaps because it seems so obvious, that modern rifles are much better, much more reliable and much more accurate than those of our grandfathers. It sounds reasonable but I'm afraid it is just not so.

Some of the most accurate rifles ever built were those legendary muzzle-loaders of the 1850s and 60s and despite technological advances their modern successors struggle to match them. I have in front of me a group shot as an experiment with a muzzle-loading percussion target rifle of about 1860. The range was 186 yards and the group size 1⅛ inches horizontally by ⅞ inch vertically. The shooter wrote that, 'While the result was by no means the best ever obtained, it is certainly very remarkable.' Anyone I know would be delighted with such a group today, even with the benefit of nearly one hundred and fifty years of 'progress'.

However, we are talking hunting here, rather than long range target shooting, and 'off the shelf' rifles rather than bespoke custom jobbies, so has the sporting rifle scene changed more than that of the target world? The answer is: no, not really. Less accuracy is expected of a relatively light sporting rifle but the comparison still holds good.

I suppose the average 'off the shelf' rifle of today might be expected to be more accurate than its predecessors simply because it can be built to tighter tolerances. However there's actually much more to it than that and I have the liveliest suspicion that any perceived improvement can be put down to the ammunition rather than the rifle. Modern rifle ammunition from manufacturers such as Norma, Federal, Remington, Winchester, or whoever, is made to such close tolerances that there is virtually no variation from shot to shot. And that, my friends, is what really makes rifles accurate. Even twenty years ago, we hand loaders could always make a rifle shoot better than it would with factory ammo; nowadays that's not so easy.

As an illustration, let's take my old bolt-action rifle. This was built by John Rigby in London in 1908 and chambered for a cartridge called 'Rigby's Special .350-bore.' No ammunition is available, of course, but bullets to the original design are made by Woodleigh in Australia and brass cartridge cases by Bertram, also in Oz.

Conventional twenty-first-century wisdom suggests that, for best accuracy, bullet diameter should be the same as the groove diameter of the barrel. (Groove diameter is measured into the bottom of the rifling, as opposed to bore diameter which is the size of the bore before the rifling is cut.)

The Rigby's barrel measures .362 inches into the grooves and the Woodleigh bullets are .3575 inches in diameter so one might be pardoned for thinking there was little prospect of decent accuracy. The bullets don't actually rattle down the bore, of course, but they're nowhere near the recommended size. However, the old lady will put three shots into less than an inch at one hundred yards with what is perceived to be an ill-fitting bullet, so there's obviously much more to it. In fact, my Rigby would appear to knock the theory of precise fit of bullet to barrel into a cocked hat.

So what is the answer? I really don't know, but my impression is that for acceptable accuracy and given a decent barrel, consistent ammunition is much more important than any precise fit between bullet and bore. For fine target accuracy, both are probably required.

When I began, I had intended to write about something else entirely but I've been rambling down side lanes so, to avoid having to rub it all out and start again, can we draw any conclusions?

First, for acceptable hunting accuracy, you don't need the latest in modern rifle technology. Ammo, yes; rifle, no. Second, some of those beautiful old rifles are very affordable, particularly when chambered for unfashionable cartridges. Many of them are things of beauty in their own right, handle like a bespoke shotgun and give their owners immense pleasure. And third, the extraordinary satisfaction of hunting with such a rifle, whether chambered for one of the old rook and rabbit cartridges or something bigger for deer or exotic foreign game, is something every true hunter should experience. If you don't, you are missing an important part of the total hunting picture.

All the best stories have a moral. The moral here is that there's very much more to hunting than killing an animal at long range with the latest high-tech rifle and 'Knock 'em Down and Stamp on 'em Magnum' cartridge. Such equipment is fine for pest control but, for me, destroys the simple pleasure of ordinary hunting.

My motto for rifle shooting is KISS – Keep It Simple, Stupid. It may not be quite so easy but it's definitely much more fun.

Uncle Sam's Got Grandpa's Purdey

DIG HADOKE

IN 1981, WHEN I began using a side-by-side 12-bore, MacDonald Hastings wrote in his useful little book, *The Shotgun*: 'Over & unders have never really caught on in Britain where shooting men feel that the conventional gun handles more sweetly.'

At that time, the average shooter still walked afield with a Birmingham-made boxlock and the better off probably carried a London sidelock. By the 1980s, most of these guns had been handed from father to son two or three times and they were the staple on all the shoots where I worked Saturdays as a teenage beater.

How times have changed! Now, when I cast my eyes around on a shoot day, all I see are foreign-made over- and- unders. Most of these have been bought new by their owners and admittedly they do the job well for the money. But where are all the old side-by-sides and why did people fall out of love with them? Where is 'Grandpa's Purdey'? It is a question that turns over and over in my mind as I walk afield with my old English guns, unable to imagine gaining half as much enjoyment from the product of a machine-shop in Brescia.

Well, the chances are that 'Grandpa's Purdey' now belongs to an American. We Brits have as a nation delighted in laughing at the Yanks for their brash vulgarity and lack of taste for two hundred years. Well I'm afraid the joke is now firmly on us, as we step tentatively into the twenty-first century, dressed in our technical fabrics and unsleeving our boring, cloned, continental shotguns, replete with 3-inch chambers and sporting laser-etched flying parrots on their alloy lock-plates.

A long time ago discerning American gun buyers woke up to the fact that British guns built before World War I are the best sporting firearms ever made and they are cheap in comparison with anything else of the quality and rarity they represent. Websites for gun stores in the USA have a better selection of old British sidelocks, boxlocks and hammer guns than most of those in the UK.

'Best' shotguns are among the finest things that Britain (or indeed any country) has ever produced. They are artistic and mechanical perfection in wood and metal; made by hand to the very highest possible standards at a time when craftsmanship was at its dizziest heights and labour was cheap. They represent our sporting heritage and a hundred-year-old London sidelock will serve today's user just as well in the coverts as it did the long dead original owner. Yet most British shooting men don't appreciate them.

I assure you the Americans do appreciate them; and they want them all. Perhaps only when you can't find a decent used English sidelock in this country will everyone begin to wonder where they all went and lament their loss. Already, finding a decent hammer gun for sensible money is increasingly difficult. All the while the British shooter is happily (though in my opinion shamefully) wandering around with his trusty Silver Pigeon.

So, how does a used English gun stack up pound-for-pound against the foreign challenger? How is it possible to make an arguable case for the superiority of the nineteenth-century British shotgun in the face of twenty-first-century opposition? Well, I believe the case is there to be made. The reader will have to decide for himself if it has true merit.

The cost of buying anything is at its highest when the item is new. A new Purdey sidelock ejector will cost more than a second-hand example in the same way that a new Jaguar will cost more than a second-hand one. In fact you can buy a top quality second-hand Boss, Holland & Holland or Purdey for much less than you will pay for not only a new model from these makers, but for less than you would pay for the gunmaking equivalents of Ford and Toyota: Famars, Krieghoff, Arietta, Browning, Rizzini, etc. Why pay £7500 for a new Italian side-by-side when you can have an 1880s Purdey for the same money?

A new gun by a top British maker (costing upwards of £45,000) offers you nothing that the old turn-of-the-century classic does not. There really have been no significant improvements in design or manufacture. The 'best' guns are the same; the only difference is a few years and many thousands of pounds. Since it is acknowledged that the best output of the British gun industry is the best in the world, why would you want something else instead? When it is also acknowledged that pre-World War I output was of a higher quality than anything achieved since, the case for buying and using a British gun of this vintage becomes even more compelling.

Working to the advantage of the owner of a vintage English gun is the fact that the sporting gun was perfected so long ago. We still use ammunition of the type first offered by Daw in 1861 and the 2½-inch 12-bore cartridge loaded with one ounce of No 6 still performs perfectly in the field. Every best gun was made for a particular purpose. Light guns were balanced, regulated and shaped to work with light loads for fast handling. A long chamber was only used where it was warranted: weight was put only where and when it was required. The nineteenth-century buyer of a 'best' gun was too particular to tolerate the 'one size fits all' mentality we now accept.

The sidelock was perfected by Beesley in 1880, the boxlock even earlier, by Anson & Deeley in 1875, and even the over-and-under user knows of no better design than those of Woodward or Robertson which date from before the Great War. If one really considers what a best gun, directly compared pound-for-pound with a new one, can offer, there really is no contest.

The buyer with £10,000 in hand can afford a vintage gun of the first quality but can only afford a new gun of lesser quality. On a cost basis, you get more for your money from second-hand British guns. They also hold their value, and in recent years have increased; shooting the finest guns in the world is actually making you money!

At the time of writing, you could spend £11,000 on a new AYA 'Number 1 de-Luxe' or you could have a 1919 Holland & Holland Royal 'Modele de-Luxe' for £9400. Go down a little with the budget and for £7,500 you can have a new Arietta side-by-side or save yourself a grand and get an 1889 Purdey instead. A William Powell Heritage sidelock looks English but is made in Italy and will set you back a pound short of £5000. For this money you could have a very good Holland & Holland Bad-minton sidelock from the 1930s.

The MacNab Highlander at £3750 seems a good buy until you compare the quality with an Edwinson Green over-and-under from around World War I for the same money or an 1890 Holland & Holland 'Royal' for £700 less. As we get into budget territory, the Beretta 'Gold E' 682 retails at £1995 and so does the MacNab Woodcock, for which you could have the best 1960s Webley & Scott 702 you can find or save yourself £495 and get a classy 1867 Grant side-lever hammer gun.

Getting right down to the bargain basement bin below £500, we have the Yildiz side-by-side with gold-coloured single trigger or a choice of boxlock non-ejectors of excellent quality by W.W. Greener or W.R. Pape, dating from around 1914. All the prices I have quoted for English guns, I have actually seen go under the hammer at London gun auctions this year (2005–6).

In each of the categories discussed, the second-hand British classic is a better quality gun than the new one of equivalent price. It will be better in a year, better in five years and better in thirty years. The myth that you keep your Purdey for best and use your AYA for hard work is rubbish. The old gunmakers became famous because their guns did the job better than anything else, for longer and without mishap. I fire thousands of rounds per year through my old guns with hardly a murmur and I use them in all weathers.

Buying a vintage British gun is an investment in your heritage and your money will be safe. New guns, by contrast, will lose value the moment they leave the shop and will continue to do so for some time. Moreover, those machine-made modern shooting tools have no history and no soul. So, if you have a British gun handed down through the family, get it fitted and use it. If you don't have one, go and buy one now. Otherwise, you may wake up one day and wonder where they have all gone.

CHAPTER FIVE

·

Shoots and Gamekeeping

Welbeck

PAULA MINCHIN

NOT MANY SHOOTING accidents could have changed the entire history of the twentieth century, but there is one well-documented near miss that came very close.

Picture the scene: it is December, 1913, deep snow covers the ground, and a party of guns are enjoying some of England's best pheasant shooting at Welbeck, Nottinghamshire, as guests of the sixth Duke of Portland.

There is a flush of pheasants and one of the loaders loses his balance on the icy ground. As he falls, both barrels of the gun are discharged. The shot passes within a few feet of the Duke and one of his foreign guests.

On that occasion the two Dukes were lucky – but the guest's luck was not to last. Just six months later, in June 1914, Archduke Franz Ferdinand of Austria, heir to the Habsburg throne, was shot dead by a Serbian nationalist. The assassination ignited World War I.

The Archduke's narrow escape at Welbeck was chronicled years later by the Duke of Portland in his book, *Women, Men and Things*. He wrote:

> I have often wondered whether the Great War might have been averted, or at least postponed, had the Archduke met his death then and not at Sarajevo in the following year.

What is certain is that the Duke and his family have taken better care of their possessions than the Habsburgs – and some of their former neighbours.

A number of estates in the surrounding area – known as 'The Dukeries', as so many of England's noblemen had land there – have decayed, crumbled and broken up. Not so Welbeck, which is still intact and vibrant, complete with a renowned shoot that is as great as it ever was. Home to the Cavendish family since the 1600s, the estate is now owned and managed by Lady Anne Bentinck, daughter of the seventh Duke of Portland.

Though Lady Anne has never shot, preferring instead to ride to hounds and be master of her own pack, she has continued her forebears' passion for shooting. The estate's twenty shoot days are still private, with invited guests.

Steeped in history, thanks to the ambitions of the politically influential and sometimes eccentric Dukes of Newcastle and Portland, by the late 1800s Welbeck was right up there on the list of most sought-after shooting invitations. Many of the crack shots of the day, including Earl de Grey and King Edward VII, were regular guests. In fact, the Earl de Grey (later the second Marquess of Ripon) had a drive named after him on the Lambing Pen beat, called Earl de Grey's Rise.

Each wood and almost every field has a name, while nearly forty immaculate stone lodges dotted over the estate are named after notable battles such as Corunna, Gibraltar and Bunker's Hill.

There are also several remises, small fields enclosed on four sides by belts of trees. In times past, the Dukes allowed their keepers to plant fruit and vegetables within the clearings and even now, the keepers come across sloes and damsons.

The most famous drive by far on this sweeping 15,000-acre estate is the dramatic Creswell Crags. The celebrated eighteenth-century artist George Stubbs was so taken by the rugged landscape that he used it regularly as a backdrop for his equestrian paintings. Stubbs's painting 'Two men going a shooting with a view of Creswell Crags', illustrates the fact that the drive was being shot as early as 1766, albeit by two guns with muskets and pointers.

Creswell Crags is a steep-sided gorge, with a man-made pond at the bottom and dense woodland on either side. The Nottinghamshire/ Derbyshire county border follows the path of the stream that runs through the bottom of the gorge. At one time, it was possible to push the Nottinghamshire side of the wood out over the gorge and vice versa with the Derbyshire side.

It was a favourite spot for the sixth Duke, who ruled the roost at Welbeck from 1879 to 1943. In his book he recalls an incident when the Duke of Devonshire shot at Creswell Crags:

The late Duke of Devonshire, then Lord Hartington, was a keen though not very accurate shot. When shooting at Creswell Crags, in company with Harry Chaplin and one or two other of his old friends, he killed an exceptionally high-flying partridge in a manner equal to that of de Grey or Harry Stonor.

His friends thereupon gave a loud cheer. When the drive was over, he said to me, 'I wonder why Harry Chaplin and the others cheered when I fired both barrels at a cock pheasant and missed?'

'Missed a cock pheasant with both barrels?' I said. 'Why, you killed the highest partridge that ever flew from Nottinghamshire into Derbyshire!'

'Did I?' Said Hartington. 'I didn't even know it was there. However, it's over now, so don't say anything about it, and let me keep my reputation.'

The seventh Duke always made sure he had enough firepower to cope with the high birds at the Crags and had a spare pair of barrels made for two of his six guns, which were fully choked especially for shooting there.

By the close of the nineteenth century, Welbeck was renowned for its high-quality partridge shooting, particularly on the Blue Barn Beat, as the sixth Duke explains:

The bags of partridges killed at Welbeck and Clipstone began to increase from the year 1887, which was the first really good year, and we several times killed over 200 brace to four guns; but at that time the sport was by walking up birds in line. In 1894 and 1895 partridge driving was first practised at Welbeck and Clipstone. Mr W Hollins suggested to me that the Blue Barn Beat should be driven over Blue Barn lane, and this has since been done with great success. In 1896 partridge driving really commenced. The peak year was 1929, when 3,349 brace were killed. 1934–35 was also an excellent season. I believe more partridges have been killed in recent years over Blue Barn lane than at any other place in England.

Blue Barn Lane is shot in the same way today and still provides the main drives on Welbeck's partridge days.

Up until World War II, there were forty keepers at Welbeck, including two head keepers. Nowadays the estate is run by head keeper Peter Betts, five beat keepers and one beat keeper cum water bailiff, plus a trainee keeper and Margaret Rowson, who trains Lady Anne's gundogs.

Peter has been head keeper for twenty-three years, but has worked for Welbeck for a total of thirty-six years, starting as a trainee at the age of fifteen. As we drive through the Park, he keeps up a running commentary about Welbeck and the stories he has heard over the years.

'When I first started as head keeper, I kept in touch with all the old keepers who could remember royalty shooting here,' he says.

'I used to pick their brains and never forgot the stories that they told me ... I would have loved to have been a fly on the wall in those days. At one time the head keeper here had two gardeners and a seamstress!'

He then regales us with a story about a gun who used to love coming shooting at Welbeck.

'He shot here with the King once, but when he was invited back for a second time, along with the King, he was horrified and apparently said that if he was invited back a third time he would be bankrupt. This was because the King set how much tip money to give the keeper at the end of the day and the rest of the guns had to follow.'

Peter says that although there are many top notch drives to choose from at Welbeck, after three hundred years of shooting there, Creswell Crags is still one they can bank on.

'We can go to Creswell Crags having not planned to shoot it and it still shoots lovely,' he says.

'We always shoot double days for pheasants, and without fail, Creswell Crags is saved for the grand finale on the afternoon of the last day.'

Family Shoot

ROBIN SCOTT

How far, or long, do you have to travel to find the sort of sport you don't get on your own shoot?

Some friends drive up to three, four or more hours to find really challenging birds in different countryside. From time to time they've even been known to take a plane in pursuit of something really special: two hours puts them in Spain, Norway or mainland Europe, another eight and they can comfortably reach North America.

But the ones who've got the job properly sorted are a handful of lads in the Nawton and Beadlam Shoot, North Yorkshire. They can be in sporting heaven inside ten minutes, five if there isn't a tractor on the lane to slow them down.

Their own shoot over rolling farmland shows cracking birds on some drives and they've enough acreage to comfortably shoot every fortnight during the season. But the grass is definitely greener just half a mile from them. In fact it's positively emerald. And once a year they put a little money aside to buy an end-of-season boundary day on it. And what a boundary it is too!

The arable land and hedgerows that typify their own ground hits an abrupt end when it meets the four thousand-acre Nawton Tower shoot. Suddenly you stumble across plummeting valley sides that offer the sort of dizzying view no photograph, or painting, could ever capture. And when your eyes, at last, adjust to the picture, the more you look, the more you see.

At each turn of the trout stream down below another secret, tree-lined little valley draining water from the North Yorkshire Moors catches your eye as the light changes from pale sunshine to deep cloud shadow. If you're lucky enough to be there while a shoot's in progress you can even look down on the backs of the birds as they head out across the valley and over the stretched gun line, way, way below.

But of course the Nawton and Beadlam boys are used to this scenery, it's everyday fare to them. What they're after on their one away-day trip of the year is taking in the view of a pheasant or two from the business end – and that's down there on the valley floor, looking up.

I daresay a few crack shots working a pair of guns could rattle up a fair-sized bag in these valleys even at the end of the season but this team look for around eighty birds, and high ones at that. They also look for some good banter between gamekeeper Brian 'Taffy' Dacey and his team of beaters. And they're never disappointed. This year a bunch of beaters listened the night before to Dennis Sharpe's proud claim that they couldn't possibly show a bird he wouldn't be able to kill. A pint or two off midnight and even we were beginning to think they'd need a JCB bucket – not a game cart – to bring back the slain.

Ah well, two drives into the day and poor old Dennis had blown a box and a half of cartridges for nil pheasants. Back to the drawing board.

Then again, after the first drive hairdresser Pete Robinson was probably wishing he hadn't brought his 20-bore but, third drive in, he began to trim a few up, as did the only other 20-bore user that day, Anthony Rooke.

On the bigger gun front, agricultural engineer Ian Otterburn had taken some fearful leg-pulling for being the only side-by-side devotee in the party. He silenced (almost) everyone by pulling down a succession of very tasty early birds from a spectacular drive called the Cocked Hat. Even that performance though didn't stop one of the guns shouting: 'Nice one, Ian – but just think how much better you'd shoot if you got rid of that bloody old tyre lever and used a proper gun instead ...'

It was thanks though to Ian and farmer Stephen Barker that a steady trickle of birds did go into the game cart over the first few drives and kept the average going. That said, the majority of birds turned out to be hens ... much to the delight of the beaters who had a cock shoot to look forward to the next day.

Lunchtime clearly revived more than just the spirits because Dennis, Peter, Anthony, Dave Snowdon and the rest suddenly hit another gear on a succession of beautifully presented birds off the steep hillsides. Ian and Stephen were in the thick of it, pinching each other's pheasants when the chance arose ... and two or three back guns were also doing an excellent job on cock birds trying to sneak over unnoticed. The only folk who didn't appreciate the sight of cocks being killed stone-dead then falling for what seemed like an eternity to the valley floor way below, were the beaters. For some reason or other they went quiet. And despite his best efforts there was still no sign of a JCB for Dennis and his bag.

For me it was the last drive that made the day. I eventually found my peg alongside a little stream in the quiet valley and looked at my surroundings in the fading light. Downstream, part hidden by trees and a thin rising mist, was a mill house that somehow looked vaguely familiar. And it then slowly dawned on me: I was pegged against the very same pool where, as a six year old in Wellington boots, I caught my first brown trout on a fly.

Eerie wasn't the word.

Pheasants poured off the hillside above but I didn't fire, I couldn't. My gaze was glued to the cascading stream and the branch under which the fish had lain forty years earlier. I could still see Dad crouched high above on the opposite bank watching my fly's progress, hearing him shout 'Strike!' when the fish rose. In spite of the mistakes I made playing this darting brownie, and the weight of the cascading water, he somehow managed to get it into the net ...

The spell was broken, as it had to be eventually, by a huge splash from a dead hen-bird dropping into the torrent just upstream. Quick as a flash Cassie was swimming, picking it under the very same branch that had given up the trout all those years ago. She turned in the current and brought it straight to hand.

Looking up, it was obvious from the number of dogs I could see carrying birds back to their handlers that a decent old drive had been underway while I'd been 'playing' that trout from so many years ago. But what did it matter? The Beadlam boys were happy, the beaters were already looking forward to their cock day and the bag had reached eighty-six head. Or rather it hadn't.

Rightly or wrongly I didn't put the eighty-seventh bird in the game cart. Like that trout, I took it home, ate it and enjoyed every mouthful.

So, if I owe you a few quid for the stolen bird, Taffy, please let me know when I'm next up. If you don't want the money I will put it behind the bar of the Rose and Crown, buy Dennis a few rounds, then sit back and listen to how he's going to kill those pheasants of yours next time around.

Make sure you come along to hear it!

Sadly, since this report first appeared in *Sporting Gun* both Stephen – Robin's cousin – and Dennis have died. They might be gone, but they will never be forgotten.

Not a Shoot for the Faint-Hearted

WILL GARFIT

Max and Tim are chums I know through our mutual interest in fishery management. They run an amazing shoot on a forgotten part of coastal east Essex. The Vikings may have landed there but few others since. It is a world of overgrown old woods where oak, ash, sweet chestnut and sycamore tangle in their fight for life. Below is a bramble, bracken and rhododendron thicket, with primeval bog in the hollows. The woodland is interspersed with undrained meadows and on the higher land more conventional arable farming. It is the most wonderful habitat for a great variety of game, wildfowl and wildlife.

To be polite it could be called a very rough walking shoot. Guns are invited for their fitness, dogs, stamina, determination and ability to shoot through the thicket or vegetation. Somewhere on the 1500 acres is a quarry species at which you may just get the opportunity of a safe shot if you are sharp eyed through 360 degrees from dawn till dusk.

Twelve of us privileged had come through the tough selection process to be invited on a day in early December. A briefing from Max and then off to a speculative duck drive should any migrant wildfowl be on the old decoy pond. Suddenly gadwall were climbing over the tall oaks and above them teal, virtually out of shot.

It was hardly surprising that we were more successful with the gadwall: thirteen were picked and just two teal. Simultaneously half the guns had gone to drive the little reservoir and returned with a tufted duck and two greylags. A successful start indeed!

Then came the first big manoeuvre as groups of us started to hunt and blank in vast acres of arable to an area of thick hedgerows and marsh. Half a mile away odd shots indicated the other team's approach. Eventually the bramble clump at the heart of the whole exercise was surrounded. Flushed by Max's Jack Russell, the wild pheasants rocketed out in all directions, producing some very sporting driven shots.

Coffee and delicious icing-topped pastries boosted the blood sugar levels before we again split into groups to walk a large woodland either side of a brook which ended in ponds and lakes of the old decoy. I was instructed to follow the edge of the water to get a chance of coot or waterhen.

[143]

Conon and I hunted the right bank but without sight or sound of anything but a squirrel which tantalisingly disappeared into the hole of a tree without the chance of a shot. Suddenly my right boot sank into stinking mud and my left boot with all my weight slid below the surface. Without any resistance I was disappearing into bottomless black slime.

I had to brace myself on my old Beesley, flat on the surface, to prevent a tragedy. This saved me from a glutinous end and gave me a chance to grab a sallow branch overhead from which I could pull myself out. It was a lucky escape with just a bootful of black sludge, the tidemark of which was nearly up to my waist. And it was all worthwhile as Conon flushed a hen pheasant which was added to the bag.

Mulligatawny soup and pork pie made a quick lunch, then off again on another big manoeuvre. I was put as the one gun in the epicentre of the exercise. This was on the point of two woods that met at the corner where they joined. The wind was right for pigeons to flight across my corner. I hid up in a thicket and during the hour-long manoeuvre fifteen pigeons and a carrion crow made my contribution to the bag.

It was dark by the time the last team arrived from the final wood back at the decoyman's old cottage. Game bags were disembowelled and triumphant stories were told of each hard-earned trophy.

What a bag it was, with eighteen species and a record total of 159 head! This was made up of thirty-three pheasants, three red-legged partridges, five woodcock, six carrion crows, two teal, thirteen gadwall, one tufted duck, two greylag geese, six rabbits, one hare, one squirrel, seventy-nine wood pigeons, one collared dove, one herring gull, one jackdaw, two rooks, one jay and a magpie.

A great day indeed, where every step could be your last or, by contrast, could produce the shot of a lifetime.

The Big One

LINDSAY WADDELL

Every keeper who is employed to produce wild game looks forward to the season when everything comes together and the sky darkens with game as they take to the wing. Well, that may be a bit over the top, but ...

The recipe for such a season is not a simple one, not where grouse are concerned at any rate, and although dealing with wild grey partridge and wild pheasants, albeit on the moorland fringes, is not dissimilar, red grouse have the added problem of regular ups and downs due to the strongyle worm. I know greys can suffer from their own peculiar strain of the pest, but not to the same extent. This is the story of my big one to date, and I doubt if I shall beat it, although you never know.

First, the recipe. A good stock of mainly young birds from the previous season, in good health, followed by an excellent breeding season, and within it a good insect supply which is crucial for the survival of the chicks for the first few weeks of their lives. Good predator control is in there of course and the final piece of the jigsaw is good weather during the shooting season, for without that the keeper cannot crop his surplus. The quality of the guns is perhaps a topic for another time!

There have been a number of springs when most or all of those ingredients have been in place at Raby during my tenure here, but there has always been at least one thing which has happened to derail the process and have us watch yet one more chance of a really big year slide by. Feet of snow at the end of April when most of our hens were sitting ruined one. We shot an average year, but how I cursed that weather which crushed not only some of our hen grouse, but partridge, lapwing and golden plover under the white blanket.

Wet springs, poor quality heather browned by biting east winds, birds carrying too many worms, all have played their part in one way or another to bring that magic tally in the book up short.

In the spring of 1986 we had two days of freezing rain which coated the whole countryside in our part of the Pennines with six inches of clear ice. For the grouse it coated the heather in an impenetrable sheet. There was no way through. Despite the efforts of many keepers using snow-ploughs, harrows and snow bikes to break the surface and allow the grouse in to feed, by the end of May there were very few birds alive in the Northern Pennines. The keeper at Barningham, Alan Edwards, told me the few remaining grouse, which had survived on the thorn bushes off the edge of the moor, were so weak that they walked back out on to the heather when the thaw came. At Raby, on the four thousand-acre Middle End beat not a bird was shot.

It was however a good breeding season, the ground was free from parasites and the few birds did well, taking the stock on the moor up to just over half of what we would have liked. The next season of 1987 was a building year. Again a good breeding season and we managed nearly fourteen hundred brace from our meagre stock, and more importantly we once again left a good stock of young grouse, but this time far closer to capacity than the previous year.

The winter was, from our point of view, a good one. There was a nice bit of snow and a decent burning season to follow. The grouse looked well, with no indication of any noticeable worm burdens. As the spring of 1988 wore on and we approached hatching time, the tiny crane flies, tipulids, which the grouse chicks need during those first critical few weeks appeared by the millions. I have never seen so many before or since. It is not only the grouse which cycle in numbers, so does their chicks' food supply. An exceptionally dry summer may well cause a crash in the population of these vital insects – which breed in the damp mossy areas on the hill – and yet it will go unnoticed to most observers since it is not obvious until the next spring. But the tipulids were here this time, and that was the important thing.

As the hatch progressed and the broods became more visible, we were aware that many of them were double figure ones, one hen had seventeen chicks which is still the largest brood I have ever seen reared. July arrived, and the time came for us to do our brood counts. These counts entail using dogs to cover the ground either side of a transect taken from one end of the butt line to the far end of the drive, then another is done back on a different line to the other end of the same line of butts.

By this means the keeper can work out the density of grouse on that drive. Furthermore, these counts when allied to the spring stock counts can give an accurate picture of the numbers of grouse on the moor, and so help to plan the number of shoot days. This time some were never completed for the grouse rolled on in front of the dogs and we could not get a 'good' count for grouse rising in such large numbers. Four, five, six, broods all lifting together, sixty to eighty grouse at times, we knew it was going to be an exceptional season.

Dawn on The Twelfth brought a horrible morning, with fog on the high ground where traditionally we always go on the first day of the season. Therefore Claybogs was ruled out. Down then to the Middle End butts themselves, with little other option for I had a west south westerly gale and rain. We did four drives – the bag: 230 brace. These were no ordinary August birds, they were very well grown and they were going like bullets.

Day two was just as windy but clear, and so we moved up to the high ground we had intended to shoot the day before. It was another four-drive day with one big drive by our standards – six or seven hundred acres. The grouse poured through; thirties, fifties, large broods into the teens, a never-ending stream. As this drive approached the end, Mr. Boller, the tenant for the first three days, was in the top butt. He had shot ninety-nine grouse before running out of cartridges.

Blue, his loader, was sent down the line to get another handful in the hope of the hundredth bird but he did not get back before the whistle went to end the drive. The bag on day two was 348 and a half brace. This was followed, on day three, by the Monks beat which produced 238 and a half. That brought the tally to 717 brace of exceptionally fast August grouse, in only the first three days off four thousand acres.

Of our first ten days we had to abandon one, yet, despite that, the ten days averaged two hundred per day. Excluding the void day and adding on the next one we shot 2500 brace. Sadly the best was over as far as weather was concerned. A moor stuffed with birds and yet day after day we could do little or nothing. It was without doubt one of the worst shooting seasons for weather that I have ever endured, only rivalled by 2003.

The latter was not nearly as big a grouse season, but the weather did its best to ruin it. As each day slipped by without the grouse being lessened I was aware I was running out of time to crop the massive packs of birds we encountered every time we stepped on to the moor. There are only so many days you can book on any given area since the more one disturbs the grouse the more difficult they become to deal with. So, there is a balance to be struck: try and give each bit a break of a week or so and hope that the weather is kind. It wasn't. Gales, fog, low cloud, you name it, we had it.

On the days we could shoot life was good for a moorland keeper, pitting your wits against grouse in the sort of numbers that most of the time you can only dream about.

The highlight of the season came on 17 September. Frustrated by large packs of grouse being turned back by the top flankers at Middle End butts, I considered trying an improvised extension to the line. All season the grouse returning west had tried to follow a ridge that ran just a hundred yards above the top butt. There had been butts up to it in the past but they were in complete disrepair.

The reason given for their decline by the previous head keeper was that if the birds were allowed to follow too high a line they left our ground, going over the march to our neighbours. I asked one of my flankers, Fred Thompson, one of the best grouse men I have had the fortune to work with, to sit well back behind the butts as an observer, and from my position on the top flank I let a lot of birds run through to see what happened. Fred reported that they simply slid down the hill back onto home ground once they were past the butt line.

My mind was made up. Between shoot days we made an impromptu extension to the Middle End butts in a washed out gutter. It could not have worked better. The birds streamed along the ridge and through what was now the middle of the line. The bag for a four-drive day was the best of the year at 376 and a half brace. It may have been many more but on that day we had at least three single guns in the line. That ridge now has a permanent set of butts in place, which have accounted for thousands of brace since.

The season ticked by, the old record fell, and still the tally mounted. On the final day of the season the staff who had helped all year had one of the best days for weather of the season: a very stiff north westerly wind, but dry. The total for the day was 140 brace of December grouse, the best you could ever try your gun on. The young to old ratio for the year was 5.5 to one. Average brood size, eleven. The final total from four thousand acres, 5,167 brace. The old record was surpassed by a quarter.

Now, will nature give me another chance?

Grey Partridge Haven

DAVID THEAKER

FRIENDS WHO COME for the day to our farm shoot on Lincoln Heath soon guess that we have a conservation plan for grey partridges. And I don't mean the way we occasionally let a covey slip away to safety over the flankers in our beating line!

We're blessed with a good stock of greys on our farm at a time when all the conservation organisations are warning us of the species' demise. Amid alarm over the sharp decline of the grey or English partridge, we've somehow managed – touch wood! – to keep their numbers up. Maybe even to increase them.

We've tried various methods over the years, with mixed results. We used to put down greys, never in great numbers but enough to drive over the guns. Those that were left seemed to end up feeding the foxes over the winter months.

Then we tried releasing mixed coveys. The greys would lead the reds to great aerobatic feats, and the reds would navigate the greys back – or so the theory went.

But it wasn't really the answer. For some reason the released birds lacked that all-important parenting ability.

Our latest method, and one that does seem to be working, is to set up grey partridge 'nurseries' on parts of our farm where we're short of wild greys. We bought pairs of greys from Jonathon Crow, a game dealer in Newport, Shropshire. During February we put them into six isolated nursery pens.

When they started to lay, the eggs were removed and put under bantams. Finally, from late April, they were allowed to establish their own nests. A key advantage of this method is that we can provide high protein feed for the chicks in the first two weeks of their lives. Normally, in the wild, they would have been eating insects at this stage – if there were any available.

The other advantage is that the chicks learn to cluck, that wonderful noise a partridge or bantam makes when guiding its young towards food or water. It's what I call 'cluckability'. The hen bird and the cock both teach clucking to the chicks, which means that if the young survive to have their own clutch they will also be able to rear them.

We've had successes as well as failures – the rat from nowhere that got

[149]

in and ate a clutch of eggs three days before they were due to hatch, the lurcher boy who kicked down one of our nurseries just for a laugh. But the successes are far sweeter, and that makes the hard work worthwhile

I'm lucky that my son Charlie, who's twenty-eight, shares my enthusiasm for grey partridges and for conservation. He also shares the work with me and Gilbert Cant, a retired tractor driver who does the keepering.

Our grey partridge chicks are left in the nursery pens until they are four weeks old, by which time they are established in the area and able to forage in the nearby field edges and hedgerows. Those that are released with a bantam head off into the sugar beet a little later, when they are five or six weeks old, but often fly home to the keeper's garden thereafter.

Close attention is given to controlling ground predators. My watchword is that 'anything that takes partridge eggs is dead' – and that includes a real loathing for rats. Among all the usual measures to counter predators, the nurseries are defended by strategically placed Fenn traps.

Fields around the nurseries are split into relatively small areas by strips of unfertilised grass and clover, which the partridges particularly like for grazing and foraging. They also like the over-wintered stubbles which are left for our predominately spring-sown rotation.

We used to release redlegs and pheasants on our shoot, but the competition for nesting space from the surviving immigrants was overpowering for our greylegs. As a result we have reduced our shooting days from five to one, but with fourteen wild grey coveys this year plus thirty poults from the nurseries we should be able to build this up.

We are part of a group of fifty like-minded farmers and countrymen, who organise farm walks and meetings relating to the grey-legged partridge. Our members have been the winner and runner up of the Jas Martin Grey Partridge Trophy for the last two years. We are all committed to 'cluckability'.

Don't Knock the French!

SUE KNIGHT

As a keeper's wife, beater and picker-up, I've been told time and again that wild red-legged partridges make hopeless parents. For some reason, people think our French friends just aren't interested in raising broods this side of the Channel. I beg to differ – and there's plenty of evidence from gamekeepers to support my case.

A shoot in Hertfordshire has put down seven hundred reared redlegs over a twenty-five year period and the keeper has always seen numerous wild pairs each year, including late broods as the result of adverse weather. The partridges are hopper fed until March or April and the wild redlegs can always be distinguished from the released ones as they tend to hover around as individuals and move away quickly when approached. Over the same period of time, the numbers of English, or grey, partridge remained at an average of ten pairs. One contributing factor to encouraging wild partridges – of both varieties – is the cover crop mix of dwarf sorghum, maize, millet and some mustard.

Another Hertfordshire keeper also reported seeing more wild redlegs than in previous years. Most had late broods, but he had seen clutches of up to fourteen older birds. The most popular location had been topped set aside but although favoured by the redlegs, there had only been one brood of grey partridge.

Kent keepers reported a similar story. On an estate of two thousand acres alongside the M25 one keeper reared redlegs in a shared rearing field with pheasants, but each year he recorded a small stock of wild partridges – greys *and* redlegs. This he felt was due to miles of natural hedgerow and not too many footpaths so that nesting birds were left undisturbed.

Of the four Alectoris partridge species – the redleg, the Barbary, the rock partridge and the chukar – only the redleg is established as a pure-bred in the British Isles. It was introduced to England in the seventeenth century by Louis XIV as a gift to Charles II who, while in exile in France, had become interested in the new sport of shooting birds 'on the wing'.

Further imports followed with the influx of émigrés fleeing the French Revolution. The redlegs or French partridge became well established in Norfolk and Suffolk and spread mainly southwards, favouring arable farmland.

Quite apart from its reputation for poor parenting – undeserved in my

view – the redleg (*Alectoris rufa*) was often
seen as a threat to our native grey partridge
(*Perdix perdix*). Maybe gamekeepers misunderstood them. The 'Frenchies' were accused of
bullying the native grey and were often treated as
vermin by keepers who trampled on their nests and
smashed their eggs.

Before the advent of driven shoots, they were unpopular with some
English sportsmen because they tended to walk away from pointers rather
than sitting tight and then flushing for the gun. On the wing, though, they
presented an easier target by passing over guns in ones and twos rather
than a covey.

While wild grey partridges went into decline after World War II, it was
found that redlegs were easier to rear and manage, being larger and more
pheasant-like than the grey.

So what of their reputation for being poor parents in the wild? Maybe
the real reason lies in their sometimes surprising nesting habits.

Redlegs will often travel miles to find a nesting site, seemingly having
unaccountable dislikes for certain fields. Unlike grey partridges, which
seek privacy in a quiet corner, nesting redlegs can often be seen strutting
around nervously in the middle of fields.

They will lay their eggs at uncertain intervals, often abandoning a
clutch for days on end. Unlike grey partridge pairs, the hen will sit on one
clutch and the cock another. Their careless reputation could come from their
habit of not covering their eggs, leaving the nest a target for predators.

It has also been shown that late hatchers will not lay until the next year
but one, giving rise to the suggestion that many birds are barren – when
in fact they are just not ready to lay.

The ideal habitat for wild partridges is open country with hedgerows
and cover crops that provide a good stock of insects. The Game Conservancy also stresses the need for good predator control and spring feeding
from hoppers.

With expert advice available, improved cover crops and a determined
effort to preserve the English grey, there's no reason why the same should
not apply to wild redlegs.

Once established, both species can live together quite happily. *Vive
l'entente cordiale*!

An Oasis in Thanet

WILL HETHERINGTON

THE PURDEY GAME and Conservation Awards recognise shoots that have either done exemplary work in encouraging threatened species or have developed an original way of best utilising the land at their disposal. The 2003 winners were Ian and Claire Smith and their Nether Hale Farm shoot on the, frankly, rather bleak Isle of Thanet in north Kent. When they won I visited the farm, which lies paradoxically close to the archetypal British seaside town of Margate, to interview this husband and wife team. Then, two years later in the autumn of 2005, I was there with gun in hand for what turned out to be a memorable sporting day.

The day of my visit was a crisp one – wonderful conditions to be outside but not perfect for shooting, with a clear sun and hardly any breeze. After the niceties of the morning in the farmhouse, a gentle stroll took us to the first drive.

One of the beauties of this compact 350-acre farm shoot is that the guns walk all day. If encouraging social interaction between the team is your main aim I think this is the best way to do it. The chat on the amble between drives is always enjoyable and as long as the distance is not too far it is ideal. Of course packing everybody into a gun bus has a similar effect but without the exercise. Undoubtedly the worst way of doing it is letting everybody jump into their own vehicles between drives. This surely misses the point completely.

Anyway, back to Kent and those unfavourable conditions for partridge or pheasant shooting. With not a hint of a breath of wind in the air and on peg number ten, I was busy contemplating what a lovely scene lay before me when the calm was disturbed by a covey of partridge that hurtled over the middle of the line and took the guns there almost completely by surprise. In fairness to them, even though they are regular visitors here, it was the last thing any of us expected on this still morning. However, as the rest of the day went on to prove, it was no blip. The element of the unexpected in the rapid appearance of this covey was a pleasing early victory not only for the partridge but for the sport of shooting. Regular visitors had been caught unawares.

At the end of this drive when Ian Smith, the boss, appeared from the cover crop in front with the team of beaters that he marshals throughout the day he explained: 'As soon as we went into the cover that covey got up and they just kept going.' Even he sounded surprised and he practically knows every bird here by name.

This is fairly unforgiving country as it is surrounded on three sides by the sea. Shelter is at a premium and I was interested to find out about the changes that had been made and what had attracted the attention of the Awards' judges. I spoke to a gun who had been shooting there for over 20 years: 'Basically it has changed beyond all recognition. Thanet is a game shooting desert and Ian has created this small oasis in the middle of it.'

Consider that the Purdey Awards attract entries from all over the country, ranging from vast grouse moors to seventy-acre shoots, and you will realise that to take first prize is something very special indeed.

Clearly there had been a huge amount of hard work, but Ian is a low-fuss kind of man and does not necessarily love the limelight. It certainly hasn't been his motivation. In fact the broad grin he wears from beginning to end is a bit of a give-away as to his real inspiration – pure enjoyment.

While Ian takes control of the beating line and the management of the shoot, Claire shoots and places the guns. The perfect sporting marriage some might say, although there might be debate about the task allocation!

My favourite drive here was the one before lunch. Here the guns line out thirty yards from a twenty-foot-wide strip of small trees and bushes – reminiscent of the classic East Anglian partridge drives – and the beaters work a large piece of cover behind at a diagonal angle. This has the effect of ensuring that the shooting starts around pegs one to three and then continues down the line in turn to number ten. Perhaps the reason I enjoyed it so much was that I was on number six – right in the thick of it. The satisfaction of being presented with challenging birds and dealing with them well is immense. This is the ultimate test of good shooting for me.

I was certainly tested here as the partridge hurtled. According to Ian there was just enough breeze above the tree-line to give them a boost but I think that the real truth is that these are wild birds that have the instinct to go. Thankfully I was able to walk away with my head held high but it was one of those drives where every gun is kept busy enough not to notice what is happening elsewhere. This is what you want when it has been a bad drive but I don't mind a few witnesses when I have held my own.

The final tally for the day was 138 head with ninety-nine redlegs, thirty-three pheasants, four greys, one teal and one wood pigeon. I didn't shoot a grey but Ian is happy for them to be shot in moderation. It is difficult to know whether he should be more proud of the number of greys he has breeding on the ground or the fact that he manages to get the redlegs to fly so well.

With excellent company and delicious food – at lunch hot soup and a delicious sausage in a bun hit the spot perfectly – Ian and Claire know how to lay on a good day. Good shoot management is about recognising the needs of the team and ensuring that everything is appropriate to the day in question.

As I drove west across Kent on the M2 heading back to Lincolnshire I was able to give the issue some thought and I was glad to come to the conclusion that a day's shooting on this Purdey Award winning farm had matched my expectations. I would suggest as an example of the minimum fuss/maximum enjoyment farm shoot it would be hard to imagine a better day than this.

They have their own wildlife paradise and the only thing that can be hoped is that others follow suit.

Group Sex and Violence

MAUREEN WOODBURN

Ever wondered why cock pheasants are particularly suicidal in springtime? There cannot be many of us who haven't had to jam on the anchors as yet another crazy cock decides to strut across the road, narrowly avoiding the same fate as his recently squashed crony. In case you hadn't guessed – it's all down to the breeding season.

Pheasants go about things in a slightly different way to most birds. The Game Conservancy Trust and other scientists in the UK have been studying the pheasant's mating habits for years now and, by tagging and radio-tracking individual birds, have gained a fascinating insight into their sex life.

The mating system of the pheasant is a complex business, since, unlike most bird species, pheasants are not monogamous. They don't pair up in the spring and raise a brood together like grey partridges. Instead, pheasants have a mating system known as 'territorial harem defence polygyny'. This means that successful males mate with several females in a system more akin to that of mammals such as red deer and elephant seals. After mating the cock pheasant plays no further role in incubation or chick rearing, leaving all the hard work to the hens. Isn't that just typical?

Early March brings the first rumblings of what's to come. Having spread out from their wintering areas, cocks start competing with one another to establish their breeding territories. Having claimed their patch, they defend it vigorously from other males, often engaging in elaborate aggressive displays. These range from the fairly mild 'walk threat' and 'peck threat' to the more ominous 'lateral strut', in which the dominant territory holder moves slowly in front of his rival, with one wing drooped and tail feathers spread, looking very big and threatening.

If intimidation doesn't work, things can start to get a bit more heated, with the dominant male starting to throw a few punches (actually, pecks) at the other. Usually the intruder realises that the dominant male means business and leaves without serious physical violence. But occasionally the sparks really do start flying when two cocks are both determined to stand their ground.

Often they can be seen crouching in face-to-face combat, making weird bobbing and pecking gestures at each other. Suddenly spurs and feet fly as they try to take lumps out of each other. These more violent encounters are generally between two territory holders disputing their boundaries rather than between a territory holder and a rival.

Eventually, by the end of March or early April, things are sorted out. Territory ownership has been decided and the losers resign themselves to missing out – for the time being!

Territories are generally set up along woodland edges or thick hedges, bordering onto open ground. In relatively treeless areas such as the Fens, reed-filled dykes make a good alternative. The number of territories in an area is related to the amount of edge available. So several small blocks of cover are likely to have more territories than one large area. But irrespective of the size of these areas, it is obvious that territories are not evenly distributed around all areas of standing cover. So what makes a good territory?

The Game Conservancy Trust's research found that shrubby cover, particularly between one-and-a-half and six feet in height, was a key component of a good territory. Species such as bramble, hawthorn and holly are ideal. The crop type in the adjacent field is also important; cereals attract significantly higher densities of breeding birds compared to pasture or other crops. Creating good shrubby habitat along edges can almost double the number of territories from one per three hundred yards to one per one hundred and fifty to two hundred yards.

There is no doubt that one of the most familiar sounds of the country-side in spring is that of territorial cock pheasants crowing, followed by the less audible wing drum. Most crowing takes place in the early morning or, less often, in the evening, but calling birds can be heard at almost any time of day. It is even possible to identify individual males by their own slightly different crowing sounds, ranging from deep throaty 'kwok-kwoks' to more high-pitched strangled sounding squawks. Crowing can help to warn off intruding males, but it is primarily to attract hens to the cock's territory; it's his way of telling them he is 'hale and hearty'.

By this stage it is quite easy to identify territorial males simply by looking at them, regardless of whether they are crowing or not. Territory holders strut about with an upright posture, head held high, and feathers fluffed out to make their chests look bigger. The red wattles on their faces enlarge as they engorge with blood, and their little ear tufts (pinnae) stick up. By contrast, non-territorial males slink around nervously or loaf about in fields together in bachelor groups. Their feathers have a smoother, sleeker appearance and their wattles are not enlarged to the same extent.

So, while the cocks are getting steamed up over their territories, the hens wander about in little groups, quietly sussing out the talent. Using individually marked hens, we found that while they may visit the territo-ries of several males during March, by April they will generally have selected which one to breed with. Thereafter, more than nine out of ten hens remain with their chosen territorial male, becoming part of his harem for the rest of the season.

The appearance of hens stimulates the males into another series of dis-plays, firstly to attract the hens to their harem and then to entice them into mating. It can be hilarious to watch the males strutting their stuff, with their bright red wattles almost bursting – particularly when they put on a

'lateral display'. This involves trotting sideways towards the hen with one wing drooped and tail fanned, while making funny little cooing noises. The hen teases by appearing interested as he approaches, only to make flirtatious little jumps at the last minute and scamper off. They obviously don't want to appear too keen too soon.

As well as preferring good genes the hen selects a male based on the quality of his territory, since she needs to build up her body reserves in preparation for egg-laying and incubation. In the early morning and evening the hens come out of cover and feed in the presence of the territorial male. He remains vigilant, keeping an eye out for predators or other harassing males and allowing the hens more time to feed. He even escorts the hens back to cover when they have finished feeding. It seems the age of chivalry is not dead yet – even in pheasants.

In return for this attentiveness the hen allows the male to mate with her and father her offspring. The territorial male has to be on his guard all the time because the non-territorial males are never far away. They are always on the lookout for the chance to snatch a quick, and often forceful, mating with a hen when her male is not looking.

High-calorie natural food can be in short supply in spring making it difficult for hens to do well. The Game Conservancy's research team demonstrated experimentally that supplementary food in hoppers along woodland edges not only improved hen condition but also trebled chick production.

The key to spring feeding as a management tool is the siting of the feeders. It is no good feeding in the middle of woods; rather, the hoppers should be placed along the edges of cover, where the males have their territories and the hens are feeding. It need not make a huge hole in the shoot budget either, since second grade wheat is good enough and certainly better than nothing at all.

Spring is the busiest time of year for pheasant biologists. In the two to three hours of first and last light we drive the tracks on our study areas, using binoculars to scan all woodland edges, hedges and areas of thick cover. We mark the positions of territorial males on a map, recording their harem size and the number of non-territorials. This is repeated several times at each site to ensure we don't miss any of the birds. To complete the picture, brood counts are done after harvest each year to assess productivity. Over successive years this enables us to show how changes in management can affect the breeding population.

There's certainly more to the pheasant and its reproductive biology than meets the eye. So, next time you see a cock 'strutting his stuff' or about to launch himself at your car, remember there is biological method in his madness. A strange mating system it may be, but it means that only the best males pass on their genes while exploiting the reproductive potential of all the females. It's certainly food for thought as you top up those hoppers!

Nature Boy

SIMON LESTER

MY NICKNAME in the school playground was 'Nature Boy', and in a way it has stuck. These days caring for Mother Nature as a gamekeeper is part of my job description – and I'm still regularly astounded by her beauty.

As spring changes to summer, the countryside once again becomes a green and pleasant land. The buds on the trees burst into life with the fresh, bright greens of many shades. The birds sing with gusto in the mornings and on a gentle summer's day wood pigeons coo softly.

I know I am privileged to live and work in such a special environment and I consider being able to get so close to nature as one of the many rewards of the job. I'm aware, though, that as gamekeepers and country people we see so much on a day-to-day basis that we're in danger of taking it for granted.

I always keep a good nature reference book handy in the kitchen to help me identify any species that I see and don't recognise. When you move around to different parts of the country, as many keepers do, you come across an even bigger variety of plants and wildlife to recognise and learn about. Some you will come to work with as game or pests, and others that brighten up your day when you see them.

Different types of soil create different habitats. Flowers that grow any-where are ultimately used in one form or another as food for insects which, in turn, feed a host of game and songbirds. There are many sophis-ticated game cover crops on the market these days, but I bet that a weedy field of potatoes or sugarbeet, full of fat hen and red shank, is just as good if not better than some of these fancy mixes.

Great oaks and chestnuts, which, over centuries, must have produced ton upon ton of food, have an ecosystem all of their own. They make me wonder about the history they have seen over hundreds of years.

It's hard to put my finger on the most marvellous natural sights I have ever seen ...

The native crayfish, which could be found on an estate I worked on in Gloucestershire, used to thrill me each time I discovered one after dabbling under the flat stones in the stream. I was just happy to know they were there. But then, I would see the armoured cocoon of the caddis fly, made up from hundreds of tiny stones, and be taken aback by the wonder of that too.

Then there was the dipper that nested under the bridge. If you sat and watched very quietly, you would see it disappear under the water searching for those little morsels of food.

In the winter, the great heaps of pine needles and litter generated by the giant Black Wood made the ground look dark and uninteresting. But, when the sun shone one day, I noticed a solid, shiny crust of ants under a tree. I stopped and looked for a while and saw that the ground in the wood was alive with these busy emmets.

Whilst I'm on my travels, nesting, trapping or searching for a fox earth, I often come across small nesting birds, such as a willow warbler on the ground, or a dunnock in some low brambles. A bird's egg still holds as much fascination for me now as it did when I was ten. It is a thing of true beauty, something that cannot be recreated by anything but the original artist.

When these tiny eggs hatch, they produce some really rather ugly little characters, with tufts of fluff and feather jutting out of strange places! What I find so fantastic, and amusing, is the way their oversized heads and beaks rise and open in unison. Owlets are also an incredible sight, with their bright blue eyes staring at you out of all that fluff. But one thing I haven't seen yet is a clutch of eggs or a nest with a cuckoo in it.

Some parts of nature are there for you to see, while others need to be looked for. But I think that the really special sights are the unexpected ones ...

Once, while I was walking by a trout pond in the evening, I sensed something above me. It turned out to be a barn owl flying over my left shoulder. It was so close, I could hear the air passing through its feathers.

It dropped on a mouse or a vole, just yards in front of me. By then I was frozen to the spot, looking at it in awe. The owl just sat there, clutching its prey as we stared at each other, transfixed, until it thought it was time to go.

On another occasion, I actually watched a hedgehog building its winter quarters, rolling and pushing leaves and compressing them into a nest. I was supposed to be pigeon shooting at the time, but I soon forgot about that as I watched this little creature at work.

Quite apart from stunning sights of animals and birds or the colours of leaves and flowers, nature can delight other senses too. To smell meadow-sweet or the haunting aroma of balsam poplar, or even ripened corn after a shower of rain, is an experience in itself as they all have their own unique fragrance.

There is nothing like the taste of a ripe blackberry or wild strawberry, and, in the autumn, the taste of hazelnuts and chestnuts is so moreish.

All in all, I am thankful for everything I have seen during my past twenty-nine years as a keeper and am hopeful that there is still time to see a lot more.

At the age of fifty I'm sad that I have never heard a corncrake, which was once so common. After having spent a great deal of time working on a wild bird shoot, trying to increase numbers of dwindling wild grey partridges, I feel it would be a travesty if the next generation never saw or heard a grey partridge, let alone shot at one.

Another thing that disappoints me is that many of the young lads now entering the profession of gamekeeper don't know an oak from an ash. Learning more about nature will actually make us better gamekeepers.

Knowledge of nature is not only good for us; it's good for public relations – especially as we are supposed to be the guardians of the land – and for country people, who truly appreciate the countryside for the wonder that it is.

SIMON LESTER is head gamekeeper on the Earl of Leicester's Holkham estate in north Norfolk.

Movers and Shakers

IAN MASON

Pheasants exhibit a staggering variety of plumage colour and behaviour – but there is one covert species that displays still greater biodiversity. These unsung heroes of the undergrowth come in an amazing variety of shapes, sizes and guises – they are, of course, the beaters.

On some shoots, the beaters sport bowlers and tweed outclassing the guns in sartorial elegance. Other beating teams bring to mind Wellington's famous comment about his troops in Spain in 1809: 'I don't know what effect these men will have on the enemy, but by God, they terrify me!'

The behaviour of these commandos of the covert is equally diverse. Some thrash every scrap of cover with enthusiasm bordering the deranged; others are content to give the tree they are slouched against an occasional tap, a cigarette cupped furtively in the palm of their free hand. Likewise, there are beaters who launch purposefully into impenetrable gorse, whilst others inevitably find the well-trodden path or woodland ride (on beat and stand days, I shamefacedly admit to inhabiting the latter category).

And what of those strange woodland calls? On shoots where beaters are encouraged to both tap and rap, each member of the line seems to have a distinctive holler. Variations on the guttural bark 'Heyyyaaaaa' and the higher pitched 'burrrrrrrruup' have evolved as popular favourites.

But whether your beaters sport bowler hats or camo tatts, one thing is certain: without them, the shoot is just so many acres of first-rate hiding places for game that would rather not take a 30 gm load of No 6 shot, thank you very much.

At this time of the year, most beaters are lovingly stripping their hammer guns or burnishing their boxlocks in anticipation of their annual treat – The Beaters' Day. Now some guns rather unkindly dub these 'tin hat days', which raises the time honoured question of whether the beaters can outshoot the guns.

'Most of 'em think they can, but I'm not so sure,' a Norfolk keeper told me. Of course, there are excellent shots in the beating line; skills honed by all-year-round rough shooting. And for sure, most beaters are swift to criticise the ability of the guns. Some years ago, I briefly owned a hugely expensive pair of digital ear defenders. They amplified the quietest sound, including the infamous 'beater banter' several hundred yards away. 'Oh

Lord, the bugger's missed another,' and 'He couldn't hit a cow's backside with a tennis racket,' still resonate. The day I lost the digitals, I slept easier.

One of the splendid things about shoots where the guns do the hard graft on beaters' day is being able to turn the tables and return these sporting compliments – especially when a low bird sedately planes the line, unscathed by furious volleys of shot.

The unusual fines levied by some keepers are another popular feature of the big day. A ruddy-faced beater well known in Southern circles as 'Bugle' (due to the volume of his voice) will no doubt recall his forfeit for shooting a forbidden white hen during an Arctic-cold beaters' day. 'Right, Bugle,' the keeper roared. 'You were warned – now drop your trousers and get your arse in that trout pond.' To his credit, Bugle waded manfully into the ice accompanied by a rousing cheer – and a colour change as his extremities turned from a very pallid white to bright blue.

One thing is certain about all beaters' days: every nook and cranny of ground cover will be probed, the dogs sent back repeatedly to flush game from every inch of covert.

Although many shoots stick to 'cocks only' for beaters' days, some permit hens to be dropped. There is also a fair amount of 'pot-hunting', resulting in a 'various' tally as long as a cock's tail. In fact, it is an unwise member of any quarry species that ventures anywhere near a line of armed beaters on their special day. A year's pent up anticipation encourages some hugely enthusiastic shooting. The bird may be mile-high or knee-high, but someone is bound to have a crack. As one Suffolk keeper put it, 'So long as the boys are getting amongst 'em and getting some lead in the air, they're as happy as Larry.'

I recently heard a marvellous story on an Oxfordshire shoot where the local 'antis' were somewhat tardy last year, and chose beaters' day to 'sab' the nearest shoot. They turned out in force, but rather than being met by eight guns in breeks and Barbours, were faced by twenty or more camo-clad hearties who had no intention of letting their special day get ruined. I am sworn to secrecy about what ensued. Suffice to say, the bag was filled, unhindered.

With over thirty years of keepering under his belt, Jack Swain has seen it all. He says that beaters' days on the Duke of Rutland's Belvoir Estate were memorable. 'We got everyone out, tenant farmers, keepers, beaters, pickers up – we could have up to forty guns split into three or four teams shooting over several days, but however they organised it, it was always a marvellous and happy occasion.'

The bottom line is that beaters deserve their day. They turn out in all weathers and stomp through hell and high water for the price of a round and if they're lucky, a pie supper. Go on lads, enjoy your day!

CHAPTER SIX

·

Shooting – Past, Present and Future

Past, Present and Future

ROBIN SCOTT

Statistics are all well and good but their only useful purpose is to keep the people who generate them in a job. I've always reckoned it's a shadowy and suspect enterprise at the best of times.

But there's more: the fruits of a statistician's research are then picked over by a vulturine marketing and advertising industry desperate to turn even the dullest 'Did you know?' into a catchy one-liner. Quick as a flash, everyone is rushing out to buy a new brown sliced bread with nutty bits in it to stave off a heart attack.

The really heavy-duty stuff though is pitched into the political arena where it re-emerges months later in the shape of new legislation. Parliamentary careers ebb and rise on them. Table the right statistics, whip up a pie chart on the overhead projector, and you're laughing; at the very least a junior Cabinet Minister's job beckons. Champion a series of no-hopers and a life on the back benches is all a wannabe MP can reasonably hope for. How sad!

Then again, I suppose the measure of any statistic is whether there's substance to it, and how truthful it is.

Whoever coined the phrase 'lies, damned lies and statistics' hit the nail irrevocably on the head. Sporting shooting is living proof of it. Can you think of a single other section of society – with the possible exception of fox hunting – that's been treated as shockingly as law-abiding gun owners?

We've been stitched up and trussed by successive administrations, pilloried, vilified and made to take the blame for that blackest of all social evils, armed crime.

Until the mid-1960s you didn't need a licence to hold a sporting shotgun or rifle. Back then you could buy one through a mail order catalogue dropped on your mother's doorstep.

It was great. For roughly the same price as a new settee you could choose a single- or double-barrelled Baikal, a Mossberg pump gun or, for a little bit extra, a very pretty sidelock Ugartechea side-by-side from Spain, by return post.

All that changed, if memory serves me right, when a couple of petty thieves murdered a police constable with a World War II service revolver. From that moment on, the 'need' to license guns took hold. Never mind that armed robbery was a minority occupation carried out by a small number of well-known gangs, legal gun owners felt the legislative backlash.

True, by today's standards that first certificate was a fairly tame affair but the fact remains, by bringing in gun licences the government targeted game shooters, rough shooters, wildfowlers and clay shooters – not criminals. Nothing has changed in the forty years since: armed crime has risen to alarming levels and with every call to 'do something about it', politicians have turned the screw on sporting shooters, not the lawbreakers. Getting a certificate to own a gun these days is a privilege, not a right. We have had humiliating restrictions placed upon us. And legal gun owners continue to act as sitting ducks for politicians hell bent on showing the electorate they are stamping on the problem and taking guns out of circulation. But whose guns?

As the saying goes: 'Ban guns and only criminals will own them.' On this count alone successive administrations stand guilty as charged – and that's proving totally ineffectual at fighting the scourge of armed crime.

Then there's the not inconsequential matter of border controls. What controls, you ask? Exactly. They're a national joke, a terrifying disgrace.

Have you noticed that Customs officers are quick to clamp down on day trippers bringing booze and tobacco across the channel? White trannie vans are confiscated at the drop of a hat and thousands of gallons of amber liquid poured down the drain in the 'fight' against smugglers. But how often do you read of illicit small arms and ammunition being found? Hardly ever. Governments – and particularly the present regime – seem more concerned about tax evasion on fags and bottles of hooch than they do an unwanted arsenal of guns being landed here.

And another thing ... so-called civil rights groups raise merry hell whenever the likes of identity cards, poll tax, DNA testing and the proliferation of roadside speed cameras crop up. But what of shooters? To own a gun sportsmen have to routinely sign away their 'rights' over confidential medical records and give police free rein to conduct checks on their suitability to possess a weapon. And that's just part of the process. Can you imagine the bloody unrest were police to trawl through every citizen's medical and criminal records whenever they applied for a driving licence – then had it refused because they once suffered a minor bout of depression, or committed a petty misdemeanour fifteen years earlier? Traffic congestion might well be cut at a stroke – but civil rights lawyers would have a field day.

Whichever way you look at things, it's a credit to gun owners that they take such injustices in their stride. The legislative obstacles they face are looked upon simply as the price to be paid for living in a country that has grown away from countryside living, and the essential role guns continue to play in it.

Neither is it fanciful to look back on pre-licence days and recognise them as a golden age – one that was slower, more understanding, forgiving, tolerant and, yes, enlightened than it ever is now.

As a village boy I remember that guns were no big deal; certainly nothing to get wound up about and lose sleep over. Everyone from the road sweeper to head teacher had one tucked behind his back door, cartridges at hand in case a rabbit or wood pigeon turned up on his carrot patch. And as soon as you were old enough (usually five) you went bush beating where you watched guns being handled safely, and put to proper use. In other words, another education had started to run alongside the usual three Rs taught at primary school.

Farmers and farm workers owned a gun as a matter of course. They hung 'em from a hook in the outhouse, shed or barn ready in case a rat poked its head out of the granary doorway or a fox fancied its chances with the free-range chickens.

By the age of twelve my circle of friends knew every rafter within a three-mile radius of home that held a gun – and if the fancy took us, we'd borrow one (with the farmer's permission of course) to shoot a rabbit or two on our wanderings. Sometimes the grateful landowner even threw in a handful of cartridges but, usually, we had to rely on 'freeing' one or two Eley Grand Prix from our father's small stash kept on a pantry shelf. The golden rule was always to take a cartridge from an opened box so that the few you took were never missed. The other unwritten rule was to never shoot game – only pests – and return the gun to its rightful rafter before nightfall.

Can you imagine that happening nowadays? Every boy over the age of ten would be serving an ASBO and those over sixteen years left kicking their heels in a Young Offenders' Institute. And as for the farmer and our parents, goodness only knows ...

What amazes me is that in spite of the problems and hurdles placed in its way gun ownership continues to grow slowly. Most of this intake comes via adults with time on their hands, at last, and money to spare. It also speaks volumes for the fair-minded civilians who now man the firearms departments in many constabularies. They're not angels, but they do try to be even-handed in the way they do business.

The list of newcomers also includes a small number of youngsters, but not as many as the sport would like, or needs. Without young blood – as the antis so smugly point out – shooting sports will eventually wither and die.

It's a horrible prospect, but true. How we resolve this dilemma requires our fullest attention, and support. We simply cannot allow it to happen.

Years ago, and for those lucky enough to be raised in a stable family environment, the introduction to shooting was as natural as taking one's first footsteps. As long as you had a dad, uncle, elder brother, godfather or grandad who shot, your seamless arrival in this enthralling, history-rich, fieldsport was guaranteed. If only that were the case now.

No, I'm not going to get launched here about the many ways successive governments have stifled participation in shooting sports for adolescents. The recruitment problem runs deeper than the easy option of clamping down on entry-level air rifles and supervision requirements where shotguns are concerned.

The stumbling block is the family unit. Like you, no doubt, I've read about the disintegration of family life but it wasn't until one of my contributors, John Gray, took me to task over an article in *Sporting Gun* that I had to stop and think. Think hard.

In it, the question was asked: 'Why do fewer fathers these days introduce their children to shooting?'

John, headmaster of a large secondary school in the Midlands, said something along the lines: 'My school is not untypical of many others in the country. Look at our register and you will find that nearly 70 per cent of the pupils here do not have a father – they're from a one-parent family where mum is the breadwinner. No way is she ever going to give permission for her children to go shooting, let alone own a gun.'

This might hold true for a school in a heavily urbanised area, but what of rural establishments? My girlfriend (sorry, partner) did a quick tally the other day on the tiny village primary attended by her two girls and the percentage hit exactly 50 per cent in her youngest daughter's year. Statisticians might say this is not a representative sample but it sure as hell frightened the pants off me.

How, then, are we going to address it? For the last few years various shooting organisations here have done what they can to encourage more young shots, and spent considerable sums of money in the process. Statistically speaking a quantifiable success rate can be attached to these noble deeds. But are we actually getting to the kids we need to? Sadly, no.

Pop along to any Young Shots' Day and you will find the majority come from families already involved in shooting. Many arrive at the shooting school in the comfort of a spacious 4 x 4 vehicle. Precious few from a non-shooting background find their way there on a No 62 bus from Camden Town.

For a number of years *Sporting Gun* magazine ran a yearly 'Introduce a Friend to Shooting' campaign, and reasonably successful it proved too. But some readers were mortified. 'No way am I going to do that,' they cried. 'It's taken me years to get the shooting I've got and before you know it they will muscle in, talk to the farmer behind my back, and push me out.' No joy there then.

So where do we go from here? I wish I knew. Hopefully part of the answer will be found within the pages of this book.

Better known and more lucid writers than me have given their time to contribute to this shooting compendium, edited by a former Reuters foreign correspondent and *Sporting Gun* features editor, Chris Catlin. The intention is, for each copy sold, a sum of money will go to introducing young people to this sport we hold so dear.

Chris, like me, has enjoyed immeasurable fun with a gun and dog over the years. So why deny potentially thousands more people – especially youngsters – the same unique experience?

Forget about that po-faced handful of tosspot antis trying to put a stop to our sport; gun ownership and shooting teaches young people more about respect for the flora and fauna of this countryside than any cockamamie university degree course ever will. Leaving aside those two idiots from Hungerford and Dunblane, the privilege of gun ownership instills a respect in community and fellow man, too.

If the anti-gun brigade disagrees with me (which it doubtless will) then let's lay down a challenge: give *every* schoolchild over the age of fourteen the chance to try a gun under proper supervision and see what happens. I bet you the majority will want to have a go again ... and in double quick time, too. They will relish the experience.

Finally ... shooting is socially inclusive and not a rich man's sport. Yes, you can spend oodles of spare cash on the finest driven game shoots available, but never forget that a greater wealth of enjoyment awaits those of us on more modest means through clay shooting, wildfowling, rough shooting and pigeon decoying. Add dog handling, picking up and beating to the equation and you will come as close as you possibly can to finding Heaven on earth.

Don't let it die.

People Power for Shooting

ROBERT GRAY

SHOOTING HAS undergone radical surgery during the twentieth century. Carefully created landscapes, vestiges of protocol and some of the very same shotguns remain in use, but other than in a few exceptional circumstances, the type of people who shoot has changed beyond recognition. More people from all walks of life enjoy game shooting now than ever before in its 350-year history.

The sport as we know it today goes back to the ending of the Commonwealth in 1660, when many noblemen and cavaliers returned from exile where they had witnessed the sport of 'shooting flying' being carried out. For many it would replace hawking as the sport of choice for the aristocracy.

New game laws introduced to Parliament in 1671 were dramatic and restrictive. The legislation limited the 'taking of game' only to those holding a freehold estate with rentals of more than one hundred pounds per annum, a leasehold estate for ninety-nine years of one hundred and fifty pounds per year, and to the eldest son or heir of an esquire or person of superior rank. In other words, yeomen were effectively debarred from shooting.

Such exclusivity lasted for 160 years until the Game Act of 1831. This Act is obviously outdated now, but in its day was a significant reforming measure. It introduced a 'general qualification' which meant every person irrespective of land or rank could purchase a Game Certificate, enabling the taking of game. Nevertheless, the cost of the certificate remained at the prohibitively high £3 13s 6d. This meant that the taking of game remained the prerogative, if not of the nobility, then at least of the gentry. However, the new laws were a move, albeit a small one, towards equality.

In the middle of the nineteenth century, three-quarters of the countryside was still in the hands of private landowners. The industrial revolution would initially lead to a wealthy period for farming due to the need to supply the new urban work forces. In time, though, a reliance on cheap imports led to a slump for arable farming. At this point, sporting rather than landed interests took increasing precedence as the new wealthy professional and industrial urban classes took up hunting and shooting.

The country house shooting party was a new diversion for Edwardian 'Society'. The twin developments of the breech-loading gun and the railway network provided the essentials. The Prince of Wales, later Edward VII, provided the social impetus. The scale of the shoots was staggering, summed up neatly by Jonathan Ruffer in his book *The Big Shots*. 'Statistics mattered in this competitive affair, and so did social style – you combined the opportunities of a Vimy Ridge machine-gunner with an infinitely better lunch.'

In the early 1900s, large shoots would continue to compete with each other to shoot large bags, and reputations were at stake. This sort of behaviour perhaps reached its zenith just before the horrors of World War I. Sportsmen of the twenty-first century would certainly agree with King George V who, having shot with Lord Burnham on the record day in December 1913 when 3937 pheasants were killed, remarked with commendable understatement, 'Perhaps we overdid it today.'

During this extravagant period, the rearing of game was carried out on large well-keepered estates and only strays reached the smallholders. This pattern continued until after World War II, which preceded the decline and fall of many country estates. These were broken up into smaller parcels of land, leaving large numbers of farmers and managers to find themselves with sporting rights.

In the coming years, the shroud of secrecy surrounding the mysterious work of the professional gamekeepers was lifted. The emergence of high-protein pellets which fed chicks and laying pen hens alike meant that the days of armies of keepers collecting ants' eggs, chopping up thousands of hard-boiled eggs and mincing rabbit meat to feed their birds were over. It seemed that anyone with commonsense and the right equipment could rear a few pheasants to a certain standard, a point which would still be robustly contested today!

It also became clear that country sports were not just for country communities. More people living in towns with more money and leisure time on their hands wanted to shoot. Alongside the anglers, ramblers, twitchers and campers, the new shooting man found that he could enjoy the countryside too. For the right price he could enjoy a sport once reserved for royalty and the landed gentry.

Demand began to outstrip supply, resulting in spiralling costs. Ironically, this meant that once more game shooting became the preserve of the wealthy. Naturally there were those who found sport by other means, whether by wildfowling, pigeon or rough shooting. Yet even here, the land available for rough shooting would decrease with changing farming practices whilst farmers who once begged for pigeon control would soon charge shooters to carry out this work.

The growing band of shooting people who wished to shoot driven game faced a stark choice. If they could not afford a gamekeeper and the costs associated with running a 'proper' driven shoot then they could either go without, offer their services as beaters or roll their sleeves up and create their own shoot. The last three decades have therefore seen the incredible growth of the DIY syndicate shoot.

In the same period, there has been a rise in commercial shooting at more reasonable prices (and some more expensive). There is a tendency in the shooting community to be condescending about 'commercial shooting' but conducted properly it has allowed a wide variety of people the opportunity to shoot, which would have been impossible for them when faced with either the 1900 shooting party or the 2000 DIY syndicate of close friends.

Admittedly, shooting is still dominated by men, but there is evidence that this is slowly changing. Either way, the shooting community has come along way from the time when Queen Victoria observed in a letter that 'Only fast women shoot' or when in 1917 the seventy-year-old Lord Warwick said, 'I have met ladies who shoot, and I have come to the conclusion, being no longer young and a staunch Conservative, that I would prefer them not to.'

Today, 480,000 people – men and women – shoot live quarry in the UK. In 2004, the Countryside Alliance, together with the British Association for Shooting and Conservation, the Country Land and Business Association, supported by the Game Conservancy Trust, commissioned an important report. The findings of the independent report, carried out by Public Corporate Economic Consultants (PACEC), were released in September 2006. According to the experts, shooting is worth an impressive £1.6 billion to the rural economy and supports the equivalent of seventy thousand full-time jobs.

The report is based on shooting activity in 2004 and reveals that there were sixty-one thousand providers of shooting. Many of these provided pigeon and rabbit shooting as well as driven or walked-up game. While most shooting is provided by landowners (67 per cent), half of these provide shooting directly with others letting to syndicates or clubs. On average each provider is responsible for sixteen days shooting, which means that there were 970,000 shooting days across the UK in 2004. Through a series of calculations, PACEC has worked out that this means there were ten million individual 'gun days' in that year.

Of the people shooting in 2004, 73 per cent had shot as a guest, just under half shot as members of syndicates and no less than 42 per cent had purchased shooting by the day. Thirty years ago, this state of affairs would have been unthinkable, but 130 years ago it would have been incomprehensible. Shooting is flourishing in the twenty-first century. While the activity is not without its problems, it does have its people. Shooting has welcomed a cross-section of society into its arms, and it must continue to embrace many more.

Fast Women

CAMILLA CLARK

'ONLY FAST women shoot,' said Queen Victoria – a remark hardly likely to send nineteenth-century women rushing out to buy a gun. Victorian society considered it far more fitting for women to occupy their time with sedentary activities such as embroidery and playing the piano. Fifty years later, things hadn't changed much as far as women and shooting was concerned. In fact, just from the title of B.B.'s anthology, *A Shooting Man's Bedside Book*, published in 1948, it is clear that women were not considered in this context at all. Today, however, an increasing number of women are flying in the face of tradition and discovering that they like nothing more than donning a pair of breeks, grabbing their 12-bore and heading off with spaniel in tow to spend a day shooting pheasants. It's a new phenomenon and, when once a 'ladies' day' was a term used only in horse racing, game shoots are now hosting these events on a regular basis in the British countryside up and down the land.

Despite the traditional uniform and strict adherence to etiquette, driven game-shooting has been pretty good at moving with the times since it first became fashionable in the mid-1850s and it has been evolving continuously. For example, the rapid development of firearms revolutionised the early sport. And as conservation has become a higher priority, the objective of shoots is no longer simply to provide guns with record bags as they did in the Edwardian shooting heyday, but much more to sustain an environment with enriched biodiversity. Likewise the sport is no longer the preserve of the gentry and in fact it is now more accessible than ever to all. The emergence of commercial shooting is another example of how the sport has developed, making it worth millions to the rural economy, so it was inevitable really that women would get involved sooner or later.

It is probably only in the past twenty-five years or so that women have really started to move from being mere onlookers and providers of the shoot lunch to participants on the shooting field – around the same time that women started becoming actively involved in other traditionally male sports such as fishing and golf. It hasn't, however, been particularly easy for women to make inroads into these traditionally man-only zones. Whereas sons are usually taught to shoot by enthusiastic fathers, daughters have been generally overlooked in this department and steered more towards ponies. This was my experience too.

I first fired a gun when I was about twelve years old when my older brother offered me a go with his shotgun. I still remember the ringing in my ears and the intense pain in my shoulder – his gun was far too big for me, I was holding it incorrectly and I had no hearing protection. It wasn't a promising introduction to the sport, but one many women experience thanks to well-meaning siblings or husbands. It is the quickest way to destroy any enthusiasm though in some cases that has probably been the intention! These days, however, more and more women are taking it upon themselves to learn to shoot by joining clubs, having lessons and taking part in ladies' days. A few years after my first experience of shooting, I had another go under the supervision of a qualified instructor at a local shooting school. Only then did I discover that it didn't have to be a painful experience and that I might quite enjoy it after all. This is now the most usual way for women to take up the sport, and it is predominantly thanks to the efforts of shooting grounds, which some years ago began targeting this huge and previously untapped market, that there are so many women shooting today.

Not everyone will relish the idea of women going game-shooting, but no one can argue that it's not good for the sport. The more inclusive it is and the more active participants it has, the safer its future will be. Hopefully in fifty years' time there will be another version of this book and it will contain as many contributions from women as from men.

Sporting Moments

JOHN SWIFT

In some ways it's difficult, and in others easy, to separate BASC business representing shooting from enjoying the real thing. Some years ago I made a resolution not to try too hard.

Part of me resists mixing business with pleasure, however stimulating the business may be and however seductive the sporting opportunity. Our sport is not a golf course where balls and deals are struck. Nor should it become one. I am unsympathetic to the notion of armed golfing that cares too little for our quarry, but try not to be too judgmental. Nature is red in tooth and claw.

For me, shooting can be a quasi-spiritual experience best practised in relative solitude away from the crowds but shared with like-minded people. Comradeship is of course a huge part of it. Man the Hunter at one with Nature and all that jazz. Laugh if you will, but for me it is real.

That's what makes shooting different from target sports and ball games. And just in case of doubt, I still do all three.

Doing the job properly demands concentration and application of skill. There's a lot to think about when 'the moment' comes. I want to get it right, for everybody's sake. It's not a golf ball I'm trying to hit.

There is always that moment, if Diana the goddess of hunting is being kind, when you think, 'It's worked. You're on!' And I've had a few such moments for which I am eternally grateful.

After a long and chilly wait at dawn, watching as a pack of wigeon leave their feeding on the distant tideline, turn to our calls and swing towards the decoy pattern.

Or following my much loved and now sadly missed spaniel, working a line of bracken cover high above me on a Welsh hill – and just then the pheasant breaks towards me.

Or sitting on a high seat as the colour fades from the landscape, and suddenly he's there! A solid animal materialised out of nothing. I'm bemused that he arrived without being seen, but he did.

Or lying on the turf straining my ancient 8 x 40s to distinguish rock from beast a mile and a half away. Then the long, wet detour and breathless climb up the burn, the belly-scramble, face in peat – and there are the deer, a couple of hundred yards further to windward.

The normal conventions of modern civilisation simply don't apply. Man the hunter has had similar experiences for hundreds of thousands of years. I always feel surprised and privileged.

And there have been moments too when I didn't want to be put to the test; there's a bit of funk in many of us after all.

Just when I'm trying to get the Labrador to sit still, why couldn't the arching cock pheasant go and fly over somebody else?

Or, waiting for moose in the lonely Scandinavian Arctic, when I make out that faint, distant bark of a hunting dog miles away; and five minutes later, there it is again, but closer.

'Oh please, go somewhere else. I know I came all this way – but not today.'

The same goes for fishing. You need rhythm and concentration. You must try to think like the fish, judging the current's swirls around hidden rocks and backing hunches. Should you go deep or stay on the surface? Then – you didn't blink – the fly has gone. The long pull. You're on!

It's even more exciting at night, alone in the Universe with ink black water. Logic says you came to fish and, presumably, there are fish somewhere. The river seems to be flowing uphill. Then all of a sudden, perched on a slippery rock, the line is taken out of your hand and mayhem ensues. You are not alone. You had better get control.

There is something magic about that heart-stopping moment. Until then it is preparation, planning and technique. You control events or think you do. The choices are yours and you have all the time you need.

But after the moment, events control you. You know you should still control things, but the choices are few and the quarry has not read the script.

The pack of wigeon swings back out to the tideway. The deer keep their rumps pointing towards you until the light has gone. The fish spits out the fly and you spend the next ten minutes replacing a tangled leader.

But if they don't . . . it's down to me! And, if I've prepared well and Diana smiles, it's just possible I won't make a complete mess of it.

Sharing these moments with friends is priceless – they should not be muddled with business. But then everybody and all circumstances are different. Long may it last!

A Sense of Occasion

BARRY ATKINSON

WHEN I FIRST went beating as a teenager in East Yorkshire there was always a special sense of occasion on shoot days – from the early morning gathering in the farmyard, through the lunchtime distribution of pint bottles of icy bitter which were often too cold to handle, never mind drink, to the almost ceremonial laying out of the bag on the wide grass verge at the end of the day.

I considered myself fortunate to be accepted as a beater because long waiting lists were then the norm. These days the number of dedicated beaters seems to be dwindling, a trend that becomes more apparent with each passing season, especially when the weather turns nasty.

New recruits tend to be those who have retired early. Young people who do show genuine interest are often influenced by relatives or friends who are actively involved in field sports; it is those without existing links whom we seem unable to reach.

If there were an effective recruitment agency for beating, the result would benefit not just shooting but the countryside at large.

The work is essentially for unpaid volunteers, without whom shoots could not function. A shoot owner once explained to me that the beating purse was to recompense beaters for travel, lunch expenses or both. So the real reward is a lifestyle that offers something money can never buy.

The obvious benefits include physical fitness and enhanced good health. Then there is the beater's direct involvement with a wide range of subjects and activities, all steeped in tradition and honed by innovation. All this, together with the company of people from diverse backgrounds, the enjoyment of good food and drink, and the 'crack' of sharp humour, contributes to that sense of occasion I remember from my youth.

There has been pressure on the British countryside and country life for a long time and I believe that we on shoots have almost learned to live with it, at times with a degree of complacency.

During my beating season I have witnessed enough to cause me serious concern about the status quo. Many are finding it more difficult to defend what is rapidly becoming indefensible. The priority of commercial profitability has obscured many traditional objectives, standards and practices; and consequently the sense of occasion once regarded as a pre-requisite is quickly becoming a thing of the past.

Overbagging is now in the public eye and invites further waves of criticism. Some larger estates and enterprises have committed themselves to intense programmes of let days which require massive stock reserves to cater for gun teams hungry for large bags, irrespective of the sporting quality of birds.

The resultant stress ripples out from overworked keepers to all involved on each drive and is even detected by working dogs. David, a colleague on several shoots, tells me: 'My dogs are not infallible and I don't think I should feel guilty if they fail to perform to field trial standards.'

All this creates a perverse equation – more revenue equals less satisfaction. In plain language, greed has crippling consequences.

Fortunately not all shoots are pursuing the same goal. And one where I went beating on New Year's Day should serve as an inspiring model for those that have lost their way.

Polesden Lacey is a National Trust property, a Regency country house set in three thousand acres on Surrey's North Downs. The small shoot of twelve guns and a handful of supporters co-exists successfully with the many other people on this much-visited estate.

Although only 350 pheasants are put down, giving a modest season's bag of about 120, they have reason and purpose to attend to estate husbandry at every opportunity – and they do just that.

In reality the shoot contributes to the estate's welfare many times more than the annual rent value, and the members are happy to have it that way. They establish and maintain ideal gamebird habitat wherever possible and carry through careful vermin control year-round.

A day's shooting or beating there has that real sense of occasion – a sure sign that a fair day's sport is on offer to everyone.

BARRY ATKINSON, from Nottinghamshire, holds the record for beating on every available grouse, partridge and pheasant day on 148 different shoots in sixty-six counties during the 2004/2005 season to raise funds for a gamekeepers' charity and cancer research. He wrote this article before the launch of the National Organisation for Beaters and Pickers Up (NOBS).

A Future for Shooting

CHARLES NODDER

THERE ARE TWO main genres of sporting literature: 'How to do it' and 'How it went'. This is as it should be because shooting is first and foremost a recreation. And common to all hobbies is a fascination for doing it well and the spinning of unending yarns about what was achieved.

Not this time, though. Instead I'd like to consider the future of live quarry shooting and suggest what should be done to secure it. Inappropriate bedtime reading, perhaps, for the sportsman easing towards sleep after an arduous day under the driven pheasants or flighting wigeon, but important nonetheless and therefore included in this collection without apology ...

Shooting is one of those rare hobbies that has an opposition. If you collect stamps or enjoy going to the theatre, nobody else much cares. If your pleasure is in using a noisy jet ski or keeping a pet skunk, you may upset one or two people but you won't encounter national, structured hostility. Should you be a shooter of live quarry in Britain in the early part of the twenty-first century, however, you face a determined, multi-million pound culture hell-bent on spoiling your fun.

I label the 'antis' a culture because it is important to understand their mindset. Whatever their motivation, which may be anything from misplaced class hatred to genuinely held concern for animals, they are every bit as passionate about their opposition as we are about our sport. They love stuffing envelopes to MPs as much as we love stuffing in the cartridges when the pigeon are piling in over the decoys. They pack a London pub after a demo to swap tales of derring-do with the placard and the loud hailer much as we gather round the whisky bottle in the shoot room to relive the best moments of the final drive.

The difference, of course, is that the antis' recreation is opposing shooting, whereas ours is actually getting on with the shooting itself, *not* attending to its defence and promotion. We have to be cajoled and dragooned into writing to our MP or going on marches. The antis do it all the time and, sad people that they are, believe it to be the best possible fun.

Over the years, of course, sportsmen have responded to this mis-match by farming the job of defending and promoting shooting out to a range of membership organisations, which they pay to do the rather uninspiring task for them. On the whole these bodies have done quite well, for despite vociferous opposition not much has been lost. The occasional species of bird has joined the protected list; the use of lead shot has been curtailed; very large calibre guns and those with the potential to fire an unseemly number of rounds have been banned but, all in all, an Edwardian sportsman would find shooting's current legal status in the UK remarkably familiar.

What might surprise him, however, is that shooting sports, which were to him an occasional pastime of the elite, now enjoy a very wide following and are the basis of a significant industry. He would certainly be intrigued that many participants now come into the sport without a long apprenticeship under the watchful eye of a parent, guardian or gamekeeper.

These developments are, on the whole, positive. It is good news for shooting's future that a boy from Birmingham can, if he wants, buy his way into the gun line alongside a member of the House of Lords. It is better news still that the money he spends will sustain a gamekeeper's job and look after a patch of countryside that might otherwise lose its physical character and biological diversity. It helps the sport that the game he shoots has an increasing chance of going to a supermarket and perhaps being cooked, according to some populist TV chef's recipe, by someone else who lives in a city.

The downsides of game shooting's expansion are, however, well documented. Commercialism brings its price. Some farms are certainly being shot too often, others too heavily, and a very few in ways that are environmentally or politically unsustainable. This is a big concern because shooting will always be judged by its weakest link. The shooting organisations have done their best to respond by setting out, in the Code of Good Shooting Practice and Shoot Assurance Scheme, the clear standards necessary for shooting to be defendable in the modern age.

The next move is largely down to us. Will shooters become more selective when buying shooting or accepting invitations? Will they be prepared to raise an obvious breach of the standards with their host or shoot organiser? Will they, through peer pressure and through buying on quality and not just price, help to give commercial advantage to the game farms and estates that are doing the job right and at the same time freeze out the places that are letting us all down? My view is that if these things don't happen, and soon, UK game shooting will certainly face some degree of direct political curtailment.

The other requirement for securing our future is for individual shooters to stop expecting someone else (i.e. the shooting organisations) to do all the defending and promoting for them and to actually do some of it themselves. However good the organisations are – and my own view, briefly, is that they are very good but need to work more closely with one another – they cannot win this war without foot soldiers.

Everyone who shoots needs to do his or her bit to explain the hobby – particularly to persons in authority or those who influence them. We need to encourage outside interest; to counter inaccuracies in the media and to ensure that our own participation is always within the agreed standards.

We should not be discouraged if the current threats to game shooting seem large. Other branches of our sport have faced similar moments of truth and survived. Coastal wildfowling was under great pressure a few decades ago when the burgeoning conservation movement homed in on the obvious ecological richness of Britain's estuaries and felt it to be incompatible with the presence of what they regarded as a bunch of gun-toting cowboys. The response was the formation of well-organised and well-represented wildfowling clubs, with entry procedures, training programmes, codes, rules and disciplinary procedures. That particular branch of shooting sports is now as safe as it ever has been.

Lowland deer stalking was similarly once something of a free-for-all and vulnerable to accusations of inefficiency. Even without the stimulus of direct and concerted opposition, stalkers have likewise become much more organised, better defended and, as a result, politically more secure.

There is one other area of shoot management that causes me particular concern. Game managers have known intuitively for centuries that the control of predators to safeguard quarry species is a necessary part of having a harvestable surplus to shoot. Research has confirmed this fact many times over and also shown how important predator control is for other wildlife too. Yet the methods allowable for controlling common pests and predators are continually whittled away by politicians here or in Brussels.

Over the years, hunting, various types of trap and the use of pesticides such as Cymag have all been banned. Currently there is pressure to increase the frequency of trap inspection and to reduce still further the ease with which rodenticides can be used. Things rarely seem to go in the other direction. Excuses are found for not testing or approving new types of trap. Progress towards the management of species such as badgers and birds of prey seems permanently stalled. This ratchet effect, making effective predator control more and more difficult, must in time have a deleterious effect on game management and therefore on sporting shooting.

So too may the similar patterns of growing bureaucracy which increasingly restrict the processes of game rearing and the handling and sale of game meat. Yet worrying though all these detailed developments are, to my mind they are as nothing compared with the overriding importance of making sure that shooting is defendable and is actually getting on with the job of defending itself.

To eavesdrop on the shoot room chat about the latest impositions from Brussels or from Defra, one might think that the greatest threat to shooting's future was from the outside. It isn't. The future lies firmly in the sportsman's own hands. It will be best served by ensuring that scrupulously high standards are maintained throughout and that we all do our own individual bit to blow shooting's trumpet.

CHAPTER SEVEN

·

Stalking

A Red Stag in the Rut

CHRISTOPHER BORTHEN

Our binoculars followed the hen harrier traversing the slopes high above the calm waters of the sea loch, searching to and fro in slow, regular sweeps. Suddenly she hurtled to the ground creating an explosion of feathers – and the grouse was no more.

It was October 20, the last day of the Scottish stag season, and my companion and I were about to join Death on those very slopes – one more stag was needed to complete the estate's cull figures.

There's no road into this peninsula and the nearest house is a good day's march inland: you go in by boat and you come out by boat, and if you shoot a beast you drag it down to the shore – there's no pony or quad bike to help you here.

Snow was covering the high tops, but we were soon warmer than comfortable with our leg muscles protesting against our forced pace up the steep slope. A couple of ravens circled a lonely crag, and we grinned silently to each other, acknowledging the old superstition among Highland stalkers that it's a good omen to see these birds in the morning as they'll be expecting to feed on the gralloch by evening.

Just at that moment, from over the brow, came a sound almost not of this world, both frightening yet somehow belonging to these hills. A testosterone-filled stag was roaring out his challenge to any adversary within earshot, while proclaiming his status as a procreator to the hind parcel he had gathered around him.

He was an even, but unimpressive, eight-pointer; typical of a poor-doer on this forest, so – whatever his own self-esteem – we judged him better in the larder now than promulgating his genes in the future. I stalked to some rocks overlooking the distant scene, but unfortunately they were in full sight of the hinds. If I moved an inch I'd be rumbled and the hinds would depart taking my stag with them. No matter how I tried, there was simply no way of closing the distance.

A shadow fell across my binoculars and I glanced up to see a golden eagle soaring overhead. For ten minutes I marvelled at his grace, all thoughts of my predicament temporarily banished. As he disappeared from view I realised time was slipping away fast and I had to take a chance if we were not to go home empty handed – but when I dared to sneak another look, the target animal was lying down!

I eased my rifle from its slip, chambered a round and settled into a comfortable shooting position against a rock. Cupping my hands I copied the sound of a roaring stag – with a double grunt at the end just for good measure. As if attached to a gigantic spring, the stag leapt to his feet and charged in my direction. Now I was worried that he might not stop in time to give me a shot. When he was a hundred yards away I gave another, fiercer, roar, which served to make him stand still to answer my challenge. For a split second he stood broadside and the 180-grain, soft-nosed bullet from my .308 thumped into his chest. His adrenalin buoyed him up as he ran in a semi-circle for fifty yards before collapsing, and I waited until the last of the hinds had disappeared before showing myself.

We stood to admire the corpse that had so recently been the monarch of this particular glen; still now, but as magnificent in death as he had been in life. The gralloch completed, we ate our piece, before my friend departed to bring the boat nearer whilst I dragged the carcass down to the shore.

Of the three species of British deer that rut in the autumn (red, sika and fallow) there can be nothing quite so glorious as the red deer rut in the Highlands of Scotland, followed closely by those gigantic West Country specimens in Devon and Somerset, to which I was introduced by my grandfather at the age of four.

The autumn rutting species – unlike roe, muntjac and Chinese water deer – are all herding animals to a greater or lesser extent; adult male herds spending most of the year away from the female-and-youngster herds, but mixing together during the rut.

Successfully calling a red stag away from his parcel of hinds at the height of the rut is one of the most exciting experiences a stalker can have. At this time of year the stags are roaring out their challenges all over their hind-holding areas, through day and night, indicating their ability and attraction as a sire to any unattached females, while at the same time – like some bellicose drunk at closing time – offering to fight any other stag bold enough to take them on.

Stags aren't quite so foolish as that drunk outside the pub on a Saturday night, though. They know that fighting in the wild can be a formidable business with life-threatening consequences for both contenders. And while fights *do* occur, sometimes ending in fatalities, these tend to involve stags of similar strength, status and antler conformation that have exhausted all other means of determining supremacy.

When challenged by an obviously superior beast the lesser of the two will generally make some hasty excuse about an urgent appointment at the dentist's or remember that his parking meter is about to expire, and depart elsewhere with his dignity reasonably intact.

Where both combatants are reluctant to withdraw, they will try every means possible to avoid aggressive physical contact. This posturing is just like the human equivalent when two men are anxious not to be seen to back down in front of their womenfolk, but where neither is particularly keen to get a bloody nose either. It will involve some or all of the following:

Assessing the opponent's antlers: 'Is this bloke bigger and stronger than me?'

Vocal challenges, by way of roaring: 'If I shout loudly enough, maybe he'll take fright and go away.'

Parallel walking, while eyeing each other up and making themselves look as fierce as possible: 'Just watch it, you louse, or I'll give you what for!'

False charges or lunges, a sort of psychological warfare used to unnerve and unsettle the opponent: 'Keep your distance. Dare to come near me, and you'll get some of this!'

If all this fails, a crude pushing or shoving match ensues. If one of the belligerents is weaker than the other, and is forced to give ground, that is usually the end of the matter. He departs – with furious intentions, and woe-betide any lesser stag that crosses his path – but neither victor nor vanquished has sustained physical damage; only pride has been hurt, and that doesn't threaten the reproduction of the species.

Only if the pushing and shoving fails to decide an obvious winner does the confrontation take a nasty turn. At this point – surrounded by hinds which are in danger of being usurped by lesser stags while the two protagonists are otherwise engaged, and having failed to substantiate superiority through more peaceful methods – they will lock antlers in earnest. Each will now attempt to kill the other with his formidable headgear.

Even at this stage death is rare; one or both will probably retire wounded before a mortal blow can be struck, but certainly neither will be in any condition to face another usurper for a while, so this is just when a young hopeful might decide to risk all for love and sneak in to grab a piece of the action. Thus is the gene pool of all herding species diluted, and spread wider than if just one alpha male bred with every female.

As the boat slid away from the shore with its antlered cargo safely stowed, my companion produced a couple of beers. As I raised mine to my lips I noticed our friends, the two ravens, flapping around near the spot where we'd left the gralloch. We glanced at one another and solemnly raised our cans to the black shapes high above, just as an osprey plunged into the loch and rose with a silver prize clutched in its talons. 'Cheers!' we said.

Out for a Buck

GRAHAM BROCKHOUSE

ROE STALKING is probably the most varied form of deer stalking in the British Isles. The roe's habitat changes totally from north to south, and stalking methods change with it.

Here in the Borders and in other parts of Scotland, many roe live totally on the open hill. Stalking them is very much akin to red deer stalking in the Highlands, except that roe are harder to pick out than red. The basic premise is exactly the same: first spot the beast you want to cull and then stalk it.

In the vast conifer blocks of northern England and Scotland, tactics have to change. Where there are wall-to-wall sitka spruce with narrow rides, the major element is luck. It's often a question of being in the right place at the right time. Only if there are plenty of open areas and plantations of young trees can the stalking tactics remain roughly the same.

Further south, where there is a patchwork of agricultural land interspersed with woodland, it is again easier to spot and select beasts as generally they frequent woodland margins or graze in the fields.

Taking the hill ground first, the selection of animals to cull will depend on the population – and this can be established only by long hours of sitting out on the hill and counting deer. Stalking consists mainly of footwork, keeping quiet and using the wind to your advantage.

The roe deer has acute hearing (personally I think this is their best sense) so silent movement is essential. The range at which most hill roe will be shot tends to be greater than their lowland cousins and, as they are a small target, accuracy is crucial.

In forest situations it is hard to assess the population. Many bucks seen when they are out of season never seem to appear when they are in season. In this situation I try to shoot as many young animals as possible. That said, where the protection of young trees is the main consideration I shoot what I see.

A lot of this type of stalking is conducted on foot, sneaking around the rides at dawn or dusk and watching paths that roe tend to use. If you have a long lease on a block of forestry it can pay dividends to erect high seats at favoured places where animals cross rides or feed on the margins. By doing this you can sometimes afford the luxury of being a little more selective.

In an agricultural environment it is far easier to assess a population and consequently much easier to decide which animals to cull. Again, stalking can be conducted on foot or high seats can be erected in strategic settings for maximum effect – and incidentally also for safer shooting where the land is relatively flat.

Having stalked roe in this kind of environment for many years, I used to split the bucks into groups once I had decided on the number to cull. Sixty per cent of my cull would be young animals of up to two years old, 25 per cent would be old animals and approximately 15 per cent mature bucks. This worked extremely well over a number of years and resulted in a well balanced population of bucks and does in the area.

Roebucks generally cast their antlers from late November through to the end of December and immediately start growing their new set. These antlers are covered in velvet and grow until fully formed. The testosterone levels in the bucks' bodies increase and with this the antlers harden. The bucks remove the velvet covering by rubbing the antlers on trees.

Old bucks tend to clean their antlers first and by April most of them will be clear of velvet and in hard horn. This varies from south to north, however, and northern bucks may be a week or two behind. Down through the age range this process becomes later so that some yearling bucks will still be in velvet in late May. The animals are generally still in their winter coat at this time and, again depending on latitude, come into their foxy red summer coat anytime from mid-May to mid-June.

When cleaning their antlers or marking out a territory roe cause damage to trees, so understandably they are not popular with foresters who generally want them removed as soon as possible. If you are fairly new to roe stalking and come across such damage, you may be pressured into shooting the animal responsible. But this can be a mistake, particularly if the animal is a buck holding an established territory.

This type of buck has already damaged a number of trees on his boundaries but will not cause any more problems as he has marked his area. If you shoot him the area will become a disputed territory with perhaps two or three more bucks fighting over it and causing serious damage to trees in the area.

For this reason I do not shoot a buck that has already established a territory, particularly in a young plantation. You may see a little more damage in the rut but this will be minimal compared with what happens if you shoot him.

It always pays to try and remove all unwanted bucks as early as possible in the season. I cull the animals whether they are in hard horn or velvet, and generally try to have most of my bucks shot by the end of May. I do this because June and early July are quiet months for roebucks with little movement taking place. Also, the cover will be getting tall by then, so that the animals are harder to see and remain hidden for long periods.

Mid-July until mid-August is the period of the roe rut, with the bucks becoming more vocal and active as they pursue the does in their area. During this period I generally account for the mature and older animals that figure in the cull. It is also the time that most continental and other trophy stalkers visit the UK as success is achieved more easily during the rut. As for me, I have never shot a gold medal animal, despite having had many opportunities, and there is only one silver medal animal in my collection of heads.

This beast – I estimated him to be at least eight years old – was shot for causing excessive damage to a young plantation. His head was starting to go back or, in other words, he was past his best after having been a classic gold for at least two years.

When stalking roebucks you will need a fair amount of equipment, but I would recommend getting the best you can afford when it comes to binoculars and telescopic sights. Most factory produced rifles are very functional and with factory ammunition will consistently produce good groups at one hundred yards, which is more than adequate. On the other hand, scopes and binoculars do vary in quality. As a lot of stalking is done in poor light, my advice is to buy the best. Remember that good sight pictures make for accurate identification and shooting.

Rifles are a matter of individual choice and for roe stalking the legislation is different in England and Wales from Scotland, so it all really depends on where you live and what you want. I would hazard a guess that the .243 Winchester is possibly the most widely used roe rifle in

Britain, but being fortunate enough to live north of the border I prefer to use my .222 Remington for roe where the situation allows.

Always remember that it is accurate bullet placement that terminates the animal's life, not the size of the bullet. I have seen animals run just as far when badly shot with a .300 magnum as they have when shot badly with a .222.

All stalkers at some time will make a mistake and it usually ends with an animal being wounded and making off. This is when the responsibility rests firmly on the shoulders of the stalker, who must follow up and despatch the animal as quickly as is humanely possible.

Experience is the best teacher and over the years the novice will learn a lot, but I feel that it is incumbent upon anyone who wants to stalk at least to try and achieve a Deer Management Qualification (DMQ) level one certificate. This is now required by most forestry companies before they will lease you stalking and does at least ensure that a stalker has a basic knowledge of deer and their biology.

I also believe that stalkers should own or have ready access to a dog that is able to track deer. Although its services may never be needed, I would not object to legislation on this point. If the stalker has shot at and wounded an animal, I feel it is incumbent upon him to find that animal whatever the circumstances.

Remember that safety is vital. You need a very good backstop for a rifle bullet, bearing in mind that expanding bullets cause horrific wounds. My advice to everyone is to think at least twice before pulling the trigger.

First Impala

ASHLEY BOON

Sunrise colours the hilltops and sets off the calling of Cape turtle doves, the continuous soundtrack to an African day. I lift the rifle to my shoulder and experience again the thrill I felt two long years ago as I stood by the fire's smoking embers in the cold before dawn. A glorious feeling washes over me, like waking up as a schoolboy only to remember it's the first day of the holidays. I'm back in Africa.

For four days I've been at Sandspruit, this northern Transvaal farm, and still haven't caught up with the impala I've come here to hunt. I've been close, but here in the hills the rains are late and so far the unseasonable weather has made it a frustrating trip.

The earlier visit was my first encounter with the continent that so captured my imagination as a boy. As I followed Brian, my host, out into the thornveld that morning, I felt like Ernest Hemingway. And all I was hoping for was to come upon the commonest antelope in Africa!

First impressions were burned into my memory ... the infinite variety of trees with wonderful names like 'buffalo thorn' or 'wait-a-bit thorn'; the plaintive call of the 'go-away' birds, the stunning colour of my first crimson-breasted shrike and the rich red of the dusty ground; the vervet monkeys whose rustling passage made us pause and whose unfamiliar form was such a surprise to my northern eyes.

My first little bee-eater, bright green and orange, flicked back and forth from the branches of an acacia as Brian paused to point to the tracks he'd found. With his clipped South African accent he sounded almost offhand: 'Look, this was a big leopard that came through here last night.'

And finally there were the impala, skittish and darting. I felt like Mole introduced by Ratty to a delightful new world. The tick-bite fever I got later wasn't so much fun, though.

Brian, who used to be a PH, a professional hunter, was disappointed that I didn't get a ram during that earlier visit, but I wasn't. There would have been something a little crass about stepping onto this new and exciting stage and shooting the first animal I saw. I was far happier that I had been able to experience this wonderful new place and could enjoy the anticipation of a return trip.

Yesterday I sat for two hours waiting for a herd to come to the dam to drink, but none did. As I sat trying to ignore the midday heat, watching the vultures and black eagles spin slowly across the cobalt sky, I could hear distant impala rams calling out the challenges of the rut.

I dropped back downwind to stalk into the source of the noise. After a long walk I came on them in the shadows of some dense thorn scrub. I got within thirty yards of the herd, all ewes. Although I could still hear the males there was not a horn in sight. So, rather than panic them, I slipped away.

Earlier, as I stalked the ewes, a greater honeyguide had found me and started to call and chur on the branches right in front of me.

Honeyguides will lead animals, including man, to a bee's nest. There the bird can feed on the leftovers once the animal, often a honey badger, has opened the nest for them and had its fill. The locals say that if you are taken to a nest by a honeyguide you must always leave some for him and not be greedy – or 'next time he will lead you to a lion or a black mamba!'

Getting more and more vocal, this one gave up on me in disgust as I continued my search for a shootable ram. It was dusk before I found a group of rams rutting and, with no chance of a shot in the gloom, I decided to back off and return in good time next day.

So, after a long walk, here we are at last, close enough to hear the hoof beats, the unlikely guttural grunts, the clack of horn on horn. The rams are still in the area where I found them in the half-light last night.

We have spent what seemed an age crossing a horribly open area, crouched and shuffling on aching calves to reach the cover of the thorns. Now we are very close. Foot by foot we approach the sound of the rams. Suddenly Brian holds his hand out in a silent, urgent gesture. He's just in front of us, he whispers.

I crawl to the nearest tree, ignoring the stabs of thorns in my hands and knees, to slide the rifle onto a branch and search for him.

All at once I make out the dark-eyed head and neck only thirty feet away. It's the only part of him I can see at all, and that not clearly. The impala is staring straight at me. Between us there is a crazy confusion of thorns, but I find a gap that gives a clear view through the scope and rest the cross hairs over his neck. Slowly I pull the trigger.

Afterwards Brian insists he said, 'Good shot!' But as we go forward a ram sets off bounding through the cover, filling my heart with thoughts of wounded game and regret.

I put the rifle up again but cannot get a shot off at the fleeing animal. Feeling sick, I walk in to look for traces of hair or blood. Instead I find the outstretched, lifeless form of my impala. It is my first African quarry.

I am flooded with relief now that stealth and silence are no longer needed. I take a long look at my first ram, run my hand over those elegant horns and enjoy a good friend's congratulations.

I wait in the gathering dark for Brian to get the backie (pick-up), listening to the calls of the pearl-spotted owls. Then comes the drive back and later, celebratory beers round a fire under a star-filled sky. True, it isn't a buffalo or kudu, but it is a first. You only get them once and now, finally, I have hunted in Africa. I wonder if I have a right to feel this happy, so much so that I doubt if Hemingway himself could have felt happier.

Artist with a Rifle

ELIZABETH HALSTEAD

EVER SINCE I was a child I have loved animals, especially deer. I used to stay with an aunt in the New Forest and often watched the fallow in all the secret places where she knew we might find them. As an adult, having spent ten years in Canada, I have painted all kinds of British and Canadian wildlife – but deer have always been a challenge.

When I met my second husband I had just completed a painting of a roebuck in a stream, an image that came from my memories of the New Forest. He was a stalker and gamekeeper and was quite critical of my roebuck. He assured me that I would get lots of chances to study them, and he was right.

On one memorable occasion, during September, we were stalking together in a big wood in the Cotswolds, a wood in which we knew most of the buck. Graham had taken out an old buck and we were going back to the vehicle when we spotted a set of legs up a narrow footpath. It was another buck. Graham challenged me to see how close I could get to him. I knew he was testing my woodcraft.

The wind was right and I slowly made my way towards the roebuck. He had his head stuck in a thorn tree, nibbling the leaves, and was oblivious to me. I crept closer and closer, hardly daring to breathe, every step an effort not to crack a twig or disturb a leaf. Slowly, slowly... I was studying the beautiful coat and the slender legs, trying to remember the muscle structure for a future painting.

I was very close now. Holding my breath, I reached out to touch him – when suddenly he became aware of my presence and turned to look. I will never forget the startled look in his eyes as he saw me. He leapt three feet sideways and fled up the path. I was shaking like a leaf and my heart was in overdrive. We laughed all the way back to the vehicle.

Roe are my favourite deer and I have any number of videos of them in my head, including one when I was sitting up in a high seat, very, very early on a misty June morning.

As the sun came up the birds were singing, the water of the small burn alongside me was bubbling and the dewdrops were hanging on the grasses. I was so relaxed I was almost nodding off – a dangerous thing to do with a rifle in a high seat.

Suddenly I caught a movement only twenty yards away – and up stood a roe doe. She stretched, and alongside her I saw her two dappled kids. The kids both suckled from her, bumping her in their eagerness. She nibbled a few leaves and then lay down again.

The trio were under the overhanging branch of a Scots pine and I watched enthralled as the kids bounced round and round their mother. Then one stood on her back and played king of the castle whilst the other tried to push it off. That image is still there in my head, as clear as a bell, and one day it will be a painting.

The memory of shooting my first roebuck is just as clear. There was a harsh frost on that early May morning and Graham had asked me to sit in a high seat on top of a bank in a plantation that was being hammered by a roebuck. I had always said I could never shoot a roe and I felt quite sure I would not see one, so I snuggled down in my thick coat and pulled my scarf up round my face.

Just as the sun was peeping over the top of the trees I caught a movement down in the plantation. I told myself, don't worry it will be a doe. Then I spotted a set of antlers above the small trees, coming closer.

I froze. I was hoping he would just go away but no, he was working his way towards me, thrashing every tree in his path. He got closer and closer and I thought, I have to do something about this. I rested the rifle on the bar and watched him through the scope. He was forty yards from me now with his back towards me and his head and neck going up and down a lovely young Scots pine.

He stopped for a few seconds and I shot him through the back of the neck. Down he went. I reloaded and waited and watched, no movement. I was trembling as I opened the bolt and gingerly made my way down the steps.

I had mixed feelings about killing him, but as we were entrusted to look after the plantations I felt I was doing a job. What's more, the roebuck would feed us and our friends; we both love eating venison.

Graham came eventually and watched me gralloch him. When I boiled his head out I found the bullet lodged in his nose.

My experiences with red deer are quite different. I have had some fantastic days on the hill in many different locations and my head is full of images which I have put on canvas.

When I look at the stag's head on my studio wall it brings to mind a stalk I had with a good friend at the top of Loch Shin. Alan is as agile as a mountain goat and he took me out one morning to try and get a stag. I followed him for an hour or more, puffing and panting, my legs aching. Occasionally Alan told me to 'bide a while whilst I go and have a little spy'.

Finally he beckoned to me. When I reached him he told me there was a stag holding about thirty hinds on the other side of the bank. The stag was old – and Alan wanted me to shoot him.

My heart started racing. We stalked over some peat hags and as we came over one of them a young stag jumped up and ran down the hill.

'Quick, quick!' Alan told me. 'He'll disturb everything. We must reach that rock as they will all run up that far bank.'

We ran to the rock and Alan set up the rifle. Sure enough the deer started running up the far bank, about a hundred and fifty yards away. All I could see was a mass of bodies. Then I spotted the stag among them. They slowed down and the stag walked out onto a rock promontory slightly above us

The hinds were above him, making their way up the hill, but the stag stopped. All I remember is that he looked like the Monarch of the Glen.

'Shoot him now,' said Alan – and I pulled the trigger. The stag toppled down over the rock and lay on a grassy knoll. I hugged Alan, who slapped me on the back. Then, trembling with excitement, we made our way over to him.

He was a ninepointer, his teeth were quite worn down, and Alan reckoned he was about twelve years old. I was elated.

I have painted him several times in different backgrounds and his memory as the Monarch lives in my mind and on my canvases, together with all the other animals I have stalked with camera and rifle.

Fickle Fallow

CHRISTOPHER BORTHEN

ALTHOUGH SOME believe that fallow were introduced to Britain by Phoenician traders, or even by the Romans, most experts today agree that it was probably the Normans who brought them across the English Channel in the eleventh century.

There are now over 100,000 fallow living wild in Britain and another 20,000 in parks and on deer farms. My first encounter with a fallow deer came when I was all of four years old . . .

The sound of a cow bellowing in the woods was a thing I'd never heard before, so something was wrong. I ran through the meadows as fast as my little legs could carry me to tell my grandfather.

Grandfather, who was in the middle of inspecting the pigs, listened with the kind of respect and sincerity that only grandparents show towards their grandchildren and with a wry grin told me to go and change into long trousers and to bring his tweed jacket from the peg out to his old green van. Even better than telephoning the farmer, I thought, we were going to visit him instead; at the very least, I'd be certain of a ginger-nut biscuit from the wooden barrel that always stood on his sideboard, and maybe some lemonade.

Instead of turning in when we came to the lane leading to the farm house, we continued towards the woods where the cow's bellow had come from. Grandfather hushed my hurried questions, parked by a disused gateway and told me not to make a sound as we entered the wood. There it was again! Powerful, haunting, somehow timeless in its voracity – it didn't sound quite so much like a cow now that I was with Grandfather, but it couldn't be anything else.

Our progress was very slow – more as though we were somewhere we shouldn't be and had to be careful not to be found out. He was certainly behaving in a peculiar manner and I wasn't quite sure I approved, but being out alone with him was always the most wonderful of adventures.

Farther and farther into the wood we went, changing directions as though at a whim, following paths sometimes and then leaving them without any apparent reason, until I was completely lost. Every now and then the sound that had brought us here would echo through the branches, louder and louder – we were getting closer. I shivered involuntarily, not with cold (it was a balmy autumn day) but with a primeval instinct that warned me to be aware; maybe to expect danger or excitement of some sort – an instinct that might have forewarned my forefathers and saved their lives when they were hunter-gatherers – and which was still lying dormant, ready to come to the surface at that very moment in a four-year-old's existence when, for the first time, he was about to witness something that would have a profound influence on the rest of his life.

Coming to a halt behind a large oak tree, my grandfather knelt down so that he could whisper in my ear. He told me to look around the trunk, very slowly and carefully, with no sudden movements, and not to make a sound. For the first (and probably the last!) time in my life I was incapable of uttering a word. On a mound, not fifty yards away, a magnificent fallow buck with enormous antlers threw back his head and gave a tremendous roar, his prominent Adam's apple bobbing up and down with the exertion. I was absolutely terrified, yet I couldn't take my eyes off the scene in front of me. His harem of does was milling about all around him, and at that point he pawed at the ground with his forefoot and charged down the mound at a young pricket who had unwisely come too close to the lord and master of the rutting stand. The pricket didn't wait for his senior's arrival, but took to his heels and departed in haste with much snapping of twigs to mark his progress.

Having lost all sense of reality, and heedless of the carefully explained instructions, I tugged at my grandfather's jacket, gesticulated wildly in the direction of the buck, and shouted for him to look.

Needless to say, when I turned around again, all I saw were a few upright tails and flared rump patches bobbing away between the trees. To this day I am still surprised at how quickly large numbers of deer manage to disappear in woodland, almost seeming to melt away.

Shortly after that we followed the Quantock Staghounds, who were meeting not far from our home, and subsequently went out with the Devon and Somerset Staghounds on Exmoor, a short drive away. I was introduced to all the masters, the huntsmen, the whippers-in, the kennel huntsmen and the harbourers, as well as all the members of the field who knew my grandfather – which was most of them. So, before I was five years old, I had developed an intimate love affair with deer and hunting that has never left me.

Some thirty years later, when I was managing the deer and running the pheasant shoot on an estate in Devon, which was also host to a large population of wild fallow, that first experience of the rut and my foolish behaviour came back to haunt me mercilessly. As my patch included some three thousand acres of pine forest, criss-crossed by public footpaths and bridleways, plus farming and forestry operations, I tended to use high seats to help account for most of my annual cull, though there were times and areas when only stalking on foot would produce the required results.

One warm, sunny afternoon in October, just before the first pheasant shoot of the season, I was returning with one of the keepers after inspecting some deer damage to one of his cover crops. We were walking past the newly-positioned pegs on a drive known affectionately by the beaters as 'Death Alley', when I heard that 'cow' bellowing in the woods again. Because of our mission, I had my rifle on my shoulder and my binoculars around my neck 'just in case', so I told him to go back for his tea on his own while I investigated the source of the sound.

Not fifty yards into the trees I encountered does that were directly in between me and my quarry. If I passed them on my left I'd give them my scent, but if I was very careful, and very lucky, I could sneak by them on my right. The manoeuvre worked.

Perfectly aware that the frequently changing positions of the does could give me away at any moment, I nevertheless forced myself not to hurry things, and moved an inch at a time to a vantage point whence I could assess my target. Gently parting the branches of a bush revealed the best fallow buck I'd seen for a long time. He was lying down with his back to me, not twenty-five yards away. I didn't need the binoculars; there was a safe backstop; and to raise the rifle and squeeze the trigger would have been the work of a moment.

I was in a quandary. A little angel hopped onto my right shoulder to remind me that 'Never shoot your best bucks' was an adage that had been drilled into me from my early stalking mentors. It made sense, of course.

Then a little devil hopped onto my left shoulder to remind me that I had diligently managed this fallow population for a number of years, unselfishly shooting only the poor bucks and leaving the best ones. Thus, quite logically, through my best efforts, this buck had been spared to reach his prime and his full potential, and to pass on his genes to future generations. I, of all people, could justify taking this trophy as a reward for all the hours spent pursuing less worthy beasts. It made sense, of course.

In the event I did neither, preferring to creep away unnoticed, because the following day I had a special friend coming to stay and I made up my mind, there and then, that he would be the one to shoot this buck.

Head stalker on a remote Highland deer forest with thousands of red deer and a few sika, he liked nothing better than a busman's holiday as far south as possible stalking our roe and fallow. His last stag-stalking guests of the season had finally departed and so this trip would be a welcome break for him while he 'rested the hill' before he and his under-stalkers started on the hinds.

At dawn the next morning we were to be found walking across the parkland towards 'Death Valley' – me keen to show my friend good sport, and he equally keen not to let my efforts be wasted. But I had made one vital miscalculation.

My foray of the previous afternoon had taken place while all the pheasants were wandering around the woods enjoying the sunshine, paying no attention to my cautious progress through the wood. Now, of course, they regarded the approach of two humans as the signal for a slightly earlier than usual morning feed.

One after the other, until it seemed that all the thousands of pheasants on the shoot had roosted in that particular spot, they fluttered down to earth, cackling and calling to all and sundry, in that annoying way that pheasants have, and beating their wings furiously to make the maximum amount of noise.

We halted – the pheasants ceased to come off roost. We took one step forward – the pheasants fluttered down again. And so it was, a sort of Grandmother's Footsteps whereby every pace forward was greeted by a cacophony of sound as a further ten or a dozen pheasants proclaimed their approval at our progress, applauding loudly.

My friend glanced in my direction, and I looked sheepishly back at him. No deer in its right mind would hang around after that little performance, and we hadn't even reached anywhere near where I had planned to start the first approach, let alone the final stalk.

I anticipated that if we were to retrace our steps immediately, without even attempting to enter the wood, the deer might decide to return after a few hours, thus giving us the opportunity to wring some success from the disaster I had led us into.

On the way back to the Land Rover I apologised for my stupidity, but he would hear nothing of it, saying how fortunate he was not to have to compete with roosting pheasants when he was stalking his red deer in the Highlands. I knew that he was more embarrassed for me than I was, and I knew that he knew I knew, which somehow made it worse!

Ten minutes later, on another part of the estate, he called a pricket by imitating the groan of a rutting buck – using some bugle-like contraption that he said could also call red deer stags – but decided not to take the shot in the end. Then we watched a couple of roe does, a mother and daughter, going about their business before shooting an unwary fox returning home from his night-time patrol. Finally, we sat up in one of my double high seats with a pair of cast fallow antlers and rattled them together a few times, to imitate a fight between two master bucks, just to see what would happen. Surprisingly enough, because I'd never had much success at this before, a couple of mature does with youngsters at foot came to see what was going on, followed by a pricket that paid the price for his curiosity, with a heart shot from my friend's .243 Steyr-Mannlicher.

We had had our fun, so after we had finished in the larder we returned home for an early breakfast before setting off for a leisurely few hours fly-fishing on the river. After a pint of Scrumpy cider and a ploughman's lunch at the inn, we grabbed forty winks before tea and set off, once more, to try to outwit the object of our attentions twelve hours previously.

Never before had I enjoyed a textbook stalk more. The does were where they had been the previous afternoon and the same manoeuvres outwitted them. The master buck was on his rutting stand, just as before, and was equally impervious to our final approach. All that remained was for me to part the boughs of the bush, indicate to my friend the natural rifle rest that a bifurcated limb offered, and the trophy would be his ... except that it didn't go quite like that, because, as Robbie Burns has it: 'The best laid plans of mice and men gang aft agley.'

As soon as he saw the large, fully-palmated antlers, my friend gasped in amazement. 'I can't shoot that!' he whispered. 'If anyone shot a beast like that on my forest, I'd be for the chop!'

'But you don't have a beast like that on your ground,' I hissed. 'Just a bunch of poor-doing, emaciated, disease-ridden, half-starved apologies for red deer that will never grow heads like this if you managed them selectively for a thousand years! Now shoot him and don't mess me about!' I had hoped that my tongue-in-cheek insults would make him see the funny side of the predicament we were in, and that this would melt away his resistance to taking the shot.

'I'll have you know that my deer are no such thing ...' and we both burst into uncontrollable laughter.

You've guessed it: when I looked again, all I saw were a few upright tails and flared rump patches bobbing away between the trees.

Baltic Boar

CHARLIE JACOBY

It WEIGHS a quarter of a ton and it comes straight for you – you're up against the wild boar of Lithuania.

Picture a cold pheasant drive. Snow lies on the ground, ice tinkles in the tree, but instead of the warning chatter of the blackbirds, you hear snuffling and grunting ahead.

As the game breaks cover, you spot another difference between it and your average pheasant. Though moving at 20 mph, it is not flying, it weighs up to six hundred pounds and is the size of a wheelbarrow. It also seems to be hurtling towards you.

The boar shooting is tremendous. Our party of four guns from the West Midlands are keen pheasant shots and insist on treating themselves to at least a week of driven boar every season.

Lithuania offers loads of game and many species compared to other

Eastern European countries. The best time is the first two weeks of November, not just because game is plentiful but because most species are in season. You can have a go at boar, roe buck and doe, cow elk, raccoon dog, fox, hare and – from high seats only – mature bull elk. The high seats rule is so you can see whether the beast is old or young.

Aficionados of the famous boy reporter Tintin will step off the aeroplane at Vilnius airport in Lithuania and say at once: 'Syldavia'. The description of the country in Lithuanian Airlines' in-flight magazine is spookily similar to the magazine Tintin read in King Ottakar's Sceptre.

Our translator met us at the airport. Like Tintin's translators Krônick and Klûmsi, Aidos Raudondvaris had the displaced air of the political officers who accompanied Intourist package holidays to the Soviet Union, uncomfortable away from a desk. Where the clothes of the beaters and 'hunt master' would have fitted in on a UK shoot, Aidos stuck resolutely to a long, padded, beige duffel coat and unsuitable boots. His English was equally suspect. 'I hope we will come very friendship,' he told us at the airport. 'If you have question, I will tell everything.'

We kept silent, in case.

After a night at a comfortable hunting lodge, the hunting day starts in semi-darkness with beaters forming a line on one side of a snowy forest clearing and shooters on the other side. At the head stands hunt master Rimantas Serys with Aidos next to him. The dogs, including Lithuania's own hunting dog the Lietuviu skalikas, sit impatiently on the snow. Twice we see them relieve themselves on their owners' legs – which detracts from the solemnity of the ceremony.

Rimantas, 36, is hunting master for the forest of Kopiskis, an important position locally. He looks after five thousand acres of forest as well as fifteen thousand acres of arable and meadow and also works on the whole Kopiskis area, which is four hundred square miles. He has been doing it for seven years. It gives him a comfortable house, a smart jeep and an impressive trophy room in a country where many houses and most of the former Soviet collective farms are abandoned.

Shooting means euros here, do not buy Lithuanian currency. But Rimantas says he works for love as much as for money. He feeds areas in the forest with maize most days; he pays off farmers who lose their wheat and potatoes to his boars; and he prays for rain. Boars like rain. He hosts nine driven days on his patch every year – six of them with parties of Germans and three with us.

There is no full-time staff but Rimantas calls on friends, including lumberjacks and a fireman, to beat. Because of their work commitments, the line-up of beaters changed often. He was too polite to ask shooters to tip the beaters at the end of every day – but we realised we should have done.

Rimantas makes a speech about which animals we hope to shoot today and emphasises safety (we use either solid slugs in 12-bores or rifles).

And then we move off: shooters in a snug minibus, beaters in a fabulous 1959 Russian lorry that the occupying army left behind when it retreated to Moscow in the early 1990s. Rimantas has refurbished it.

We line up on one side of a block of forest, one hundred yards apart and often on high seats. We wait. The drive is longer than one of our pheasant drives. Beaters take up to an hour to blank in each patch of forest. Experienced boar-hunters in the party wear walking boots. Tyros like me wear wellies. Warmth and grip on the ice is the key, so the others are right.

The first game to break is usually the roe deer. We also see hares, foxes, wolves, raccoon dogs and the occasional animal the size of half a Land Rover – an elk – who trots past in majesty, barely breaking a branch.

We had excellent sport. You usually hear the boars grunting in the undergrowth ahead. Then they hurtle through the line of guns. We once saw more than twenty, running along the side of a big ditch, like a fast-moving black carpet. A big pack nearly bowled over one of our guns, Tony Taylor . . . he shot one of them going away.

Tony had a dream week. His bag included a big old, male wolf – the first killed in the area for twelve years. It made the Lithuanian newspapers as a 'good news' item. A travel agent had organised the trip and promised wolf shooting. The fact this wolf made the national press allowed the guns to question whether the travel agent was not perchance over-promising on this trip. Aha – said the travel agent – but you got a wolf, didn't you?

The European wolf is not endangered. At the time, the IUCN listed the Italian subpopulation as vulnerable and the Spanish population as lower risk, but the huge population in Russia and Eastern Europe suffers not from shooting but from expanding human populations.

Our day ends with a similar ritual to the start. We form a line, the beaters form a line; the dogs are so tired many are now lying down. Our bag is laid before us and fires lit around it. A bugler plays a lament for each animal shot. He didn't have one for a wolf, so made up a triumphant one that owed a lot to Glenn Miller.

By the end, we had taught Aidos some juicier phrases. After one drive he sidled up and asked: 'Please? What is "foo kinbar starred"?'

We grew to like him.

Kudu Bull

TONY JACKSON

Let me whisk you far from our soft and gentle climes, south to that distant land once known as the Dark Continent. For a good many years now I have hunted in Africa from top to toe, from the Sudan, through Zambia, Zimbabwe and down to South Africa, invariably seeking plains game and bird shooting, for big game have always been beyond my pocket. Today I look back in sheer disbelief at my innocence in the early days. How I survived is still a mystery!

Take, for example, the occasion when I was sent to the Caprivi Strip by the South African Tourist Board on a promotional trip. The Caprivi lies to the north of Botswana, running from east to west and is dissected by a substantial river, the Chobe. It is wild, remote Africa, a country of elephants and buffalo, of leopards, lions and hippos in the river pools. This is not the sanitised Africa.

This was only my second trip, or safari, in Africa and I still had a blind faith in the knowledge and abilities of those who lived and worked there. In the majority of cases my faith has always been more than justified but just occasionally the system fails.

Let me explain. A travel agent, named Rod, and I had been flown by Cessna into a bush landing strip on the edge of the Caprivi and then driven to a hunting camp scenically sited on the southern bank of the Chobe river. Our mission, for want of a better word, was to check out a large island some twenty miles downstream with a view to assessing the potential for visitors, both hunters and tourists, in a camp which was under construction. So far, so good and for a couple of days all went well, apart from a cobra which I found in my hut and which I tried, and failed, to shoot with a 9 mm automatic pistol someone lent me.

On the third day Rod and I, together with our guide, embarked in a fibreglass dinghy with an outboard, to head down the Chobe. We were armed with only a side-by-side boxlock 12-bore, a box of shells and the automatic pistol with a dozen cartridges. For supplies we had coffee, milk and a bag of biltong made from dried impala meat. It was, to say the least, basic.

However, in our innocence we embarked and, for several hours, chugged along the still river waters between tall beds of papyrus reeds. Occasionally we would see a hippo, while jacanas or lily-trotters, chestnut-coloured birds with white throats and long blue legs, scampered across the lily pads and, once, we spotted a crocodile basking on a muddy bank.

And then it happened! The boat struck a sandbank, the propeller was ripped off and, to our horror, we found ourselves drifting downstream away from the camp with absolutely no means of propulsion. At one point we floated round a bend into a wide pool where, to our horror, we saw a dozen or more vast hippo heads staring beady-eyed at us as we drifted by. Now hippos are not the gentle giants of popular imagination, but have a nasty habit of upturning boats, thence to chomp in half the unfortunate occupants. Suddenly a massive water-horse ducked under the water and appeared to be heading for us. I loaded the 12-bore and fired two barrels of No 5 at roughly the point where I expected him to emerge with the result that either the noise or the shock wave must have had some effect because we remained in one piece and, hearts thumping, carried on with our helpless and hapless journey.

The only answer, we decided, was to land at the nearest stretch of clear bank on our left-hand side, leave the boat and walk back the seven or eight miles to camp. It seemed a good idea at the time!

Another half mile and an ideal landing place appeared, and with the one paddle we had on board, we managed to beach the craft and take stock. Armed and with our supplies, we set out to find the nearest track. For half a mile or so we trooped through the grasses, passing baobab trees and thick clumps of bush, until we came to water. More bloody water! It stretched on either side of us, with no apparent end and was about a hundred yards across.

Suddenly the horrid truth dawned. We had landed on an island and the only way of escape was across this murky arm of water which, for all we knew, was croc-infested. We were so desperate that we even tried to make a raft from dead timber, but on launching it immediately sank! There was no alternative but to make our way back to the boat and think again.

That night we slept, or tried to sleep, on a small hillock overlooking the river. I had fired three shots from the pistol in the hope that someone from the camp might hear them, but as we were not due back for twenty-four hours, even if they were heard, no one was going to take any notice.

Across the river a lion played havoc with a troop of screaming baboons, mosquitoes attacked us and the biltong and coffee did nothing for our appetites. To cut a long story short, for three days we camped out, while I wandered about shooting the odd dove, and a spurwing goose for the pot, while all the time listening and hoping to hear a rescue craft chuntering down the river. At last one of us had the notion of writing a message in huge letters on the sandy shore. 'Prop Lost – Help'.

On the third day a small plane droned over, circled and vanished. Three hours later a rescue craft turned up and, to our joy and embarrassment, we were rescued and relief swept through the South African Tourist Board, who had been going quietly frantic at the news of our disappearance.

A year later, undeterred, I was back, but this time to hunt in the Zambesi Valley, courtesy of one Mick Rowbotham, an ex-Kenya hand and professional hunter, then based just above Harare and running a hunting company called 'Hunter's Tracks'. Mike had invited me to hunt in northern Zimbabwe to try for a kudu.

My professional hunter was an old friend, an Englishman called David Willey who was based in Harare. From the capital we drove north for hours to the hunting concession close to the Zambesi and here, in a typical grass-thatched hunting camp, I spent a long and exhausting week in what, as day succeeded day with only the occasional distant glimpse of kudu, appeared to be a fruitless chase. The bush was dense and in heavy leaf and though we saw numerous impala, buffalo and a good many elephants, by the Friday, my last day's hunting, the chance of catching up with a kudu, in my opinion the most beautiful of all Africa's spiral-horned antelopes, appeared slight.

All morning David, two trackers and I worked through thick mopane under a blazing sun until at last we came to a hillock overlooking the jungle and, slowly and somewhat dispiritedly, clambered to its summit with a view to spying the bush below. We saw in the distance a small herd of elephants tearing at the trees, but of kudu there was not a sign. Slowly we started to descend and then, suddenly, one of the trackers hissed and stood still. Quietly David and I looked to where he was indicating and there, perhaps seventy yards away and below us, a bull kudu and two cows were grazing in thick bush.

I was using a borrowed .30-06 and was nervous but there was no time to waste. The tracker knelt and I took the downhill shot off his shoulder. At the report the bull lurched and then vanished from sight. We paused for breath and then clambered down the hill to where the animal had stood. There was not a sign of it and no trace of blood. I was sure that I had hit the animal, but was it merely a wounding shot? The trackers moved away, heads down, following the faintest of tracks. Fifty yards, one hundred and then a shout from one of them and, to my relief and astonishment, we dis-covered the kudu bull, dead with a bullet hole in its neck, but not a spot of blood. The neck bone had not been touched, but it seemed that a major artery had been cut and the animal had suffered a massive haemorrhage. It was a fortunate shot, for I had aimed at the low shoulder!

This was an old kudu with a magnificent, beautifully balanced three twist fifty-two-inch head, a trophy which I had shoulder mounted and which remains an evocative reminder of that once magnificent African country, Zimbabwe, now destroyed almost beyond recognition.

Charge of the Heavy Brigade

MICHAEL YARDLEY

THE CAPE BUFFALO is allegedly the most dangerous game animal in Africa and, as I discovered, on the bushveld the hunter can easily become the hunted.

Like many shooting men, it has always been one of my ambitions to hunt big game in Africa (too many Gregory Peck and Stuart Granger movies at an impressionable age). I have been there to trek, to climb Kilimanjaro in 2005 and, four years previously, hunted plains game and shot birds in Namibia.

The latter was an especially interesting experience, leading me to stay for six instead of the planned two weeks. Funds ran out and I ended up hunting meat for local butchers to pay for living expenses, and developing a taste for springbok in the meantime.

There were other adventures: tracking a cattle-killing leopard on a remote farm about two hundred kilometres from Windhoek, but never finding it, and an interesting encounter outside a hut with a puff adder, resolved by my Beretta 303. But no big game.

Last year, I resolved to go to Africa again, with one mission – Cape buffalo, *Syncerus caffer*. I am not especially inclined to shoot elephant or lion. Rhinos are on the quarry list again, but only for those with squillions – well, £50,000 to £100,000 – and the inclination to shoot something remarkable without much purpose. Leopard can be shot too, but they tend to be baited at night from hides. Not my thing.

No, it had to be a buff – because it's big, it's mean, and because it can be processed into excellent steaks and sausage. I have my own shooting philosophy. One should shoot things for only two reasons: because you can eat them, or because they're a pest. I have no trouble in justifying my sport as a result.

Big game hunting is not inexpensive. Although buffalo is one of the most challenging species to hunt – and some would argue the most dangerous – it is the cheapest of the Big Five. Nevertheless, do not budget on much less than five thousand pounds for a very basic no-frills hunt.

The first problem was to decide on a country and, next, to find the right PH (professional hunter). The first decision was made for me, happily. I had work in South Africa in the Johannesburg area. Asking a friend, a local gunsmith there, Bruce Wentzel, for some contacts, the name Jeff Smith was suggested.

Much would depend on Jeff. As one of his colleagues remarked: 'Our job is to keep you out of your coffin.' It was a reminder that buffalo hunting is something to be taken seriously.

When, eventually, I got Jeff on the phone, he was quietly spoken, almost shy, but something clicked between us. We met in Jo'burg and confirmed a deal.

Jeff might have had an English name, but he was an Afrikaner with great pride in his language and heritage. I subjected him to quite a grilling – as any prospective client should.

He was a full-time professional, a dangerous game specialist, and had been for fourteen years. He came across well and was no braggart. 'I don't sell dead animals, I sell experiences,' he had noted seriously at the beginning of our first meeting. The photo records of his many hunts inspired confidence in his skills, both as hunter and photographer. I liked his manner too. The fact that he brought his partner, Ronell (a keen huntress), and stepson to our first meeting also impressed.

Jeff, it transpired, had shot all his life. His father had a small farm. Before he took up full-time hunting, he had been a soldier and an electrical technician. He had hunted in Zimbabwe and Mozambique as well as South Africa. He favoured the .416 for dangerous game (owning a double and a bolt gun in this much-respected calibre). He didn't like the city, he loved the bush.

A couple of weeks later we were heading towards it in his Land Rover. Our destination was a property about five hours from Jo'burg in the Hoedspruit area, close to the vast Kruger National Park. There were kudu, blue wildebeest, impala, duiker and warthog on the place, not to mention cats. Of course, he wanted to see me shoot and note my reaction to the bush so the plan for us was to hunt a wildebeest bull, so that

Jeff and I could work together in a non-threatening situation before tackling dangerous game.

Shortly after our arrival, we zeroed my rifle on an improvised range. Jeff had loaded some 400 grain Woodleigh soft points for my .416 because our gun laws prevent me from possessing them in the UK. These were slightly slower than factory ammo, but accurate and, relatively, pleasant to shoot, in so far as a thundering .416 can be.

Having proven I could shoot tolerably well, we began to hunt. Not much into the first day – and I suspect as part of my rapid apprenticeship – I was left by a waterhole for an hour: 'You're not going to get lost and lonely are you?' I didn't, but had an interesting encounter with a troop of baboons that involved me backing off rifle in hand from a very large dominant male and his mates. I was pleased to see Jeff and his vehicle return.

After a couple of days of driving, glassing, walking and looking for spoor – the usual African routine – we had not seen much. Eventually, just when it appeared that we might have to leave empty-handed, a sudden chance arose for a wildebeest bull. The shot was free-standing at about eighty yards. I could not see the beast's head clearly, but it was broadside and a heart/lung shot offered itself. Up the front leg . . . steady . . . steady . . . boom.

Jeff watched the strike. 'Good shot, Michael,' and patted me on the back. Thank goodness for that. But, we had to find him yet – the wildebeest had run forward as the bullet struck, as well-shot beasts often do. We followed the blood trail pushing thorn branches out of the way. But some twenty minutes and no bull later, we squatted down: 'I don't understand it, he's here,' Jeff mused. Then we saw him, a few feet behind, dead under the shade of a tree. The bullet had impacted a little too far back in his boiler-room, but it was a one-shot kill.

After dealing with the carcase, and winching it aboard a vehicle, we returned to the farmhouse to dress it and recover the bullet (most PHs in Africa like to recover bullets to add to their ballistic knowledge).

To anyone who might criticise the fact that we were hunting on what was in essence a fenced ranch, one might note that the finding of the game had been extremely difficult. An enclosed hunt does not have to be 'canned' any more than a pheasant shoot with reared birds needs to be unsporting.

Enclosed hunting is the reason why the numbers of previously endangered species are looking very healthy in Southern Africa. It all depends on who you hunt with and what philosophy they follow.

Having passed my first test we moved to another location. Jeff had found a buffalo breeding project where there was a need to cull two beasts. By selling this opportunity, funds for the project were brought in. He had found me the chance not only for a good, young bull, at reasonable cost, but for a good hunt too.

The next morning, the hunting was harder and the psychology quite different. The gates of the project opened, and we drove into a real-world version of 'Jurassic Park' at sunrise. We were there, in the present, looking for something that could kill us.

The routine was the same as for plains game, however: driving, glassing, looking for spoor, trekking through the bush. We saw lots of signs. Buffalo tracks, the prints of a very large leopard and all sorts of impala spoor. The buffalo were scarce. We saw an old female standing alone. There were other sights to savour, though – giraffe with their young, zebra, and a giant monitor lizard swimming in a dam.

We carried on and followed buffalo tracks to what seemed difficult ground – densely covered and undulating. You could only see a few yards ahead and there were many spots that a beast might hide.

I had had some back pain, and popped an 'aspirin' in the morning. Some hours on, Jeff had turned as we went through some pretty unpleasant stuff and looked me over – assessing, I suspect, how I was coping with my first day's buffalo hunting. He seemed satisfied. I looked uncommonly laid back. The only problem was that I had taken a muscle-relaxing sleeping pill by accident, not an aspirin. It had been in my pocket from the overnight flight a week before. I realised the error of my ways as I struggled to keep my eyes open and chuckled softly. 'What are you laughing about?' he asked.

'I'll tell you later.'

We began to suspect that the buff were going doing to the river bed and the surrounding long grass to hold up.

For the third day of the hunt, an older local man called Atcha joined us. He knew the ground well and together, Jeff and Atcha were a formidable team. The tracking pace became more intense.

The buff had crossed our tracks at one stage. We saw very fresh spoor and hot dung. We drove by the river bed once and Jeff noted, 'I'm going into the long stuff to have a look, it's dangerous, you stay with vehicle for now.' Not more than a few minutes later, Jeff came bounding out, rather excitedly, having bumped into one of the great beasts: 'They're in there, they're in there, I knew it!'

Things were building up. I started having an internal dialogue with myself – 'just put the bullet in the right place, the right place.' I was calm, and relatively collected, but there was fear too.

We moved to more open ground. I spotted some members of the herd; we stalked in very slowly. There was a chance of a shot, a close one at about forty yards, maybe less. What happens if they charge? (Shoot the one coming at you first but don't shoot too soon.) It didn't happen. The beasts got wind of us.

Later, we saw some buff getting ready to cross a track at the edge of some cover. This was a longer shot, maybe ninety yards. I was ready, relaxed, rifle up, cross-hairs on the heart. 'STOP!' Wrong beast – a female.

We moved back to the river-beds in the Land Rover. Nothing now. Morale was a bit low after all the hard work. Were we going to shoot a buffalo? ... I can't quite remember what happened next.

We had been moving quite slowly, when there was an explosion from the bush. Suddenly three buffalo bulls were charging us – three abreast. It was as if the gates of hell had opened and three demons on horseback were coming for us. Jeff floored the accelerator and steered with his right hand (his left having been incapacitated by an ill-timed spider bite the day before).

The buffs were gaining. Should I shoot one? We were coming to a hairpin bend. The back end slid, Atcha and I were hanging on for all we were worth. Was the vehicle going over? The buffalo changed course. They galloped parallel to us. Then, we hit the riverbed. The Land Rover went down like a roller-coaster and joltingly up the other side on our bushveld switchback.

The buffalo turned for another broadside. It was like something from an Indiana Jones movie. And, as in all ripping yarns, they didn't get us. It was bloody close though!

Jeff parked up a few hundred yards away, 'Now, let's go and shoot one of them,' he said in a determined voice. 'You're kidding,' I replied, 'they're enraged.' He wasn't. Who was I to argue?

When, at the end of that very memorable day, I did shoot my buff it was, in truth, an anti-climax. We came upon the beasts grazing just before sunset. The shot was easy. A youngish bull was broadside at fifty yards, I put the Woodleigh into the right spot (the heart/lung area), and from the moment of impact you could see it was a mortal wound.

Mr Buff went eleven paces and was dead. Nevertheless, I put in an extra shot – a solid – on my final approach to the carcase. I had learnt that buffalo are clever, schizophrenic creatures and that .416s work.

I had gone to places, metaphorical and physical, that some never visit – and some might not want to. I had resolved never to consider anything other than a heart/lung shot unless my life depended on it. I had determined to take out a second mortgage to get back to Africa as soon as possible.

I am planning to shoot another buff and an eland with Jeff this year. I'll give him the last word: 'It was very difficult, they were pretty elusive, the brush was quite dense, we had to get right on top of them before we could see them and they stuck to the thick stuff all the time ...'

The Buffalo

PAT FAREY

IT WAS LATE afternoon and a warm breeze drifted through the grass towards the hunter as he stealthily closed the distance to his quarry. He left his two native guides behind as he moved forward. There was little cover between him and the Cape buffalo, yet it didn't appear to be aware of him. It just stood stock still, with its forefeet in the water and its dark mass silhouetted against the rocks behind. Even so, the hunter eased down onto his belly, and crawled the last few yards 'knees and elbows' with his rifle held well clear of the ground. The grass was still damp from a midday shower but the late afternoon sun was baking it dry, leaving only a deep heady scent that seemed to be attracting even more flying pests than usual. The hunter ignored the flies buzzing around him and continued his slow silent stalk.

He was close enough now to see the buffalo's glowering red eyes, sharply contrasting with the shiny black coat flecked all over with mud and a dull grey spatter. The young hunter knew this terrain well and had already claimed a lion at this same spot at the water's edge; the quarry he now stalked was potentially just as dangerous – maybe more so. The hunter was close enough to the beast's left flank to take his shot, yet it still showed no sign of being aware of his presence. Every second he imagined that the buffalo would turn its head, discover him and charge, but its painted red eyes just seemed to be fixed straight ahead, glaring across the water and beyond in a baleful unblinking stare.

Carefully the hunter raised his rifle to his shoulder, judging the distance and checking the elevation of the simple open sights, then he lined them up on a point behind the left foreleg of the beast. It still hadn't moved. Taking a deep breath, he took up the travel on the trigger to the breaking point as he consciously tried to relax the beating of his heart. Then, while keeping the sights firmly on target, he slowly released his breath while squeezing the trigger at the same time – just as he had been taught. The trigger broke, the rifle nudged back into his shoulder; he hardly noticed the muzzle report. The lead projectile left the barrel and crashed into the buffalo, knocking it sideways with the initial impact, before the beast toppled over and fell stiff-legged into the water.

The hunter slowly stood and surveyed the scene with a feeling of satis-faction. A perfect stalk, a perfect shot. The buffalo was on its side with half its body and both its right legs covered by the water, the two left legs were parallel with them but in the air – rigid and awkward looking – pointing towards him. The wind had dropped and everything was still. He walked towards the buffalo, but just as he bent down a loud shout came from behind him – 'Michael, come on in, your tea is ready!' It was his grandmother, standing at the kitchen door. Unlike his parents she actively encouraged him to shoot – had taught him in fact – and he spent hours with his air rifle in her garden.

The boy walked the few yards to the puddle beside the rockery at the end of the lawn, and retrieved the small toy buffalo from the water. The lead pellet from the air rifle had 'welded' itself to the side of the model's metal flank. He picked the pellet off, leaving yet another dent and a grey smudge on the buffalo's sparse black paintwork. The buffalo had been shot many times before, only the head with its gaudy, red painted eyes remained unmarked. Michael placed the buffalo along with its compan-ions in a battered biscuit tin full of Britain's Zoo figures, other animal models and all manner of toy soldiers – many of which had been targets at one time or another. He cracked the barrel of his old BSA air rifle, to show it was safe (as his grandmother demanded), pocketed the matchbox full of Marksman pellets, then walked back up the garden path for tea, stopping only to pick up his two plastic 'native guides' – actually 'Zulu warriors' – and depositing them too into the biscuit tin. It had been a good day's shooting, and hopefully there would be many more.

Struggling with Roe

IAN VALENTINE

I WAS ENJOYING a pint in the King's Head last week, when the conversation round the bar turned to roe stalking. It turned out that the chap next to me had shot his first roebuck the evening before.

'I couldn't believe my luck,' he said, wiping froth off his moustache. 'I was only in the high seat for ten minutes before this buck turns up. We were back home by 8 o'clock. Have you ever been fortunate enough to get one?'

Checking my watch, I signalled to the barman for two refills. It was only 10 o'clock, so there was plenty of time to pour my heart out. Besides, talking about it might do me some good.

My first attempts at roe stalking took place on ground belonging to Sparsholt College in Hampshire, where the head tutor Martin Edwards manages the deer across a few hundred acres of fields and woodland. Clients pay top dollar for big bucks, so I was invited to bag a youngster or runt that would add little to the gene pool.

We were out at dawn that first morning and saw plenty of deer in the half light. At least two were browsing within range, but the rifle remained on my shoulder throughout. 'That's a tinkler, not a sprinkler,' Martin would say, as one doe after another appeared in front of us. The females were out of season and they seemed to know it well. In the three hours it took for the sun to rise, we saw not one buck.

'I'm afraid that's roe stalking for you, lad,' my guide said. 'You'll learn soon enough that one shot in three outings is a good ratio. The rest of the time you can simply enjoy a mug of tea and watch the world wake up or shut down. You'll always see something, whether it's a fox or stoat, owl or bat. If you don't like that, then you're better off elsewhere.'

I decided I did like that, so a month later I returned, brimming with optimism. Bucks were sparring for supremacy at the height of the rut, so there stood every chance that Martin would call a yearling close. 'They've only one thing on their mind at the moment,' he said drily, 'and it isn't self-preservation.'

This time we climbed a high seat and waited in silence as the shadows shortened with the rising sun to reveal a roebuck on his morning forage. Martin squeaked twice like a fawn to grab his attention. The buck was grazing more than two hundred yards away across a clearing and I watched him react to each squeak as if he was leaning on an electric fence. His ears pricked and nose twitched as he entered sensory overdrive. This suitor was in the mood for love!

The high seat Siren squeaked twice more and our bewitched buck trotted around the wood-lined field, stopping every thirty yards to check his bearings. One seventy yards ... one forty ... one ten ... I took a deep breath and then exhaled, settling myself for the shot. 'No no, not this chap,' the stalker hissed, 'He's far too good for you.'

The buck eventually approached the foot of the high seat, his broad chest heaving in anticipation. His deep hazel coat beamed summer's vitality, while the loveliest of heads exuded a class and condition that I did not merit. I could only watch in fascination as Martin interacted with this wild creature in its natural environment.

Over the next months I went out time and again, searching in vain for a cull buck or doe. We saw deer every visit, but rarely the right one at the right time of year. When we hunted does, there were bucks; when bucks came back on, we could hardly move for barking does. There had been close shaves, like the evening we crawled over a dung heap for seventy yards to get within shot of a small buck. But just as I set up for the shot, he chose to move behind a hedge.

One frosty morning in early February, as bitter a dawn as had risen all winter, our teeth clenched and toes clawed while we waited for a doe to appear. We were contemplating a premature breakfast when a travelling party of a buck and two following does appeared in the gloom. Martin nodded his consent and adrenalin flooded my body with warmth. 'Wait until that first doe reaches the gap in those trees then fire in your own time.'

For five long minutes I studied the buck through the telescopic sight as it stood in the gap. Finally, he moved on and the doe edged forward to take his place. Yet, as I brought the crosshairs down behind her slender shoulder and moved my finger onto the trigger, fate decided I still did not deserve my first roe deer. Maybe it was sixth sense or a sudden surge of testosterone, but the buck chose that moment to chase his does to safety. Two seconds later and my story could have ended there.

Throughout these near misses, I would watch and learn about roe stalking. We had seen bucks chase each other across fields and surveyed countless deer from the vehicle like safari tourists. Often, we would find the perfect spot, only for the wind to change. Once, for a wonderful half hour, we studied a doe fuss over her two tiny fawns.

It may have been the same family that we spied from a high seat as the sun rose the following April: a mature doe with two yearlings. Bucks were back in season again and a pair of short spikes pricked from the nearest deer's brow. I was in business. For what seemed an eternity, the cull buck mucked about, either pestering his mother or standing adjacent to his sister. Eventually Lady Luck granted me a reprieve as the buck advanced towards us along the hedgerow. At 140 yards, he turned to stand broadside on. His mother and sister were no longer in the line of fire. 'Take your time, now,' came the calm voice over my shoulder.

PFFFFTTT went the bullet through the sound moderator. A brief pause and then three perfectly healthy roe deer disappeared across the clearing. 'Ah well,' Martin said with genuine sympathy. 'You're not the first and you won't be the last. At least it was a clean miss.'

Three weeks later and I had recovered enough pride to face my demons, this time with my father Danvers Valentine in Perthshire. My roe troubles had at least given me a valuable insight into a sport that my father has enjoyed all his life and it would be a neat ending to my tale if I could bag my first roe with my old man's .243. He orchestrated a textbook stalk, approaching a young beast from beneath the brow of a hill, marching in line to minimise our silhouette, before creeping forward on hands and knees under the cover of a dyke to within a hundred yards. He set the rifle up and I crawled in behind it. Again, I missed a sitter. 'Ah well,' sighed my father, as the buck scampered off into the woods unharmed, 'there's a lot of Scotland around a deer.'

My neighbour at the bar glanced from his half-finished pint to my own untouched glass. 'Maybe you're just a bad shot?'

Perhaps, but then honestly I can hit the centre of a paper target at one hundred and fifty yards and further, whether lying prone, sitting or standing with sticks. I have shot other species of deer. The unavoidable truth is that on both occasions I came down with a heavy dose of nerves, jitters, hoodoo, buck fever, call it what you will. In the heat of the moment, I had lost my bottle. One day I will get a roe and I will cherish it forever. Indeed, next week I am going out in Hampshire again. Surely, it will be third time lucky?

CHAPTER EIGHT

·

History, Humour and Memories

Dead Guns' Society

BILL HARRIMAN

Over the years, I have had a variety of strange assignments from commissioning editors and I have now learnt to take requests for articles on weird subjects in my stride. However, I must confess that I was somewhat taken aback when one editor asked me to assemble this particular team of guns to shoot at a country house party in the grand style.

At first, I couldn't believe my luck. I was being asked to host some serious shooting in pleasant surroundings with my choice of guests and with the magazine picking up the tab. Like most offers which sound too good to be true, it was!

On asking if I might ask anyone of my choice to shoot, I was told 'Yes', but with one condition. 'No problem', I enthused. 'Just name it!'

'All of your guests must be dead.'

My hearing ain't what it used to be and the line was a bit crackly so I said, 'Come again.'

'Dead,' he said, 'You know, bereft of life, resting in peace, shuffled off this mortal coil, joined the choir invisible.'

Now I enjoy the Monty Python Dead Parrot Sketch as much as the next man, but this was plainly ridiculous.

'So you want me to compile a guest list of dead people for a shooting party?'

'That's right, you have always said that you would give anything to be able to speak to famous shooting personalities from history.'

I protested: 'I know that I have been blessed with a host of talents, but I don't number necromancy amongst them. Besides which, it's probably still illegal and carries the penalty of being burnt at the stake on conviction.'

He was unmoved by this appeal and so here I am taking you into the Twilight Zone of our shooting forebears.

Naturally, I had to square this with the authorities in the Spirit World. You wouldn't believe the bureaucracy involved in getting a weekend pass for nine deceased people to join the land of the living again. A strange man who smelt strongly of sulphur appeared from nowhere with a contract to sign.

'I suppose you want this in blood,' I quipped, instantly regretting this frivolity. 'Of course, it wouldn't be legal otherwise,' replied my shadowy companion and, reluctantly, I rolled up my sleeve.

Having squared the formalities, I set to choosing the members of what I came to regard as the Dead Guns' Society. I wanted interesting people from a wide time frame, all of whom excelled in shooting of one form or another. The dull, irascible, rude or mediocre would have no place in this gathering. Also, members would be chosen according to the level of contribution that they made to Britain's sporting heritage.

My first choice was easy; Colonel Peter Hawker is regarded by many as the father of modern shooting. His classic book *Instructions to Young Sportsmen* ran into numerous editions during his life. Hawker can be dogmatic at times, but throughout his writings there is an unassailable spirit of *enthusiasm* for the sport.

I have always admired the variety of activities to which he applied himself and at which he invariably excelled. He did well during the Peninsular War as a regimental soldier, showing considerable courage in battle and great powers of physical endurance. By contrast, he was an accomplished musical composer and performer and had a broad knowledge of classical literature. His knowledge of ballistics and precision engineering was masterful and in many ways he personified the scientific and industrial spirit of the early nineteenth century.

As we shall try for duck, I shall ask him to bring his famous Manton 4-bore gun, which he christened 'Big Joe'. Manton was his favourite gunmaker and Hawker was a great publicist. Less welcome was his interference in Manton's workshop which once resulted in a fire after an over-enthusiastic application of the bellows at the forge. Perhaps the Colonel will agree to entertain the company at the pianoforte after dinner.

By natural progression, my next guest will be Sir Ralph Payne-Gallwey, Bt. His writings have enthralled me since I was a boy and I would like to repay him for the inspiration that he has always given me, particularly in the study of archery and siege engines. He played a round of golf against a professional by using a bow and arrow instead of a golf ball and clubs, coming a close second.

Sir Ralph could hold his own in Edwardian society and was something of a wit and raconteur. He once tried to induce a very frosty lady travelling in the same railway compartment to share some conversation. She declined and both parties nodded off for the rest of the journey. On waking, Sir Ralph remarked to his taciturn companion that whilst they hadn't said much to one another, at least they could say that they had slept together! Let's hope he comes out with more like that during dinner. Also, I shall try to prevail upon him to demonstrate his ability with the Turkish composite bow when we are not shooting.

And now for my first lady guest, the famed exhibition shooter of Buffalo Bill's Wild West, Miss Annie Oakley. In her time, Annie Oakley was an international superstar and athlete who excelled in a male-dominated world. Whilst Hollywood has often portrayed her as some rough country hoyden, in reality she was petite, very feminine and sweetly natured.

She also knew a wrong 'un when she saw one. When presented to Edward, Prince of Wales – a renowned lecher – she deliberately shook the hand of Princess Alexandra first, in direct contravention of court proto-col. To his credit, the Prince did not hold that against her. She revelled in fieldsports: 'Truly, I long for the day when my work with rifle and gun will be over with, and when I can take to the field and stream as often as true inclination may lead me there.'

Annie Oakley's greatest contribution to shooting in the UK came from her shooting lessons for ladies given at Lancaster's shooting ground in 1887. Such was her popularity and respectability that stuffy Victorian Britain came round to accept that shooting was a proper pastime for ladies. Modern lady guns remain ever in her debt for this. With a bit of luck, we may persuade her to give an impromptu demonstration of her skill with rifle, revolver and shotgun.

Next on the list is Robert Churchill the gunmaker, shooting instructor and forensic ballistician. He and I will have lots to talk about and I look forward to swapping case notes with him. I would like to know more about his quarrel with Sir Gerald Burrard over forensic matters, but I don't want to embarrass him by raising such a delicate matter. If any of the guns are off form, I am sure that 'the other Mr Churchill' will oblige them with a spot of remedial tuition.

Her Grace the Duchess of Bedford rates as one of the most outstanding guns in British sporting history. Sir Hugh Gladstone described her as one of the twelve best game shots in the country. Sometimes, she shot as many as 4800 head in a season.

On one occasion at Woburn, she killed 273 high pheasants with 366 cartridges and followed this with eighty-four pheasants for ninety-four shots in a single drive. Her Grace bemoaned the fact that lady guns were hampered by what was considered modest costume: 'It is impossible for a woman to do a long day's walking in comfort over the moors or in turnips in a skirt which is longer than eight inches below the knee.' Hopefully, Her Grace will be able to gain some inspiration by Annie Oakley's shooting dresses which she designed and made herself. These were not only modest and practical, but very feminine as well.

Colonel Thomas Thornton made an extensive sporting tour of Scotland in 1786, in which he shot, fished, stalked deer and hawked (amongst other things!) He is mainly remembered for his work as a falconer, but he was also a very fair shot. The Colonel was court-martialled for an incident in 1794 when he commanded the West Yorkshire Militia. This gave him a bad reputation which was compounded by his Francophilia and admiration for Bonaparte.

Like most true sportsmen, he abhorred mere slaughter and forbade himself to take a double shot at blackgame. 'Humanity then cried stop, would you destroy the whole race?' Thereafter he gave up double guns with the comment that, 'I look upon all double barrels as trifles, rather knick-knacks than useful.'

By 1793, he had obviously thought better of this as he commissioned a gun with fourteen barrels from the London gunmaker William Dupe. He must certainly be invited to bring this mighty gun and to demonstrate it to the company. I shall encourage him to bring his cross-dressing mistress Alicia Massingham (aka the Norwich Nymph) who was famed for beating a crack jockey in a race at Knavesmire in 1805.

John Mytton, Squire of Halston in Shropshire, was everything that an English huntin', shootin' and fishin' country gentleman ought to be. Expelled from both Westminster and Harrow, he then proceeded to knock down his private tutor and failed to matriculate at either Oxford or Cambridge.

From an early age, he was a prodigious gambler and often owed huge sums which he was incapable of paying. This did not cramp his style and he went through his short life (thirty-eight years) at a hell-for-leather roistering pace. He drank port as if it were water and had an iron constitution. On one occasion he stripped naked to pursue some ducks into icy water with no apparent ill effect. He also had a great partiality for filbert nuts and ate huge quantities. His madcap behaviour manifested itself in practical joking. Once, after entertaining a parson and a doctor to dinner, Mytton disguised himself as a highwayman and ambushed them on the road, firing blank charges from his pistols. The unfortunate pair were pursued as far as Oswestry before Mytton gave up the chase. He also rode a bear into a dining room to cries of Tally-Ho, Tally-Ho!

When confronted by a ferocious dog loose in a farmyard, Mytton caught the animal by the back of the neck, sank his teeth into its nose and pummelled it into submission. Needless to say the animal never showed any disposition to attack a human ever again.

Mytton is said to have been so skilful with a rifle that he could hit the edge of a razor at thirty yards and split the ball. He is said to have lent his name to the savoury dish known as Mytton of Pork and we shall honour his presence by serving it cold for lunch. For all that he was a hellraiser, John Mytton was a kindly sort of man who was generous to a fault. The Dead Guns' Society welcomes him with great enthusiasm. (Hopefully he won't get his kit off while retrieving duck, though.)

Another sporting squire of the old school was George Osbaldeston, who was known as 'The Squire of England'. Like Mytton, his greatest fame is as a foxhunter but he was also a phenomenal shot. In Scotland he once bagged ninety-seven grouse with the same number of shots, twice killing two birds with one barrel. He also killed twenty brace of partridge with forty shots on one occasion.

Such a performance would be considered remarkable today using a breech-loading gun with quick-shooting cartridges. The fact that Osbaldeston performed such prodigies of shotgun marksmanship 'with a flint and steel of 18 bore made by the celebrated Joe Manton' is nothing short of miraculous.

He was also a noted live pigeon shot and won matches against the best shots of his day such as Horatio Ross, Lord Kennedy and General Anson. His prowess with firearms was not confined to shotguns and he was mustard with a duelling pistol, once putting ten shots in the ace of diamonds at thirty feet. No wonder people treated him with careful courtesy. He was a great card player and once played billiards for fifty hours solid. On that basis, it looks like we are in for some late nights.

He was also a very gallant gentleman, both in terms of physical courage and in his dealings with the ladies. An example of the former was the rescue of a barge boy near Lincoln who had fallen into the Witham. Osbaldeston rode his horse into the water and brought the boy safe to land. As for the latter, he heard a sensitive young lady being subjected to some catty comments about the quality of her corsage at a hunt ball. Making his excuses, Osbaldeston slipped away and four hours later returned with a magnificent orchid, which he presented at the supper table to the discomfort of the young lady's tormentors. In order to obtain the bloom he had ridden a twenty-five-mile round trip. I like his style.

In order to bolster the ladies in the Dead Guns' Society, I am minded to invite the Hon. Mrs McCalmont. She was a keenly competitive shot in an overwhelmingly male-dominated sport. As early as 1882, Queen Victoria had written to her daughter the Queen of Prussia to the effect that 'only fast women shoot'. Her Majesty's words had no effect on Mrs McCalmont who not only shot well, but also hosted the odd ladies-only shot at Mount Juliet in Kilkenny. Anyone who was prepared to thumb her nose at royalty in Victorian Britain gets my vote.

You may be surprised that Lord Ripon is not invited. Not a hope! Although a phenomenal shot, he was dull, anti-social and practised with his loaders after dinner. Very bad form.

Sending the invitations seemed problematic at first, but a Ouija board solved any difficulties there. Now, I sit alone by the fire in the comforting darkness of the large and rambling house where we are pledged to meet. Outside, a barn owl flits like a spectre between the trees and I hear the sound of horses and carriages on the drive. I had better go and bid my guests welcome.

The Iron Wolf

JOHN HUMPHREYS

In 1827 there lived near Thetford in Norfolk a farm labourer who made a few pence making nets for the bird catchers. With the permission of his employer he gleaned scraps of hemp from the fields which he wove into delicate nets and sold. Taking a batch to fulfil an order he was stopped by two gamekeepers who searched him, found the nets and dragged him before the squire, accusing him of assaulting them. At the Norfolk Assizes he was convicted of having in his possession 'engines' for the taking of game and for resisting arrest. Despite his pleas of innocence, he was transported to Australia for seven years, the standard poaching sentence. On his return from the colonies in 1835 he strolled out into his old haunts and was almost immediately caught by a man trap. His leg had to be amputated at Thetford hospital.

Such was the way of game preservation in the first thirty years of the nineteenth century. In 1805 there had been a poachers versus keepers battle at Aylesham in Norfolk after which six young men were captured: many of the 'watchers' had been wounded by them. The poachers were condemned to death, a sentence reduced to transportation when they came to trial. On their way by coach to the hulk which was to take them overseas for ever, they made a desperate effort to escape, overpowering the guard, whose pistol misfired, and running off. Hampered by the chains in which they were shackled they were recaptured and all were hanged.

This was a terrible and disgraceful time in the history of game management. The large-scale rearing of pheasants brought in its wake temptation for starving village folk who survived on little more than turnip tops and hedge fruit. Those in Parliament who made the rules and those who sat on the benches in judgment were the selfsame men who owned the great covert shoots and would go to any lengths to preserve their precious pheasants. It was they who passed a series of Game Laws each more cruel and savage than the last. The Game Laws filled the gaols and the convict ships and made criminals out of honest labourers. To ease the Game Laws would be to open the flood gates to democracy – not at any price.

The spring gun was the first 'engine', as they were euphemistically called, to find popularity with estate owners. This was a fearful device whereby a heavy pistol loaded with crude lumps of lead, or in some cases a four-inch iron bolt, was set by tracks in the woods. A series of trip wires led from the pathways to the weapon which, being on a pivot, would swing round to cover the human target which caught the wire. Most were aimed below waist height but the more sophisticated models had an elevating screw by which a keeper could direct the charge at a trespasser's head. Col Hanger devised a small cannon to be fired from the roof of his house when poachers were suspected of being in the woods. It fired clay balls and marbles, some with holes in so that they made a terrifying whining sound. He used clay not for pity of the poachers but in order not to damage his standing timber with lead.

This was a monstrous and criminal device for it was totally indiscriminate and most of its victims were innocent ramblers, women and children. Mrs Righon was gathering mushrooms on the Rushbrook estate in Norfolk, ironically intending to sell them to the kitchen at the big house. She trod on a spring-gun wire and fifty-five shots lodged in her upper legs, which were dreadfully damaged. A small boy climbed into a hedge to cut himself a droving stick and he caught the full charge of a hidden gun. A gardener was sent to prune a tree, set his ladder and he too was cut down by a gun set by a keeper. It was not unknown for a landowner to be caught by his own booby trap and a Captain Chatworth shooting on his father's estate in the absence of the gamekeeper was shot badly in the thigh.

In his standard work *Rural Sports* the Rev. W.B. Daniel, obviously a true man of God, gives sound advice and many tips about the setting of traps and guns. He suggests deploying them in remote coverts and lightly covering them with moss and leaves. He was opposed to the large, steel-toothed mantrap, not on humanitarian grounds but because 'not one in twenty will throw the jaws of the trap close after remaining on the stretch several nights together'.

About the only people who were not caught by spring-guns and traps were the poachers themselves. They were up to all the tricks and would drive a herd of cattle before them to discover the wires or carry long poles which they used to feel their way in the dark. It was not unknown for the more desperate of them to drag a keeper from his bed and make him walk before them and not only witness their poaching but be the first to stumble on one of his own spring-gun wires. In case of mantraps the poachers would strap wooden slatting round their legs as protection.

Mr Lawson, a respectable sixty-five-year-old curate of Needham Market, was strolling in the woods one day studying the wild plants. He stood on a mantrap and was caught. Passers-by heard his shouts but could do nothing until the keeper came with the key to unlock the machine, which took some time. The clergyman was much damaged. If the spring gun was the left jab the mantrap was the right hook of game preservation. A giant version of the gin trap then in common use for vermin control, the mantrap came in various designs, each with its own chillingly folksy title. There was 'The Crusher', 'The Body Squeezer' and 'The Thigh Cracker', each with its own peculiar arrangement of teeth or cutting blades designed to do the greatest damage. I have one here at home. It is five feet long, almost too heavy to lift and its interlocking shark's teeth meet just below knee height. A monster found in the West Country was eight feet long and weighed a hundredweight. Richard Jefferies coined for them the collective title, 'The Iron Wolf'.

Other types included 'The Boy Trap' and a razor-toothed ankle job, light, movable and devastating. Many caught in such traps were lucky to escape with amputation. Often the victim lay for the whole of a winter night undiscovered; usually gangrene, shock, exposure or loss of blood set in and in those days of primitive and unaffordable medicine many died from an encounter. The view of the squires and lawmakers to such tragedies was 'Serve 'em right!' The early traps were knocked up by village blacksmiths but later they were produced commercially in Black Country iron foundries and featured in their catalogues alongside cast-iron stoves and kitchen ranges. In 1821 a West Brom ironmonger proudly announced his invention of the 'humane' mantrap. This had no teeth but merely held the poacher firmly until the keeper arrived with the key to release him. It was in such a 'humane' device that the poor Rev. Mr Lawson was caught and so badly hurt.

By far the greatest deployment of these 'engines' was in Hampshire and East Anglia, especially Norfolk where game preservation was at its most obsessive. It was in Hampshire that an observer in 1785 described 'the most shocking sight I ever beheld.' ... [Fifteen poachers]....

disregarding the notice of what was prepared for their destruction, ventured that night, as had been their custom, into the wood where no less than four of them were found in the morning caught by these terrible engines; three had their thighs broke by the crackers and traps and the fourth was found dead in a body squeezer ... I saw the poor wretches immediately after they had been taken from these destructive engines.

Traps did not always deter for poachers had their way of finding out where they were set. One landowner came down one morning to find all his mantraps sprung with bolts of wood and his pheasants gone. Signs were posted, 'Man Traps and Spring Guns on Theife Premifes' and one landowner went as far as to display a trap suspended above such a sign, the trap holding a severed human leg. Passers-by were not to know that the son of the house was a medical student who specialised in anatomy. Not only game was protected by the fearful machines. Ronnie Crowe gave me a copy of an undated sign which reads, 'Trespassers Beware. During the Fruit Season Man-Traps and Spring Guns are placed in this Orchard'. It is worth mentioning that such notice boards were no more than conscience salvers to those who set them for I doubt if one in ten poor villagers could have read them.

By the end of the third decade of the century humanitarians had triumphed and the cruel engines faded slowly away. Here and there they lingered. Dear old Jimmy Wentworth Day reported a poacher caught in a mantrap in the 1920s and losing a leg. Another record by F.M. Denwood records a man being shot by a spring-gun near Cockermouth in Cumbria in 1932. Neither case came to the attention of the public. It is still possible to come across a rusting trap or a spring gun round which a tree has grown. One trap was found in the thatch of an old cottage and not long ago I heard of a ferreter finding one still set deep in a patch of brambles and half covered with the soil of 180 years.

Then it was the mantrap; today we have the Right to Roam, a long road indeed from one deranged extreme to the other. I can think of a few, wicked, reactionary old keepers who might have strong views on which era they preferred.

Don't Strain Your Barrels!

SAM GRICE

You need a sense of humour to survive as a shooting coach. Otherwise how could I cope with the likes of a young man who came to me for a lesson a while back? Serious, keen to impress, you know the sort . . .

He was new to shooting, he told me, but had read all about it in a book and decided – there was a pause for his words to take effect – to shoot 'with maintained lead'.

Well, I said to myself, this bloke sounds as if he knows what he's talking about. So I gave him a chance to show me. He had a couple of shots. Then a couple more. And so it went on until disillusionment set in.

'I don't think I'm getting it quite right,' he said. I could see what he meant. Every target was missed a good three feet behind.

It was maintained lead all right. But there was a snag: he was making sure the target maintained the lead, not the gun.

I explained to him gently – you encounter some fragile egos in this business – that it was generally better to keep the gun ahead of the target, not vice versa.

After this astonishing revelation, he quickly got the hang of it. He even smiled. I can probably claim to have made his day.

I often think of my young friend when newcomers arrive at the shooting ground and tell me they have read a shooting book, or perhaps been coached by an expert shot.

It all begs the question: so why the heck have they bothered to come to me? I much prefer those few honest souls who turn up and say: 'I've got a problem. Start me again from scratch. Right now I'm effing hopeless.' Now, those are the people I can usually help.

Most of you will say you would never be so stupid. Maybe so, but in less obvious ways many shooters make similar mistakes.

I've lost count of the number of shots who reckon to know a thing or two but still haven't got into the habit of mounting their gun properly. Or those who lift their heads to make extra sure they're on target. Maybe I should be grateful they keep on making the same mistake. It keeps me in business.

Not long ago a middle-aged professional came to me for a lesson. We got talking. He hadn't read a book or been to another coach. Instead, he told me, he had worked it all out for himself. 'I shoot straight at the target and swing the gun incredibly fast so that it spreads the shot just as it leaves the barrels.' He racked his brains for the right analogy. 'It's like water from a fireman's hose.'

Hmmm ..., I thought, this should be interesting. He had a few shots at some clays, then a few more. Soon he had emptied his fireman's hose without wetting a single clay.

Only then was it time for me to have a quiet word. He could afford to slow down a little. There were one or two basic principles of ballistics he might care to consider. Perhaps he would like to try a more conventional technique?

Which is just what he did. And it worked.

Then again, his little theory was far from being the most outrageous I've heard over the years.

At one time I would occasionally have shooters telling me with a straight face that they didn't like to try long range shots because 'they will strain the barrels'.

It took me some time to puzzle out the origins of this amazingly resilient myth. I reckon it must go back to the days of black powder, when a shooter would quite simply use more powder to increase his range – and risk bulging or bursting his Damascus barrels.

Probably someone's great-great-grandfather passed this advice on to his son, and so it went on from generation to generation. The advent of nitro cartridges did nothing to dent its popularity.

A regular visitor to my ground is kept fairly busy during the season as a loader. He likes to tell the story of one of his customers (whose name is never, ever mentioned) who fired seventy-three shots on the first drive 'for one and a bit birds'.

One and a bit? Well, the gun was sure he hit the bit – and he should know.

It was a day with an expected bag of four hundred birds or so, and this particular shooter was a man of about fifty, well-dressed, well-heeled, well-spoken, and armed with an impeccable London gun. Sadly he was a truly hopeless shot.

All day long he thrashed the air with his barrels and finished up with no more than a couple of brace.

My poor loader friend had to hump around barrow-loads of cartridges. The hapless gun kept asking what he was doing wrong. Every time he gave it both barrels. Boom-boom, straight into thin air.

My friend could do very little to help him. He just wouldn't change. To his eternal credit, the frustrated shooter never lost his temper and gave my friend a very generous tip at the end of the day. Probably he wanted to buy his silence.

I suspect he had also listened to some duff advice from an elderly relative. Myths about shooting – like the one about straining your barrels – are often hard to dispel.

One of the worst is the old line that whatever you do, you must shoot with both eyes open. Oh yeah?

Tell that to a pukka shot I know who used to make a real ass of himself in very exalted company. They all joked that he couldn't hit a barn door from inside the barn. And worse.

The truth was that he was a right-handed gun but had a very strong left eye. As a result he was missing everything up the left hand side. It was a mistake just about any coach would have spotted.

I told him to close his left eye. The problem was solved in a single coaching session. From then on he shot as well as the next man. No more barn door jokes.

Talking of things that open and close on farms, how about the famous five-barred gate? As in the classic piece of advice: 'You need to give it plenty of lead – about as much as a five-barred gate.'

I often wonder how anyone can look forty yards up at a high pheasant and imagine a five-barred gate, miraculously unhinged and moving through the air at fifty miles an hour. When did you last see a farm gate doing that?

The only way to get it straight is to forget the bloody gate and remind yourself that accurate shooting depends on experience and practice. Perfect practice, that is.

Good shots result from an almost magical, instant computation based on all those occasions when you have got it right before.

As soon as people start squinting down their gun at airborne five-barred gates – and this is as sure as death or taxation – they're going to miss.

So what should fathers tell their sons on the rare occasions when they're actually listening?

Me, I put on a CD and let the great Duke Ellington do it for me.

It's the one piece of shooting advice I'd like to leave for my grandchildren. And it's all in a song: 'It don't mean a thing if it ain't got that swing.'

The Bath Bird

BRYN PARRY

To say that I was a beginner was true. I had used a shotgun before when I had borrowed an ancient piece and walked up an old railway line with a friend and had even potted one or two pigeons, more by luck than skill. What I had never done was take part in a proper driven shoot.

The invitation was typically relaxed and gave the impression that I would be strolling around with a group of friends whose main aim was to enjoy each other's company and a very good lunch; shooting was included but hardly mentioned.

I borrowed a gun, a side-by-side with a lump of rubber taped onto the trigger guard and a stock with a slight dink that would be fine, I was told. Two boxes of cartridges were thrown in, which would be more than enough to see me through the day I was assured, and I was set to go.

I followed the instructions to the rendevous. The journey took longer than I had anticipated, the feeling of panic slowly building as the traffic crawled along. I finally turned off the main road onto the country lane and with anxious glances at my instructions and my watch I drove as quickly as I dared. At last, I saw a group of countrymen standing around with guns and dogs. Relieved that I was only twenty minutes late and that they had not moved off, I parked the car, grabbed my kit and walked over to the group to introduce myself.

Everyone was very friendly and I started to relax as I shook hands all round. As I greeted the last of the group he looked a little perplexed as he asked me whose guest I was. My response brought no enlightenment, the group had never heard of him; wrong man, wrong shoot.

Ten minutes later I found the correct shoot as I turned into the drive and started the long journey up the crunchy gravel towards the big house. I parked my red Suzuki next to the seven green Range Rovers, pulled on my black wellies and went across to introduce myself ... to the beaters.

Redirected, I took my wellies off and went up to the house. The door was open so I walked in. No one was around so I coughed and said 'Hello?' No response so I walked past the stuffed bear and beneath the stuffed deer towards the distant sound of laughter.

'Ah, here you are, at last!' said my host, clapping me on the back, 'no, don't worry Old Boy, we are all terribly relaxed here, help yourself to a bacon sandwich. Cup of coffee? Good, now let's introduce you to the guns as we must get on.'

The sandwich and coffee were untouched as I was introduced to the guns, polite but cool as they shook hands with this late, new boy. Looking around the group I realised that I was literally the boy, the youngest by thirty years, and of course they had all been shooting together their whole lives; very relaxing.

We drew for pegs; I drew number four and there was a collective intake of breath from the group. My offer to drive round in the Suzuki was declined and I put my kit in the back of one of the green Range Rovers, 'Don't worry about him, he's very much a one man dog, it'll wash off.'

I took my post on the peg at the bottom of the valley and craned my neck as I looked up towards the distant skyline. 'Bit of a hot seat this one,' said my host, 'have fun.'

I looked behind for pickers-up, checked my barrels, acknowledged the guns to my left and right and loaded my gun. I could feel my pulse throbbing at my temple and my hands were damp with sweat. I trod down an area of mud to make a firm footing and practised mounting the gun a couple of times until I noticed my neighbour's wry smile. I told myself to relax and stood with my gun in the crook of my arm.

Birds! Thousands of them! The skyline was suddenly dotted with birds that seemed to rise vertically from the cover and soar into the stratosphere. I chose one and raised my gun and fired, twice. I broke my gun, stuffed in fresh cartridges and fired again; and again and again. On either side of me the guns calmly pulled down screamers, the fallen thudding in front while their dogs watched impassively. I didn't hit one, not a single one, not even a possible. The squadrons flew in unbroken line over my peg as the smoking cartridges piled the ground at my feet.

I tried looking in front of the bird, I tried ambushing, I tried mounting on the tail and then pushing through, I even gave it a 'five bar gate', whatever that means. It was hopeless; I couldn't touch them. The odd cry of 'yours' rang out along the line, two shots from me followed by a single one from my courteous neighbour and the thud of a bird hitting the ground well behind; humiliation. God, give me a bird or let the earth open and swallow me up.

Finally, thankfully, the whistle blew and it was over. My hands burnt from the hot barrels and my second finger was bruised from the trigger guard. All around me dogs with names like Purdey, Snipe and Drum hoovered up the dead birds.

I stood with bowed shoulders and looked around as my host came up and shouted, 'Never mind Old Boy, there are days when I shoot like a drain! As long as you are enjoying yourself, that's all that matters! Come here, Bomber, you bloody dog!'

At least on the second drive I was number six so there were marginally fewer birds to miss but miss I did, every single one, not a sausage, total and absolute disaster. The third drive I was in a wood at the end of the line and a beater grinned as he walked past. I grimaced in return, my face unable to force a smile, let alone form a greeting. Being in the wood did not improve my shooting but at least it was hidden. My record remained unbroken and then I ran out of cartridges.

We gathered around the host's Range Rover while soup and sloe gin was passed around. The atmosphere was jovial and relaxed, the guns invigorated by a wonderful morning's shooting, comparing notes and joshing amicably. I stood silently as I contemplated faking a heart attack or inventing some pressing reason to race away from this ghastly day.

One of the guns detached himself from the laughing group and wandered over to the dunce's corner where I stood miserably.

'Do you get much shooting?' he asked with raised eyebrow, clearly knowing the answer but too well bred to show it.

'Not much,' I said, stifling the urge to cry, 'mostly rough shooting. This is rather out of my league, I am afraid.'

'Nonsense,' said my new best friend, 'I'm sure you have been having a lovely morning. I think the trick is just to relax and enjoy yourself. Stop that, Sniper, bloody dog! Sorry about that.'

'Oh, don't worry, it'll wash off,' I said as we were told to mount up and get off to the next drive.

During lunch I asked advice from Sniper's handler. 'Oh, Lord,' he said, 'I've really no idea, I just sort of look at the bird and then, you know, sort of look ahead of it: Bob's your Uncle if you see what I mean. I think the secret is probably just to relax and enjoy the day. I'm sure you will be fine. Pass the port would you, Old Boy, there's a good thing.'

The final drive of the day came along at long last. I had given it my best but now realised that shooting was not the sport for me. I was back at school and the boy left out of the team, the outcast; the abject failure in life. Not one bird had fallen to my gun and no one had even asked me for a joke at lunch. Frankly, if they had, I wouldn't have been capable of telling one, so deep was the gloom. My shoulders were sore, my head ached and my hands were blistered and bruised. The end of the day just could not happen soon enough for me and my spirits lifted at the prospect of getting away home and out of this world forever.

'Yours!' Bang, bang went the gun at number four. 'Bugger!' he said.

'Yours!' Bang, bang went number five and the cock bird flew on.

'Yours, Brigadier!' Two more shots followed the bird as the wind caught the cock and curled him along the line.

Number seven gave him both barrels and the bird flew on unscathed.

'Yours, Bryn!' came the cry and my gun went into my shoulder, as I looked way, way in front of the archangel. I don't remember the shot but I do remember the way the bird's head snapped back and he plummeted to the ground way out on my right.

The whistle went, I broke my gun and ejected the single spent cartridge and put it away in my pocket. I took out the unfired cartridge and noticed that as I put it back in the bag my hand was shaking. My heart was beating, jumping, thumping, leaping and I felt invincible. I had done it. I had shot a driven bird, finally. What a simply wonderful thing shooting is!

'Bryn,' my host said as he came along the line, 'that was a Bath Bird.'

Noooooo! What had I done now? Shot some special rare protected species, killed the Marquis of Bath's bird? The shame, my heart stopped, the elation fled, the misery returned.

'A Bath Bird,' he said with a huge grin, 'is the sort of bird you lie in your bath and dream about. Well done, Old Boy, time for a cup of tea. Lovely shooting, we must get you back next year.'

'I'd love to,' I replied, 'I'd really love to. I've had a wonderful day.'

The Major's Woodcock

PETER WHITAKER

There are times when two woodcock may be observed flighting quite close together, offering the chance of a right and left. I have often wondered whether any of the *Shooting Times* Woodcock Club owe their membership to such a situation for, although demanding a degree of stage management, the opportunity seems too good to miss. However, although it may be a way of shortening the odds, there is no guarantee of success, as experience has proved.

Major Handisyce-Dick was the last of the great shikars. Little had escaped his aim in all the world's continents; his trophies graced the walls of schlosses, palaces and hunting lodges in Europe, Africa and Asia. In Bangalore, he shot a tiger with a single ball from a slipping howdah – but he had never shot a right and left at woodcock.

I met him at a Game Fair in the members' enclosure on the outside of several Pimm's and the other side of Isla Havimova, a Russian princess (allegedly) whom he had met some years before in a shooting party at Zidlochovicich. She had asked him to pull off her boots; it had not stopped there and they were married in Paris on the stopover flight back to Tunbridge Wells where they now lived. He greeted me warmly with: 'What about these woodcock?' By the time we parted he and the lovely Isla had invited themselves to stay and I had promised to set him up for a bottle of Balvenie and another entry in the record books.

They arrived in a weather-blasted safari Land Rover the colour of desert sand and with much of it inside. In the back, guarding a mountain of kit sat Beowulf, a grizzled Labrador/husky cross.

For three nights I had watched two 'cock in close single file following the line of a withy hedge behind my big pond, and sited my guest where they would be clearly outlined against the last light in the western sky. But it is the law of the jungle as well as Sod's that things are not as easy as that, and on the two following evenings only one bird showed. The wily old shikar held his fire and we decided to give it one more go. This time instinct told me to place him on the island in the pond's centre for an all-round field of fire, while the princess and I watched comfortably from a garden seat. Beowulf attended his master anchored to an alder with a rope that would have stopped a tugboat sailing.

This time Diana's smile was sweet. Two birds came and the shots could not have been softer. At the double report one 'cock fell dead at the water's edge where I grabbed it before Beowulf could close the suitcase, while the other fluttered earthwards towards the road that runs beyond my boundary. Clearly it was mortally struck. The Major's roar of triumph was drowned by that of Lawrie Driver's truck taking him on his annual holiday to haul tates and sugar beet in East Anglia.

In spite of Beowulf's best efforts, aided by my two springers and Labrador, we never found that second woodcock. Only a speckled feather clinging to an elder branch betrayed its passing. We concluded it must have picked up and gone on. The Major was distraught. Even the consolation prize of a single malt failed to dispel his gloom. When he had gone I wondered whether this was the way rights and lefts at woodcock were not meant to be.

Much later, on his way home, Lawrie called to see me. He thought I'd be interested. On his way up he had stopped at Membury Service Station where a mate gave him a shout. 'Hey Law,' he cried, 'what's that little old brown bird caught on your tarp?' It was, said Lawrie, a woodcock, trapped under a rope.

'What did you do with it?' I asked him, suddenly excited. 'Oh, I binned it. Any good to eat, are they?' I never dared tell the Major.

Sporting Hotels

RICHARD PRIOR

WHERE SPORT IS the driving object, one stays in whatever accommodation happens along, if any. In the course of a chequered life, sport has taken me into some strange and unfamiliar places, from the plush comforts of the Ritz in Madrid to a cowshed in Siberia. Even if the details of the actual sport concerned tend to fade, many roosting places carry with them some lingering flavour, pleasant or toe-curling.

I was sent to Spain with my reporter's hat on when the Ritz was promoting partridge-shooting weekends. They may do still. Anyway, a limousine took me out into the parched countryside in company with the organiser. In conversation he gave some fascinating, but quite unprintable, figures for the relative kill-to-cartridge rate of the different nations who came to shoot there. So many for the Germans, so many for the French and so on.

'Ah! But you haven't said how the British do!'

'You're different – you only shoot at your own birds!'

It was obvious there was some distance still to drive, and time was getting short when to my surprise he suggested stopping for a cup of coffee. I had to say that in England shooting was the only invitation where you could turn up early with good manners. 'Oh, in Spain it would be extremely rude to be punctual!'

We had a very good day, and at the end, trudging up a desert track, we were met with the startling sight of the major domo of the Ritz waiting for us, resplendent with tails and white gloves holding a silver salver charged with brandy glasses. That's a picture which lingers.

At the other end of the scale – a *pension* in Northern France which a party of English had been persuaded to visit for one of a series of pheasant shoots. This organiser had been very insistent that his enterprise should be duly reported on by *The Field*, and all else having failed, I was sent. I forget what the shooting was like, but our reception at the hotel was more than a little frosty. On the second night dinner seemed very late and, after a while, a formidable dame commanded me, as apparently the only broken-French speaker, to her sanctum. She explained in trenchant terms that not only had the bill for this trip not been paid, but neither had it for the previous trip and – with rising indignation – neither had the one before that! We did get some supper, and did not, as I feared, have to do the washing-up, but it was a near-run thing.

The organiser didn't get his write-up in *The Field*. What a pity: I would have liked the job of writing it.

Most sporting hotels go to amazing trouble on behalf of their guests. We ran stalking courses at a fantastically hospitable hotel at Walkerburn on the Tweed. No matter how boring my daytime lectures, at least everyone could gather in the bar and talk them over afterwards. The people who came were always enthusiastic, but even they were stretched one year. The hotel had some forestry ground for roe stalking where we had rifle shooting practice. The range day was a blizzard. At times one couldn't see the target at all, but everyone had a go, and our host dosed each snow-covered competitor with Highland Dew as soon as he finished, bless him. It was a surprisingly cheerful party.

What is it in Scottish water which makes whisky taste so wonderful? My stalking trips to Scotland always involved filling large containers with local water to take home for our evening libations. Local produce too. I was often tempted to stop at one hotel in Kingussie, not because of its particular comforts, but to call at the butcher opposite who made the most delicious haggis. There was some merriment in a bar in Blackford near Perth when I was there because a visitor asked for a particular brand of mineral water in his whisky, when the bottling plant of the kind he wanted was over the road and used the same supply.

One of my stalking clients was a considerable gourmet. A number of his friends in Brussels had a tasting of thirty different bottled waters to see which tasted best in their whisky. It must have been a good evening! The eventual winner was something labelled 'Scotteau', which came from Glasgow. I might have bought a couple of bottles to try ... he purchased the export rights for Europe.

There was an attic bedroom on the Solway where the icicles hung like stalactites from the small cast-iron skylight, but one was young and any discomfort was worth it for the chance at a wild goose. We had two or three schoolboys in the party, one of whom alone had failed to score as the days went by. It mattered to him dreadfully. On a freezing night we ferried across the River Nith and hid in various creeks, giving the gooseless one the best place. Frozen hours later the cry of geese electrified us, and to our joy a small skein flew straight over him. No bang. We trudged over to see what had gone wrong – and found the blighter sound asleep. Words failed us.

Hotels in Scotland have been revolutionised in recent years but it was not always so. Even if one was 'a bona fide traveller' as was necessary to get a drink on the Sabbath, bars were not the well-lit, warm and welcoming part of many hostelries they are now. In one where I stayed in the 1950s, I believe a bar did exist, concealed like a gents' loo behind some shrubbery in the yard, but I never found it. If you wanted a drink, you asked for it. I was hind-stalking at Gaick Forest for a week, coming back each day tired and muddy. The bath water was hot and beer-coloured. Marvellous. Catering, too, was ample if a bit strange. Once bathed, there was tea, with all sorts of scones that the Scots do so well. That might have been at half-past four. Then at half-past six there was Tea – which started with soup and a meat course and finished again with tea, but after that there was nothing – nothing at all – until breakfast next day.

My transport in those days was a 1934 Ford 8, from which all but the driver's seat had long gone. Before the motorways were built, driving up from Devon meant threading a succession of towns, including a so-called short-cut through the Liverpool tunnel. In that vehicle one had to stop somewhere for the night on the way, but even then it was something of a marathon. Heading for home at the end of my hind-stalking week, with six hundred miles to go I pulled in to the garage next to the hotel for a fill of petrol. The attendant said grudgingly, 'I can let you have half a gallon'.

Did he think I was going to walk the rest? Immersed in my stalking, I hadn't heard of the Suez Crisis.

How Not to Do It

PIFFA SCHRODER

I KNEW IT WAS a mistake but – old friends of many years – they were so persuasive, so cheering and warm and enthusiastic: 'No problem, yes of course we know that darling, but you've got your gun now and you have to start somewhere haven't you, and this is the perfect way ... last day of the season ... very relaxed ... it's just family and a few chums staying whom you know anyway ... there's nothing to worry about ... so you will come won't you, Friday evening, that's smashing ... .'

As a total novice, I knew this was an extraordinary invitation – you just don't get invited to shoot, even by very good friends, until you've been tried and tested for a couple of years and, moreover, on 'other people's shoots'. Which I hadn't, and which 'other people' usually don't much encourage .... However do novices, all agog from the shooting school, manage to get onto a proper shooting day unless it's via their friends or their family? Those initial shooting days with strangers are terrifying enough anyway, as the crustier old bulls tend to saunter up to inspect the newcomer – look surprised, mutter about 'officers' shoots' and then make some sort of crack on the lines of – in my case – 'Well *well*, a *lady* shot, heavens to Betsy.'

Later, after the first couple of drives perhaps, it's either 'Bless my soul, never seen that done before' or 'Not at all, it really wasn't my bird' or, far worse, the rather pitying 'I say – just a thought – why don't you shoot where it's going rather than where it's been?' And you have to grit your teeth and remember that a) everyone, even them, has had to begin somehow and b) it's meant to be fun. Meanwhile you can see them all watching your every movement and flinching rather ostentatiously whenever you raise your gun . . . (If you're a novice *and* a woman, it's absolute hell: men are anyway deeply distrustful of any female who pretends to shoot. The only females that gentlemen willingly tolerate on shooting days are silent, biddable and preferably Labrador, which may account for the fact that, for many years, before every single first drive, I always had to disappear and throw up behind the nearest bush out of sheer terror . . .)

Anyway, having spent the interim weeks panicking – frantically ringing the shooting school for more practice, then worrying about what I might forget to take in the car and making lists of everything imaginable – I arrived, a wreck, on the Friday evening as bidden. Lovely house party of all ages, all of whom were friends, cosy and relaxed and the fires blazing while a good January storm lashed outside. Having spent the drive down sick with terror, I went to bed that night praying that perhaps it would snow, or that a tornado would strike – anything which might entail the shoot being cancelled . . .

I slept intermittently and Saturday morning finally dawned. The storm had gone through and there had been a very hard-freezing frost. No hurricane, no mist (a white-out would have been nice) but bright, cold and clear. By 9 o'clock everyone had started gathering outside in cheerful pandemonium. Dogs tear about madly, galvanised by bellowed admonitions and the cold. The house party crunches out into the bedlam, booted furred and armed, chatting and laughing; the hostess appears with thermos flasks and goodies; keeper and beaters congregate in the yard, huffing ghosts marking time impatiently from foot to foot and our host trying to impose some sense of order to the proceedings.

'Morning everyone ... ah good ... here come the gallant neighbours ... well done ... over there by the barn would you ... think you know everyone ... Now, anyone missing? If not, all over here for a minute please? ... It's no numbers today, I'll place you ... Soph, you've got Mummy's 20-bore? And Jack and William have got the twelves and ... what? Yes, of course darling, anyone else need a cartridge belt? Now ... everyone sure they've got the right cartridges? Owen, just the man, check them for me will you please ... somebody watch those bottles *Christ* who's let the puppies out... ?' A small terrier, quietly intent on his own affairs, looks round shiftily and, squatting, tidily empties his bowels into a guest's open cartridge-bag on the gravel. '... *Right* ... that's about it then ... anyone under twenty-five onto the tractor – *watch the* ... Oh well, it had a dent in it anyway ... everyone else follow me in the Land Rover, darling you take the girls in your car and I'll take whoever's left and the dogs – OK everyone? Then *let's go.*'

First drive was brilliant – woodcock flitting about, dogs skidding over thick ice on the pond, bright sunshine but a good wind now, lots of barracking and everyone in high form and shouting unhelpfully at their chums down the line – the most perfect morning. I didn't hit a thing.

The next drive was even better; tall woods on the side of a vertical hill, ponies galloping furiously round the field below, pheasants like starlings and some spectacular hat-doffing shots and the valley spread out below. And I didn't hit a thing.

Two more drives before the bull-shot and the King's Ginger. Sophie had got her first pheasant, the young men were brilliant, the old hands stood behind and shouted, 'Well done,' and now the pale midday sun had emerged for the last drive before lunch, at the end of all of which I still hadn't hit a thing.

Some two hours later, fortified by a tremendously good osso bucco – didn't drink of course – I took out my gun again with feverish determination for the single, last, drive of the day. All those ridiculous nerves of the morning … just go for it everyone said and I thought, right, think positively, I can do this, this is going to be it …

The last drive was magic. Standing down by the river in a huge valley below the woods and the birds were as tall as steeples. It was the time for the old and the bold. We watched and cheered and then a couple of the boys connected and then everyone else seemed to get their timing right too and the birds kept on coming out higher and higher and sailing down from the great dark woods. And as the light started to fade the snow came, gently at first then in thick soft drifts, muffling the river banks and shawling round the trunks of trees. And finally the whistle was blown, and the dogs and the pickers-up took over and the guns began walking the slow contented walk of a well-tested party at the end of the last day of the season, congratulating the host, the keepers, the beaters and each other on a truly wonderful day in which, I knew, I hadn't hit a thing.

Over dinner, my total failure was summarily dismissed. 'You'll just have to come back next season, right? You'll show us all up with what you've learned at shooting school – promise? – no stopping you then – meanwhile what's *far* more important is that your glass is empty, hang on a sec….'

The following day the party split up. There was the usual disorganised flap – chaos in the boot room, suitcases being lugged noisily downstairs by complaining males, coats untangled, guns retrieved. The cat had been discovered locked in the larder, happily ensconced in the remains of the kedgeree; we all felt wonderfully well, very spoiled, and loth to leave. The cars were packed, there were hugs and kisses all round, lots of 'safe journey' and 'bye darling' as we climbed into our respective motors and revved up – it was like the start of Le Mans. Backing smartly away I swung the steering wheel round with the heel of one hand in a highly professional manner and waved merrily out of the window with the other. The wheels skidded, there was a small interval which you could have measured in nanoseconds followed by the most ghastly crunching noise – everything came to a halt. With unerring accuracy, I'd backed slap into the corner of the barn.

It was, of course, the only thing I'd managed to hit all weekend.

How it All Started

RICHARD SHELTON

FOR MOST OF those old enough to remember it, 1953 stands out as the year that Edmund Hillary and Sherpa Tenzing conquered Everest and a very young Elizabeth II was crowned Queen. For a shy eleven-year-old living in the lee of the Chilterns, 1953 was an *annus mirabilis* for quite a different reason.

For some years before, my brother Peter and I had been the proud owners of Webley air pistols. A young starling, spit-roasted the same afternoon over a fire of dead hawthorn twigs carefully selected for their tinder dryness from the top of the hedge, was our first success. Sizzling over the rather too high flames, the tiny fowl soon acquired a crisp brown coat and droplets of fat, some with a pinkish hint of Good Friday about them, made their own unwelcome contribution to the hawthorn fuel below. The wonderful aroma of the scorched meat was signal enough to the two young sportsmen that the starling was cooked to perfection. The quality of patience is but poorly developed in the minds of small boys and, in roughly snatching the bird off the cooking fire, it fell off its greenwood spit and into the ash. Singed fingertips brushed off the worst of the grey crust but an attempt to cut the starling into equal halves was nearly defeated by the bluntness of my penknife and the curiously rubbery quality of the flesh. There was nothing wrong with the flavour though and, after a few minutes of determined chewing, only paper-thin bones remained.

Parental advice, reinforced by our own experience, honed our cooking skills and convinced us that the house sparrow, like the starling classified at that time as a pest, was the best eating of the smaller fowl. Corn-fed in the stack yard, its flavour in autumn rivalled that of the grey partridge. We learned how to supplement our hard-won bags by trapping the sparrows using five bricks and three twigs. About twenty were required for a pie or, even better, a suet crust pudding. Both were traditional ways of cooking sparrows in country districts, living memories revived during the bleak years of rationing at a time when only the better-off had access to larger game.

Advance the calendar to 1953 and my dear father, who had a keen eye for a bargain, had, for ten shillings (50p) obtained a single-barrelled, folding .410 shotgun. At that time, most guns of this sort were hammer guns crudely made in the back streets of Liege. The family's new prize was unusual in being both hammerless and of British manufacture. Along the top rib it bore the proud legend, 'Army and Navy Stores', not the name of the Birmingham maker but that of the famous London shop set up as a co-operative in the nineteenth century by British Officers keen to equip themselves for foreign service at minimal cost to their inadequate allowances. This was the good news. The bad was that the little gun lacked a stock, a deficiency remedied by Papa by the construction of a sort of pistol grip made from the right front leg of an old mahogany chair. In his strong hands, the little gun was soon doing deadly work among the young rabbits lying out around the local beech woods.

Much as we enjoyed our 'shooting in miniature', with the advent of the .410 in 1953, greater prospects beckoned. Shortly, with a parental brass case home load in the breech (correctly closed of course by bringing the embryonic stock up to the barrel) and a young rook 'sitting on' the fore sight, I prepared to take my first shot with a 'proper' gun. I pushed the safety catch forward with a nervous thumb. The result of snatching at the trigger was a surprisingly loud report and a cut lip as the knobbly little stock crashed into my face. As to the rook, it flapped uncertainly away on what I have no doubt now was its maiden flight.

There was to be no more shooting that day but a few weeks later the .410 reappeared wearing a full stock of sycamore to which my father had screwed a raised comb of pine. The result would probably not have passed muster in Purdey's famous Long Room but the little gun now fitted and, after a successful shot at a feral pigeon pecking innocently on the leavings of the harvest, it was to account for both my, and, a quarter of a century later, my eldest son John's first pheasant. Like me, he soon grew out of the .410 and passed it on for the use of my youngest brother's boys at their farm in Oxfordshire. For all that the little gun was going to the best of homes, the pangs of parting with a piece with such vivid associations proved stronger than I realised at the time. For John also, the thought that our first fowling piece was no longer in pride of place in the gunroom left a gap we thought we would never fill. We were wrong.

Although my official duty at the Scottish Game Fair is to help man the stand taken by The Atlantic Salmon Trust, of which I have the honour to be the Research Director, the highlight for me is always a walk along Gun-makers' Row. This year, tucked away in a corner of my friend Graham Mackinlay's well-stocked stand was a rack of .410 shotguns. Three were finely-crafted double hammer guns, wonderful examples of the great days of British gunmaking but far too grand for me, or at least my current bank balance. The fourth was identical to the one that had left such a gap at home and not only did it have its original stock but all of the finish with which it had left the factory in Birmingham over seventy years ago. Despite Graham's generosity and allowing for the effects of inflation, it cost me rather more than ten shillings. However some things in life are priceless, none more so than the early memories of sportsmen of all ages. Can I still point it in the right direction? A rabbit and a wood pigeon hanging in the game larder and the 23 Eley 'Fourlong' cartridges still in the box say 'Yes'!

Dear Diary

GRAHAM DOWNING

ONE ADVANTAGE of getting older is that I never need to tell my wife what I want for Christmas. She knows that there is nothing I will appreciate more than having a further volume of my Sporting Diary leather bound and gold blocked, so that it can sit on the gunroom bookshelf to remind me of yet another batch of shooting days they can't take away from me.

I have kept a sporting diary since I was fourteen years old. That was the year my father and his shooting buddy took over a small rough shoot just a couple of miles from where we lived on the edge of Norfolk's Broadland. The arrangement was that the spoils, if any, were to be divided three ways, between the two shooting partners and the landowner. To ensure that all was properly recorded, somebody had to keep a diary, and that duty was allocated to me.

Immediately, the diary was expanded to cover not merely the proceedings of that particular little shoot but my entire range of shooting, and indeed hunting, activities. I can honestly say, hand on heart, that I have not failed to record a day since. Well, almost. Admittedly in the first few years it was sometimes several weeks before I wrote up my diary, painfully trying to recall the exact details of some half-remembered evening flight or an afternoon spent trying to outwit those wild marsh pheasants, and I daresay the odd sortie may have gone unrecorded. At times I had to force myself to commit dates and descriptions to writing, poring over the calendar a month later to work out exactly which day it was that I had shot over a particular wood or marsh.

In time, however, completing the day's diary entry became a ritual, a duty as important as cleaning the gun or feeding the dog. I found that, once I had completed two or three seasons of entries, the thought of giving up the diary was impossible to entertain.

A sporting diary is not merely a game book. I do not keep columns of birds and beasts killed, arranged by species and with little notes about the weather and the identities of my companions. No, I write copiously and at length about the day in a large notebook, covering just as many pages as I see fit. In the early days, entries were rather brief, but nowadays I might write a page about a simple trip to the saltmarsh, while an invitation to some new shoot that I have never visited before normally warrants two or three pages of description, sometimes more. Even a blank evening flight gets a few lines.

We are not talking Bridget Jones stuff here. I do not go in for gut-wrenching parades of self-doubt, indecent exposure of innermost thoughts or vindictive spite against my sporting comrades, although I have on a very few occasions made one or two pointed remarks which I have invariably regretted afterwards. The object of the exercise is not to comment upon the failings of others, but to enable me, years later, to recall with clarity a particular day in field, fen or marsh.

My diary has done all that has been expected of it, and more. It gives me enormous pleasure to select a volume, sink back in an armchair and read my own account of some long forgotten exploit. Invariably the narrative takes me instantly back to the time and place in question. Once more I am ghosting in my gunning punt through a misty dawn on the Blackwater estuary, catching the whiff of decaying marsh litter as I wait by the edge of an alder carr for teal to drop in at last light; lying back in the heather under the hot August sun after a morning's walked-up grouse shooting; hearing the spine-thrilling cry of a pack of hounds across plashy meadows as the December daylight fades or waiting quietly in some oaken hollow for a single cock pheasant to soar overhead, its bronze feathers glinting in the low winter sun. The experience is fresh once more.

Little incidents come back to mind – the snow drift which I stepped into whilst pigeon roost shooting; a succession of retrieves which old Teal made in the pitch dark of the Hundred Foot Washes, perfectly judging direction and distance from the sounds of the splashes made as the birds tumbled into the floodwater. These are things which I might have remembered in isolation, but in my diary they are placed in their proper context.

Not surprisingly, my diary follows the unfolding chapters of my life. Teenage years rough shooting in Broadland and fowling at Blakeney, then hunting with the university beagle pack. In my mid-twenties the focus shifts to the Essex coast, where my wife and I made our home when we were first married, and punt gunning starts to feature strongly. Then come the Scottish trips, walked-up grouse at first, then hill stalking, followed swiftly by roe, fallow and muntjac in East Anglia as the stalking bug bit. In my thirties, now living in Suffolk, I started to shoot driven game – something which I could only dream of when I was a boy – and first one, then a second small syndicate shoot makes its appearance amongst the pages.

Meanwhile, the Hundred Foot Washes link the years together like an unbroken thread, from my very first visits there in the 1960s to the present day. As I sit here and write this on a bright December morning, my shooting gear still lies in the hall where I dumped it last night on my return from an evening spent on the washes, standing up to my knees in floodwater amongst the willows, waiting for the moon to rise and hearing the wigeon calling all around me.

In more recent years I have been fortunate enough to have travelled more widely to shoot – Ireland, France, Sweden, Lithuania, Poland – and these expeditions give scope for description of new and unfamiliar scenery, sporting practices and hunting companions. Today I might think that I could not possibly forget what it was like to hunt capercaillie in the forests of central Sweden, so striking was the experience, but memory is a funny beast, and in twenty years' time, I may be glad of the written record.

It could be, of course, that such things will not be possible in twenty years' time. After all, the capercaillie has now been protected in Britain, and who is to say that the left and right at wild grey partridges which I shot a few seasons back in Norfolk may not be my last? Otter hunting featured in my diary right up until 1977, and that has long been consigned to the history book and fading photograph. In my diary, however, I can still smell wet hounds and see the sunlight twinkling from the buttons of the blue uniforms.

The diary marks notable occasions – a dog's first retrieve, a son's first goose, a wife's first pheasant. I can use it for inspiration or for reference. I can record exactly the numbers of birds shot on a particular marsh over a given number of seasons, as I had to do recently when compiling a management plan, or detail the changes which have occurred at one site over a decade or more.

The trophy which hangs on the wall or the photograph in its album is nothing but a snapshot, a moment frozen in time. But, provided that it has a date against it, I can refer to the day on which it was taken and recall from the written page how I crouched in a ditch at dawn as the geese flew over me or how the hounds slowly puzzled out the line across a cold, ploughed field before pulling down their hare in a hedgerow.

My sporting diary currently runs to eleven volumes, each one nine inches by seven and covering about three years' worth of entries. It will never be published, at least not in my lifetime, for diaries, on the whole, do not make good reading. But one day, perhaps, my grandchildren will enjoy finding out how field sports were enjoyed back in the good old days. When that time comes, I don't suppose I shall be around to worry about what they make of it all.

The Coldest Day

JOHN HUMPHREYS

IN THE MID-SIXTIES we had a sharp snap which lasted from Boxing Day almost until Easter. Every morning it took a hefty clout to break the water in the dog's drinking bucket, car windscreens were permanently frozen over, the water pipes like iron, the ground perma-frost. It was a plumber's dream. Birds had a hard time of it. Herons, bitterns, kingfishers and tree creepers died in droves and experts said they would never recover: they were wrong as usual and apart from bitterns the birds returned to strength in a year. Migratory birds were luckier for they could move to the coast and easier pickings but those tied to their own little parish were hard pressed.

I drove fifty miles to shoot on a secret place I knew on the river Little Ouse in Cambridgeshire. This was a wild and lonely marsh on a bend in that meandering river where brown frozen reeds stood starkly and the wind whistled as sweet as a razor. I was lucky to make it. The roads were as glass with deep rutted frozen snow which no machine could clear. In my mini pickup truck I scooted along, for in callow youth you feel immortal and despite skids and sideways shimmies those little wheels and front wheel drive got me out of trouble. It was a hazardous journey at a time when all the advice was to stay indoors and 'Is your journey really necessary?'

Necessary? You bet it was with every duck in creation crammed into the open leads of water between ice floes, pushed there from frozen ponds and lakes. Hard weather bans did not exist. I parked in a snowdrift and pulled on my kit. This was before the days of quilted body warmers and hi-tec coats. I had a sheepskin flying jacket which its previous owner boasted had flown over Dresden and had a shrapnel hole in it as proof. When I got it there was a mouse nest compete with incumbent in the sleeve. I soon had him out, rubbed in some dubbin and that was my fowling coat. Corduroy trousers, long underwear and black rubber waders looked after the bottom half, a balaclava helmet on my head and thick fur-lined gloves kept out most of the biting cold. My nose was red and raw, and where my cheeks met the wind they stung and glowed; eyes watered and even inside the gloves fingers were numb.

It was a mile slog to my favourite place tramping on the high flood bank, breath coming like puffs of cigar smoke. I was hot and sweating when I reached the oxbow in the river where many times before I had lurked. The air was electric with the cries of wildfowl. Wigeon whistled continuously, the sound silver needles sharpened by the cold. Mallard quacked, teal whistled and shoveler and gadwall grunted. A herd of whooper swans fluted delicately. The river was a black speckled ribbon of duck, stretching as far as the long bend. I had the place to myself and snuggled into a stand of heavy-headed giant reed mace, each topknot crowned with a cap of frozen snow. My dog of the day, a dear old thing named Drake, sat at my side and shivered, his teeth chattering.

The pale light faded. The birds would get up and fly around as the sun set for such is their custom. They would surely float over me as they swirled and give me a chance. A grey cloud grew in the east, yellow fringed and ominous, a cloud which spoke of snow, lots of it. With a grunt and a whistle a pack of wigeon came from the landward side and called to their friends on the water, 'Wheeeeo wheeeeo'. I rose from the reeds and fired two shots from my old BSA magnum loaded with the dreaded Western Super X cartridges, 'Yankee Rippers', they called them, an ounce and fifteen sixteenths, no less, in a gun proved for an ounce and a half. That was how it was in the foolishness of youth and the search for more and more fire power but it was all part of the fun of growing up in days of few restrictions, shortage of advice and easygoing shooting laws.

I received the usual thump on my forefinger which as often as not drew blood even through gloves. I was used to it and have the scars to this day but how lucky not to have a blowout. Mr BSA made his guns stoutly for fools like me who overloaded them. Three wigeon dropped out, two dead and one that slanted down to the river. Not the steadiest of dogs, Drake was out and had one back immediately, hunted for the other and plunged his snout into a snowy tussock where it lay buried, just a startling red speck of blood on the snow to show where it was. He went on for the one on the open water between ice floes. This was a bad moment, for a dog falling through the ice in the middle would never get out. Deaf to my urgent shouts to 'Stay', Drake went to the edge of the river, saw the duck and set off across the ice where it was thick near the bank. I screamed at him to stop, dropped the gun, rushed down and just managed to grab him by the tail before he had gone too far, I hauled him out backwards and rebuked him. That duck would have to lie where it fell. My friend lost a dog in that way and another crawled out on a ladder laid along the ice, a length of rope round his middle and managed to save his Lab. It was risky and he got a wetting but it worked. He had a companion with him to help.

Crisis passed and I knew I could shoot only birds which fell on the bank. It grew duller, clouds welled up and the first frothy snowflake hit me straight between the eyes. In five minutes there were swirling blobs, cold on my lips, catching in my eyebrows. Drake was two-toned, a white shelf on his back, jet black beneath. I peered up, eyes screwed tight, trying to penetrate the bewildering, skirling flakes black against the sky, turning white when they settled. More duck were on me before I knew it, mallard chattering gutturally, and in a reaction shot I dropped a drake which almost hit me on the head as it fell. Had it stunned me I would have lain there until the thaw. The next twenty minutes were desperately exciting with duck coming from all directions, flying round purposelessly, startled by my shots, reluctant to go far in such conditions, banking round no more than twenty yards from me, aiming to land on the river until another shot had them flaring once more.

I pulled off my glove and wrapped a sticking plaster round my cut and bruised forefinger, a thing I ought to have done before I started but – you know how it is in the excitement. I had taken fifty cartridges and had only three left. At my side lay a pile of mallard, teal, wigeon, gadwall, one shoveler and two wood pigeons. It was almost dark and snowing hard. The chill was seeping into my bones, the dog stood up and twirled his coat sending a shower of snow flying. The guard hairs on his belly tinkled soft as fairy bells for each point was a miniature icicle. A single teal came from my left and caught me by surprise but I fired instinctively and saw it flutter down onto the flood bank. Wearily Drake set off again, ploughing through the drifts and came back with a woodcock, a rare bird in those parts and a bonus. The poor thing was flighting out to feed in the forlorn hope of finding a place where the frost had not penetrated.

Two shots left and I fired a double at some mallard now barely visible in the murk. I missed with both and the fiftieth case fell red into the snow at my feet. I packed the ducks into my postman's bag and found I had picked thirty-four for my fifty shots, as good a flight as ever I was likely to see. The birds were in good condition; later they would grow razor thin as the cold gripped and wildfowlers adopted a voluntary ban, far better than Government-imposed restrictions which were unwieldy and unfair. I heaved the bag into my shoulder and very slowly trudged up to the top of the bank. Ten duck I had tied onto a cord and slung it round my neck. I guessed I was carrying the best part of a hundred pounds of meat and, a step at a time, I dragged through fresh drifts of snow, staggering over hidden tussocks, once falling full length and heaving myself up again. My hat was a shelf of snow, the dog plodded at my side, a startling pinto of black and white.

The truck was a white mound. Thankful and exhausted I dropped my burdens in the back and spent ten cold minutes scraping off the snow and shovelling it from beneath the wheels. Would I ever extricate myself? A moment of anxiety, what if the engine failed to start? No worries for she fired immediately and fter a species of skidding and sliding I managed a ten-point turn and found the track back to the hard road. There was a bottomless dyke on either side. Thankfully my truck was one of the latest models with a heater, not all were so well blessed. I had it roaring and Drake lay in the well on the passenger side and melted snow dripped off his back and onto the floor. The heat set my face on fire and the windows steamed up but we kept going and through swirling snow doing a steady ten miles an hour I made it to the old vicarage where my parents lived and a log fire awaited.

The next morning they closed the road to that bend in the Little Ouse and it remained impassable for ten days.

Farewell to Arms

DONALD ISLES

Giving up shooting! Re-writing one's will leaving the old guns to grandsons; not knowing exactly what to do with all the paraphernalia associated with the sport – boots, breeches, cartridge bags to mention but few. The awful knowledge that never again will one experience the sheer thrill of all that the shooting day involves; the almost sleepless night before, the early breakfast and loading of the 4 x 4 to be off in good time to meet at the rendezvous with friends.

Never thought it would happen to me after over sixty years shooting on and off all round a world that used to be coloured red when we had an Empire. Yet, during the last season a dangerous unsteadiness on my feet, coupled with inability to negotiate barbed wire, hedges and ditches all combined to make me realise that the beaters and pickers-up would be in much more danger than the birds, should I venture forth with the trusty 12-bore. Thus – rather than emulate Willy Whitelaw and, more recently, Dick Cheney – I have given up and shall shoot no more. All that is left are memories and a distinct tendency to read yet again the old Game Books while cursing the advent, indeed the actual arrival, of old age.

Reading the books, remembering and gazing into space bring back veritable floods of memories. My army service commencing from 1943 in the Italian campaign to 1978 when I retired from my appointment at the Ministry of Defence in Whitehall gave much opportunity for occasional shooting, but it was the season of 1992/93 when I was first able to belong to a syndicate and this continued until 2003/04. Statistics are boring but my Game Book tells me that in those twelve seasons I was out 240 days, shot but 1451 head amongst a total bag of 18,582 at a cost of the not

inconsiderable sum of £43,254. My below-average cartridge count was
3.47. All this shooting was in England and Scotland and takes no account
of the shooting around the old Empire.

Remembering the Empire takes me back to the Game Books of the 1st
and 2nd Battalions of my regiment – The Duke of Wellington's (West
Riding) – the old 33rd and 76th of Foot. The 1st Battalion book is well
known to me because during my service I had made a modest contribution to its pages, but that of the 2nd Battalion was unknown to me. Some
few years ago I repaired myself to our Regimental Depot in Halifax in the
old West Riding of Yorkshire and retrieved the book from our Archives.

A heavy, dusty tome, gold-tooled and bound in red morocco, it was
presented to the Officers' Mess in 1922 by an officer who had won the
DSO in the Great War. Only seven pages are completed, but they cover
eighteen years of shooting in India, Singapore and Egypt. The bags com-
prise black and red bear, ibex and marmot (not strictly game), panther,
boar, tiger and bison, together with many duck of all varieties. Game
was abundant. Even with a small number of guns, bags numbered from
sixty to one hundred plus; a typical example being fifty duck and twelve
snipe to four officers in India in 1938. After the last entry for 1940, the
Battalion was engaged in the pursuit of much more dangerous quarry in
the Burma campaign when the Battalion provided two columns for Orde
Wingates's Chindits in the jungle.

By contrast the Game Book of the 1st Battalion covers in detail a
wealth of shooting from 1907 to 1963, with obvious interruptions for the
two World Wars. The first entry for 1906/07 written at Tappa Khajuria
in India carries forward the bag from 1905/06 as 472. Apart from conventional game, the second entry, so descriptive of the shooting scene of
that time, includes twenty-one black buck, four nilgai (antelope), five
mugga (crocodile), and under 'Various', of all things, a wolf.

Most of the shooting recorded is in India but, after the Great War,
when the Battalion was serving in Palestine stationed at Sarafand, a major
entry for 1921 is 331 quail shot by four guns over four days. Devonport
in 1928 produced only a meagre total of nineteen pigeon, but in the 1950s
when I first appeared in the pages we had a good go at the duck, and
pheasant too, on the marshes by Colchester.

The Battalion was flown out, somewhat hurriedly, to Kenya in 1961
because of Ian Smith's UDI in Rhodesia but I must say we didn't relish any
sort of fight against our white brethren, and certainly not only because we
had a Rhodesian-born subaltern as a brother officer! But it didn't stop us

shooting and also fishing for brown trout in the Aberdares. Quail, guinea fowl, francolin and Thompson's gazelle made their entry into the Game Book.

They did so again in 1962 when once more we were flown to Kenya to take the place of the 24th Infantry Brigade which had been deployed to the Kuwait/Iraq border to deter the very first threat from Iraq to that country. In 1962/63 I was with my reinforced company battle group, some two hundred strong, in British Honduras (now Belize) where we faced the threat of invasion from Guatemala seeking an outlet to the Caribbean.

It wasn't much of a threat and certainly did not interfere with our shooting duck over the rice paddy fields at Boom. We were right on the flight path for migrating duck from Canada and the USA. I had a fellow Duke in the High Commission in Ottawa who signalled me top priority that the duck had left him and were *en route* to us. Whistler duck, teal and some muscovy came in huge numbers.

With no dogs, picking-up necessitated much wet and muddy discomfort for us in the paddy, and mosquitoes took a terrible toll on our bodies. Wild muscovy, tree perching as they are, present quite a sight on their approach to the gun line and resemble the wartime German Dornier planes. I shot one only. We had it for dinner in the company Mess. Somewhere along the way I have forgotten Khartoum in The Sudan in 1947. Again many duck on the Nile and also the slightly barbaric spearing of huge Nile perch making their passage through the dam sluice gates – a practice that was anathema to the dedicated fly fishers in the Mess.

Returning to the old Game Books perhaps one of the saddest things is to appreciate how many of the guns fell in action in both wars. It is also salutary to recall their careers and achievements; many of them became battalion, brigade and divisional commanders. Among the more picturesque was the great Peake Pasha who shot from 1907 to 1913, eventually leaving the Battalion to serve alongside Lawrence of Arabia in the desert. After the war he was a prime mover with Glubb Pasha in the raising of the Transjordan Frontier Force.

I served twice as a 'diplomatic' soldier; once at the Paris Embassy as Assistant Military Attaché and secondly as Defence Attaché at our embassy in Washington, DC in the States. I never fired a shot in these two countries as, perhaps meanly, no one ever invited me; but a year or so ago Piffa Shroder reminded me of shooting in France.

In her book *Cocks Only* she relates a delightful tale of one occasion on the French President's prestigious shoot at Rambouillet. After the customary sumptuous shoot breakfast the guns awaited the first drive. They continued to wait and clearly something had gone wrong.

At last, the Head Keeper came up to the President and in a barely audible whisper announced, 'Desolé, Monsieur le Président, mais les faisans ne sont pas encore arrivés de Paris.' I was amused to read Piffa's story because in my days at Paris the story was different but very similar. It goes that our Ambassador was invited to shoot at Rambouillet by General de Gaulle and that, while awaiting the train at the Gare de l'Est, His Excellency was astonished to see crates of pheasants being loaded into the guard's van of his train. Not wishing to annoy my good French friends I have to say that both stories must surely be apocryphal ...

As I say, I never shot in the great USA. At the time I wasn't sorry as on the turkey shoots I would have had to don a yellow phosphorescent jacket to ensure that no one mistook me for a turkey.

The below-average of birds to cartridge of one to 3.47 over twelve seasons tells one story. What it doesn't tell is of the most glorious shots or of the simply dreadful and mortifying misses.

Of the latter, seared in my memory is one appalling drive at Lockerbie. Perched on a smallish hill, with the beaters below me working a field of kale, there arose a solitary cock – my bird, flying straight at me, not difficult, and no other gun within range. The beating line stopped, watched and regrettably hooted as I missed with both barrels. I still cringe at the memory.

But, on the other hand, I have had some most memorable shots. One at Freeby when even Peter Hornbuckle, a first class shot, said it was the shot of the day. Several at Stoke Rochford when our host was driven to say that Isles was 'taking no prisoners'. However, I suppose the misses and the good shots all pale into insignificance when considered against the whole panorama of the shooting day. I just have to hope that my grandsons will be able to continue where I have had to leave off.